To Diane
with Love
Gabriela

NUMB

A True Story of Undue Influence

G.V. Cora

NUMB

ALL RIGHTS RESERVED

This novel is based on a true story. Names and perhaps the names of places have been changed to protect the privacy of other people involved. Despite being told in a fiction style, the events and history in this book are as accurate as memory would allow.

All trademark names were used with the knowledge and capacity that none of the companies endorses this book or its contents.

NUMB

Copyright ©, 2019 G.V. Cora

Editor: L. Elliott

Cover Art By: WM Productions

Trademark Disclaimer ™

The Trademark names used in this story do not reflect the opinion of the author, nor do they endorse this book.

Thank You to Wikipedia and Law.com

Undue Influence

un·due in·flu·ence

noun: **undue influence**

"The amount of pressure which one uses to force someone to execute a will, leaving assets in a particular way, to make a direct gift while alive or to sign a contract."

Law.com

"Undue influence is a crime and it is punished by law"
- Joe Prokof - Mary Rita Wish's attorney

NUMB

This Is Mary Rita Wish's life Story... A life dedicated to her Catholic Faith, love for God and love for the needy. From the beginnings of when her grandparents were poor immigrants coming to America to Mary Rita acquiring a mass fortune which led to a Religious Cult using Undue Influence to rob her of her life's work.

INTRODUCTION
FROM MARY RITA WISH

When my friend and neighbor, Gabriela Voiculescu, asked if I liked to read, my answer was: *I love to, I'm an avid reader, but I do not read fiction, love stories, killing and action stuff and when I enjoy a good book, I just can't put it down.* She gave me a book. She said it was a true story and a new book, just released. I thanked her and started to read it.

After a few chapters, I turned the book over to read the description on the back cover and realized I was reading a book Gabriela wrote and it was a true story.

Now, I really got into the book and just could not leave it alone.

I stayed up two nights to finish "ESCAPE."

I told my friend, Paula about Escape and she borrowed the book.

I suggested it might not interest her as much as it did me, because I was a friend and neighbor of Gabriela. Paula didn't know her.

A few days later, Paula finished Escape and she said she felt exactly as I did in reading Escape. She just couldn't put the book down and she said it wasn't important to know the author.

We both decided my story of "undue influence" needed to be told and Gabriela, my friend and neighbor, should be the one to write the story.

Mary Rita Wish

NUMB

A Note From The Author

When I accepted my friend's request to write the story of her life, I had no idea the task I would be dealing with.

I thought she was going to give me dates of the most significant events of her life and I would develop the story.

Well, the first stock of files almost gave me dizziness and I was ready to give up. Then I remembered my friend trusted me, she believed I could do it, so I reconsidered it. I sorted all her files by decades, many, many decades, did lots of research online, from Giuseppe Garibaldi to the Pope and the Vatican, from Krakow monasteries to non- profit organizations and I studied the 'UNDUE INFLUENCE' law. Once I got the idea of what the undue influence was, I realized that families with members, who are getting older, are disabled in any kind of form, having home care agencies, being in assisting living facilities and ALL the elderly persons should be aware of the existence of a unique type of "sharks" swimming around them. They are predators chasing their victims in order to rob them of everything they had and the worked hard for, robbing them of all their physical and mental possessions. Yes, mental possessions, because their process starts by using their victim's mind and the rest just follows.

It was an interesting journey, a lot different from my ordinary life and the things I'd been exposed to, but in the end, it gave me a sense of accomplishment, a victory over evil.

During the time, I wrote this novel, I had a few incidents happen to me and my family that made me consider if I wanted to finish writing at all, but I decided to do it.

It was a way of fighting evil; my book is a victory against Satan, just like my friend Mary Rita Wish's life.

During the writing process and I should say, all my life, God helped me, He walked next to me and so many times He had to carry me, that's how heavy my steps were.

Let my triumph, my victory and Mary Rita's victory bless you till the last page and after, and follow you wherever you go.

NUMB

Acknowledgements

Writing a real story of someone's life is a surreal process. Each word I wrote gave me a sense of a legacy to pass on to Mary Rita Wish's family, where one didn't exist before.

Mary Rita Wish, my friend and neighbor, honored me by "filling" my hands with her soul, trusting me to make her notes become the real story of her life.

At ninety, she has led a long and fruitful life, dedicated to God and charity, helping the needy. At least this is what she intended to do.

Mary Rita's life and all the events that shaped her fate blew my mind, making my words to come like an avalanche in my brain.

For two months, my husband did not have a wife; my children did not have a mother as I performed only the absolute necessary duties. Everything else was Mary Rita Wish, her unique life and the mission that I had to accomplish, writing this book that you now hold in your hands.

I thank my husband, Eugene Voiculescu, who was able to get over his first shock when I told him about my new passion: writing books and not only writing books, but writing books in the English language!

How did I find the nerve to do this? I asked myself, how I dared to do the unthinkable. Do you know what? After writing my first novel, Escape, God sent me an angel helper, and God told her:

"Leanore Elliott, did you see what that Romanian woman did? She dared to write books in another language other than hers and I don't want to stop her, she is so stubborn, so I am asking you to help her by turning her into an author who is able to write readable books."

And this is what she did. Thank you Leanore, You needed a challenge after writing and editing hundreds of books.

Thank you my family and friends for encouraging me to write and to stay firm to my new passion.

G.V. Cora

The Beginning

The Carones

Palermo, Sicily 1896....

It was a cloudy and sad day when Giuseppe Carone and hundreds of compatriots boarded the ship that would to take all of them to America.

The historic city said goodbye to the young men willing to face an unknown future. These were men whose dreams were to make money for their families.

They had so much sadness to leave the land of their ancestors behind, families, neighbors and friends, for a land where they had no roots.

Fear of the unknown was stronger than the hope Giuseppe had in his heart. Hundreds of women were saying goodbye without knowing if they would ever see their husbands, sons, or brothers again.

Everyone was aware of the danger of crossing the Atlantic Ocean with the ship being exposed to full winds and high seas.

If Rose knew how hard it was crossing of the Atlantic, sleeping in the same clothes alongside our luggage, how hard it was to keep food in your stomach. How sick all of us had been all the time we crossed the Ocean. I think she would lose her courage to step on the ship, even if I know how much she wants to be with me and to be together as a family.

I will never tell her how hard it was when the storm hit the ship, how strange I felt when I was mixed in with Neapolitans, Italians from Abruzzi, Apulia and Calabria. We all spoke different dialects and sometimes I couldn't understand what they were saying.

NUMB

A hostile atmosphere and angry looks, that was what Giuseppe Carone had found when arriving in New York.

The boat that brought him to the 'Promise land' had been stormed by inspectors as he noticed how many Italians who'd sailed with him, had been marked with symbols that he couldn't understand the meaning of.

He answered all the questions at the port of entry. Then after approximately three hours, Giuseppe was ready to leave the ship being grateful he wasn't sent back like other Italians he was on the same ship with. He saw how some of them had been separated from their group for reasons he didn't understand.

Coming from Palermo, Sicily, he didn't choose to farm in America, like most of his immigrants friends did. He decided to make money as quickly as he could and farming required time, too much time. He wanted to be closer to other Italians, to be able to speak his language and this way, he would be understood.

Giuseppe knew he had to learn English eventually, but at the beginning, he needed his compatriot's help. Once he got on dry land, all those immigrants who had been accepted to enter the country had formed a long line.

A man who spoke Italian, approached Giuseppe when his turn came. "I am Antonio. You do know what a 'padrone' is, right? I'm a boss, a middle man and I can help people like you to get a job or I can provide some lodging, handle some savings and this way, I can help American employers also. Did you know that you're part of the new immigration?" His padrone' asked. "And this isn't a good thing."

"Why is it not a good thing?" Giuseppe asked, being curious.

"Well, America liked more of the 'Old Immigration' which meant Germans, Irish, British and others and this was before you," the padrone said.

"How did you become a 'padrone' Antonio? How long did it take you to get there?" Giuseppe asked even as his mind was busy with all the novelties he saw around him

"I have been in this country for a long time. The English language is a must if you want to be a padrone, or to be successful, make a good living. I didn't want to stick to the Italian communities. I wanted to make good money and fast, like you want to do. Learn English and you can do what I do now, in a couple of years."

"Do you think I will be able to make money? I'm healthy, strong, and young. I'm willing to work day and night and save the money."

"It seems like you're in a huge hurry Giuseppe. Take it easy. We have to find a place for you to live first and a place to work," Antonio said.

After more paperwork, Giuseppe noticed his 'padrone' wasn't as busy, so he said, "Yes, you're right. I want to learn English and I want to be successful. I had heard on the ship and here at the port that Irish people can't stand us Italians, why? What did we do wrong? I have never met an Irish person."

"Italians are taking jobs that pay a lot less, you can live on poor fare, and we, the Italians are more economical. Now, the Irish are the ones doing the 'hod-carrier' jobs, the days of the hod-carrier jobs are still strong, but now, it is your turn to try it."

Giuseppe was all ears, but his thoughts went to what Rose, his wife that he left in Sicily. He wondered how she was doing and when he would be able to see her and their son, Ed again. Once Rose and Ed occupied his mind, a wave of questions

NUMB

invaded him about his decision to come to America as he worried if it had been the right one.

His beautiful wife might be so scared to be alone with their one year old son, Ed. He tried not to think of this on the journey over but again and again, this worry over her and his child assailed him.

How could I do this? Why did I do this? Hopefully, the day I bring the both of them here will come soon. I miss them; especially my son who had just started walking all over the house. I know he will have a much better life in America. I have to believe this. I cannot turn back now.

While he viewed the huge city and all the people, bustling on the roads and in the shops, Giuseppe's mind was full of memories that he had from his own country, from his city...He remembered things that had happened that changed its history. Of how bad his side of the country began to be after 1871, he had been only 10 years old but even he could see how many family members complained about the conditions they lived in.

The Southern part of the country had long been neglected, even if the taxes had been increased. The land wasn't looked after properly and nothing had been done to improve the quality of the soil.

Young Italians, even younger than me, hundreds, maybe thousands, left their families behind to find work in America because of the years of decline in my country and now I'm one of them.

The same moment he was thinking of his city, exactly the same moment, Antonio, his padrone, the man designated to help him, asked, "Oh, my lord Giuseppe, you were born a year after Giuseppe Garibaldi entered Palermo, your city, right?" He looked back down at the papers full of Giuseppe's information.

"Yes, I think this was the reason my parents called me Giuseppe." He smiled. "How did you know about this?"

"Everyone knows about General Giuseppe Garibaldi and his troops called 'Thousands' they were famous. I had some schooling and I learned about him. I love history, but I had to come here to make money."

"So, you know about the plebiscite that was done later, the year Garibaldi entered Palermo, 1860? I liked to meet and talk to somebody that knows about my city Palermo, Antonio. I love my city, but like you, I need to survive. Did you know that the year I was born was the year that Palermo and the entire Sicily became part of the new 'Kingdom' of Italy?" Giuseppe asked.

"Of course I know, but let me tell you something. I'm not even sure why I'm telling you this, maybe I see myself when I look at you. If you want to succeed and have a future, think less of your home, this is your country now, and you have to learn English like I said and the money will come. I have an idea, give me a couple of minutes and I'll let you know what this is all about." Antonio then became quiet.

He had a long list of names he was responsible for. All those people worked hard to save the money for the crossing and for the padrone, the person who would help them find jobs and places to live.

The young men called by Antonio, formed a group keeping closer to each other. Later that day, the young men were able to put their heads down. They fell asleep instantly, being exhausted.

Antonio's job was to interview them, to find out what skills everyone had in order to place them to the right employer.

NUMB

Giuseppe was the last one to be placed because he asked his padrone to find him a place to work hard and make money fast.

The factory Giuseppe was sent to work was producing 'Italian pasta and macaroni.' Giuseppe never worked in a factory, but he learned fast.

One day after Giuseppe started working, Antonio went to the factory where he worked and sat down to talk. "Giuseppe, I was thinking of your future, now that your family will get here soon and I came to talk to you about my idea. To see if you like it. I have many American employers in Chicago, people I know who want to hire Italians for their business. Do you know where this city is?" he asked but seeing Giuseppe's confused gaze, he continued, "Well, Chicago is a rail center, an industrial center and it is American's fastest growing major city. At this moment it is a 'Mecca' for German and Irish migration and a good place for Italians too."

"Antonio, you talk like somebody who really knows this city, where is this Chicago?" Giuseppe asked.

"It's somewhere north of here, a large city, friendly with many immigrants like you. What do you think if I help you to find work there?"

"I'd like to go to a place where there are more immigrants like me but you know better and I'll do what you say. For me, you are my eyes and you know what is out there." Giuseppe was nervous, waiting for a decision that would take him to a new life, the reason that he came to this country. He hadn't expected to have to make a decision this soon, but he was ready for what life was offering him. "If you say that going to Chicago will be the best for my family, my answer is yes. I will go there and start fresh."

"I'm glad you trust me, Giuseppe. Yes, Chicago will be your place from now on."

Giuseppe did feel nervous and worried as his heart was beating faster. He'd just made a decision that would change his fate, his life, but he trusted the man in front of him.

"I will make arrangements for your new work place. As soon as I finish, I will let you know all the details, hopefully soon. I wish you the best and maybe later on in life, you'll come and visit me with your family," Antonio said, shaking Giuseppe's hand.

Antonio had to turn his back and leave Giuseppe in a hurry, because he was getting emotional. Giuseppe looked so much like him, when he was a lot younger, when he, himself first came to America.

After a few days, Antonio came back and talked to Giuseppe to let him know about all the 'new' things he'd arranged for his favorite immigrant. "In Chicago, there are lots of Italian communities, they have their own churches, schools, grocery stores and everything you need, like you had at home, back in Italy, but starting now, Chicago is your home."

"Did you send many Italians there?" Giuseppe asked.

"I just told you, it's like a Little Italy there," Antonio said. "I'm afraid you'll never learn English because you won't need it, but you can ask any questions you might have, you can buy anything, discuss any problems, all in the Italian language. I know because most of the people that live and work there, do not speak English. You are a smart guy though, don't do what they did. I mean there are other compatriots that learn the language spoken in this country. You can too. This is what I advise."

NUMB

Giuseppe knew Antonio meant well, but he'd tried to learn English and he just couldn't understand it. He had to rely on his wits and instincts in most things. Like the signs and the laws were all in English and he would just ask people that he thought would know the meanings of these things to help him get along.

Not too long after their meeting, Giuseppe was getting ready to start the journey of his life, the journey of his future. A new city, a new work place, different people, churches, it seemed like everything was waiting for him.

Giuseppe said goodbye to the wonderful people he'd worked with at the Italian pasta & macaroni factory. He'd gathered the things he had and next day he was heading to the railroad station to get on the train of his new destination, the city of Chicago....

The train took him through many places with amazing landscapes, beautiful hills and rivers that made Giuseppe imagine if their outskirts looked so rich and welcoming, how would those cities look like inside. But nothing and no one prepared him for what he saw...a city like he never saw before; so huge, so large. A city that looked to him, like his entire country of Italy, the feeling was just overwhelming.

Chicago was spreading its landscape under Giuseppe's eyes. What a town, what a huge majestic and impressive metropolitan place, ready to be explored and loved. It seemed like he was dreaming with his eyes wide open.

The wide river, tall buildings, streetcars, the way people were dressed made Giuseppe feel excited but lonely and different. He kept wondering how long it would take for him to be able to bring Rose and his son to America, to be with them again. Even if he lived and worked in the big city of New York, he hadn't spent enough time exploring to see all the beauty surrounding him. Now, being on the train, he could enjoy the beautiful landscape this country had to offer.

His faith was strong and he knew God wanted him to do well. Otherwise, He would not have allowed him to be here. When he arrived, the first thing he saw was Little Sicily. It was exactly what Giuseppe expected and what Antonio told him it would be. Everyone spoke the Italian language, the shops were stocked with things he was familiar with, and he felt comfort with what he saw. He knew right away that he would love this place and do well.

He was placed in a clean area where most of the Italian immigrants lived and he was pleased to find out the winery where he was sent to work, wasn't too far away from the "dorms" where he lived with other young Italian men. Antonio had really done well in helping him and again, he felt grateful to the man.

Time went by, as he was getting familiar with the surroundings and the people around him.

Every day, he did the same thing. Work, come back, and clean up. Eat then sleep. The next day, he would do it all over again. He knew if he just kept at it, he would achieve what he needed... Enough money to pay off his debt to Antonio and for the passage of his family to come here to be with him. He thought of little else but his wife and son every night when he fell into an exhausted sleep.

"Giuseppe, why don't you come and play cards with us?" one of his roommates asked him, even while already knowing the answer he would get.

"Thank you, but I'm going back to work," Giuseppe said, putting his things in order, ready to leave.

His roommates laughed at him, seeing how much he worked, and how he did nothing else with his time. Most of

NUMB

the young men there weren't married and they wanted to enjoy the money they made.

"We have really good food," another guy said. "Do you know the small restaurant that opened up last month, at the corner of our street? "

"Yes, I ate there twice, when I didn't have the time to come home," Giuseppe said. "I felt like I was at home! I wish my wife could have such a good food, but I know for sure she will once she comes here. I intend to take her and my son there as soon as I can after they settle in."

Work was good and plenty, Giuseppe's employer liked him because he was such a hard worker. He was feeling appreciated and this gave him a sense of accomplishment.

One day his boss even said, "I wish I had more workers like you. If you have friends who want to work, bring them here as I pay better than other employers."

"I know a lot of people back in Palermo, but I don't know how to communicate with them. I wish there was a way to let my compatriots know how much work they would find in America, but I am going to tell the friends I live with."

Most of the money he worked so hard for was going to his padrone to bring Rose and Ed, his family to America.

His friends, who lived with him in the same dorm, even commented on this. "Giuseppe, soon you'll be a millionaire, you make so much money, a lot more than us, but we want to have a little bit of fun too, not just work, work, and work! Did you notice the beautiful young woman that comes every Saturday and offered to spend a few hours with us? Well, you should pay her and she can 'please' you, too."

"I didn't see her and I don't want to see her or any other woman. Soon, I will be able to finish my payments to our padrone and he will make arrangements for my family to come here. I love my wife. Yes, I need a woman, but I want *my* woman, my Rose," Giuseppe said, proud that he could resist temptations.

His friends stopped insisting, seeing how much Giuseppe loved his wife. Not too long after that conversation, Antonio came to see him. "Are you ready for the good news? Soon, your family will be here. You have two months to find a place for you and your family to live and my job will be done. Giuseppe, I still believe you can be a good padrone but do you see that I was right? Did you learn any English? Not at all! This is the problem all you guys have, work, make some money, but they're not thinking any further, being satisfied with less. Life is not only work, eat, love and sleep. There is so much more. I wish I could do more with my own life, but hopefully, my kids will."

"Antonio, if you look at all of us, you did the most, you achieved the most, we cannot even compare with you. I can only hope to achieve what you did. It's true that I'm kind of fresh in this country," Giuseppe said with admiration for his mentor.

"You're right but I know and I feel like I could do a lot more. Okay, I've got to leave now," Antonio said as he seemed ready to end the meeting.

"Can you help me find a place? I have no time to go and check, please?" Giuseppe asked.

"Of course I can, and I think I already know of a small apartment. Usually, I charge a fee for doing this and you'll be the first immigrant I've helped without charging to find an apartment. I believe in you. Like I told you before, I see myself when I see you. In a week or so, I'll be back and I'll let you know."

Giuseppe would always remember how much Antonio, his padrone, his mentor, helped him.

NUMB

The apartment Giuseppe rented was small but a lot bigger compared to his home in Palermo. He was ready to bring the love of his life and the fruit of their love, their son to America ... He felt truly excited and hopeful. Everything was finally happening the way he'd hoped. His love for God and his love for his family had gotten him through all the months of worrying and working.

The big city didn't intimidate him so much anymore, maybe because he knew he had many places to explore, many new places to enjoy. He thought of it this way now, instead of feeling so overwhelmed like he had in New York.

The big day came, the day when he would have his family close to him. He could barely sleep the night before, as he was too full of anticipation for the arrival of his family. He'd missed his wife so very much and had worried all the while that she'd been on that ship with their young son. He couldn't do anything to make it easier or anything to protect them and he'd prayed every night for God to watch over them.

Giuseppe was waving his hand to people on the deck of the ship, knowing Rose was there, holding their son in her arms.

Then yes, Rose was *actually* there, holding her son in her arms, exactly like Giuseppe imagined her doing, waving her hand to the crowd waiting on the dock. She couldn't see her husband but she knew he was there waiting for them, to hug them, ready to start a new life.

Ed Carone was almost 3 years old, his dark hair contrasted with his light colored skin. He was such a handsome boy. His eyes were inquiring into everything: the boat, the water, and all those people waving their hands.

He looked at his mother with curious eyes and she kissed him saying, "Ed, your father is waiting for you to play together. We just have to wait to be called for the medical inspection."

Ed grabbed his mother's skirt and didn't move from her, being scared of so many people around him.

The medical inspection was faster than it had been for Giuseppe, two years ago.

Soon, Rose and Giuseppe were holding each other with kisses while tears were rolling down their faces. It took awhile for them to look in each other's eyes; their hugs had no end...

Giuseppe was holding his wife so close that his nose sank into Rose's hair and the salt water aroma reminded him of the time he'd crossed the Atlantic Ocean, the time he put his feet on America's shore.

Poor Ed was crying because his parents were crying, but then he was wrapped around his father's neck with his little head resting on Giuseppe's shoulder and he seemed to calm down and feel a bit calmer.

Rose had two bags that she'd traveled with and she had to wait to get them, and be ready to follow Giuseppe to their apartment where a new life awaited them.

Giuseppe's love was spreading waves taller than the ocean waves, waves of love...

After a while, all the papers were ready, so Giuseppe Carone took his wife and his son to the place where a new life would begin with hope and love.

NUMB

The Murtaughs

Ireland 1898...

Patrick Murtaugh loved to study, and after long years of hard work at school, he became a teacher. His passion for teaching children made him choose a profession that he loved but teaching didn't provide enough money for his family.

One day after he came back from work, he sat down at the table for dinner and told his wife, Catherine, "Have you noticed how many people are leaving Ireland to go to America? I'm tempted to do the same thing to have more money for our kids. I mean the ones who will come in our family, hopefully, soon."

"What do you mean if I noticed it? That's all I see every day. I didn't say anything, but I'm glad you noticed too," Catherine answered while setting up the table for dinner. Like every evening, Catherine cooked for her husband, to show him her love. It was the way she always welcomed him home.

The couple was so much in love with each other and they had great hopes for the future, but unfortunately their country did not offer too many opportunities. Patrick's feelings were divided, the love for his job and for his students versus the pressure to be able to raise a family, to have what he needed to raise kids and be able to offer them a good education. He'd been debating about going to America, a lot more often than he'd wanted.

Catherine was ready with the food and both of them prayed before eating, feeling preoccupied with the new thoughts that were digging deeper into their minds.

NUMB

"Patrick, I find myself thinking about leaving Ireland and going to America, a lot more than I want."

"I know love and I feel the same way. Every time I'm not busy, even for a few seconds, my mind gets busy with the same subject. So maybe it's a sign that we have to do something about it?"

America was a dream as many of their friends and neighbors had already put it into practice by leaving Ireland and moving to the U.S. It seemed like a wave of migration headed there by the thousands.

The scare of the unknown was less frightening than the fear of not having enough money for their children, once they would be blessed with them.

"Patrick, I want you to know that I'll go and be with you, wherever you want to go. The fact that we speak their language would make our life a lot easier than it is for the other immigrants that have to learn the English language. We already have an advantage and I'm not scared if that is what worries you."

Patrick felt relieved to see his wife so determined. "T's just that I get less and less money from my work instead of getting more, but I hate to leave the country I love, because of this. Let's say we're going to have at least three children, how can we raise them with the money I bring home Catherine? I look around me and I don't want to live like this. Poor and living with hardly anything to our name. I want to use my teaching knowledge and be able to make more money. Actually, you helped me with what you just said. Maybe in a few days, I'll come home and say, Catherine, we're moving! We're leaving Ireland and going to America. Who knows?"

"Perfect, I'll start packing," Catherine joked.

A few weeks after that dinner, Patrick Murtaugh came home from the school where he was teaching and hugged his wife. "It's done. I paid for our ship to take us there."

"There?" Catherine asked. "What are you talking about?"

"We're going to America!" Patrick exclaimed.

Both of them started jumping up and down, like two young kids who'd gotten new toys.

"We cannot pack much, you know. It's not like we have much, but we're allowed to have two bags each, so think about it and I'll look for all the necessary documents to be sure we have everything. I am happy Catherine. I want to make our lives better."

"I know and I'm sure it will be a lot better for our kids, they will be born there. I'm not scared Patrick. I thought I would be, but being together, I'll feel a lot safer. I never wanted to be apart from you. I will stay by your side." Catherine was already busy choosing things to pack.

They both got all their things in order. Then after saying goodbye to their families and friends, the couple boarded the ship that would take them to America. Patrick and Catherine Murtaugh were ready to face a new future, full of hopes.

The weather wasn't friendly, strong winds kept hitting the ship making huge, dangerous waves. Passengers and the crew were saying prayers for the wind to stop, for a smoother sailing. They were all were getting sick but nothing could stop them from dreaming of their new life in the Promised Land. That land was getting closer day by day and everyone counted up the days like they never did before.

"Catherine, are you feeling okay? Soon, we'll put our feet on the American land. We're so blessed to be together, most of the men here on the boat, came alone. They left their families behind, to try it first, but we're different, we'll fight together. It will be a lot easier, I hope" Patrick talked to his wife, but

NUMB

mostly to himself. He needed validation for his decision now that the seas were rough and people were getting sicker and nothing but groans could be heard whenever the wind shifted and the boat creaked and heaved to and fro.

Through the roughest parts, he and Catherine encouraged each other, holding hands and praying. They held a strong love for God and they'd been taught by their parents to keep a strong faith.

The ship made it even though it took three extra days to get to New York, but they finally arrived, Most were peering out at the tall ships and buildings when they got up to the deck, worse for wear after such a trying journey. They all as one crowd looked out at the land of freedom, America.

Patrick and Catherine Murtaugh passed the quarantine inspection, both being young and healthy. After that, her husband grabbed her and held her close to his body. "I don't think this is the right place or the right moment, but I want to tell you how much I appreciate your decision to come with me and to not just wait back in Ireland for me to bring you here. I love you and I promise I'll do everything I can make a better life."

"I wouldn't have it any other way Patrick Murtaugh and I love you too." She wrapped herself around her husband, the man she trusted so much that she left her life behind. Lifelong family and friends became part of her past and she believed in a brighter future, next to the man she loved.

Patrick looked around. "I have noticed other people, immigrants like us that came here with other ships. How hard will it be for them to make people understand them, because they don't speak the language? I'm glad we don't have this problem."

Next, they were guided to the train waiting to be filled with Irish immigrants. The train took them from New York to

Chicago. For most of the trip, they were quiet, holding hands as their dreams became one, their hope for a better life started to bloom.

When they arrived, they were welcomed by tall buildings, large streets and bustling, busy people. The both of them liked it right away. It was a wonderful sight.... To see two big cities in such a short time was overwhelming for Patrick and Catherine.

Then after they exited the train, all their worries vanished because the Irish community opened its arms for the newly-arrived, welcoming them.

The South side of Chicago was the place of their new future. Patrick and Catherine found a nice neighborhood in the Parish of St. Rita Catholic church and school. A few days after they settled in, they met their neighbors. People they never knew were greeting them with fresh food, blankets and household items. Soon, they had almost everything they needed to cook and to sleep on. Their neighbors were doing the same things other immigrants did for them when they'd arrived in Chicago. It was a chain of help. The newly arrived couple was overwhelmed by such generosity.

"You'll love this place Catherine. We will have what we need to raise our family."

"I already love it. I'm glad we came here," Catherine said making plans in her mind for how to arrange things around in their new apartment, she felt like she'd gone shopping, that's how many necessary things they'd received.

The following week after he'd been hunting for work, Patrick came home and told Catherine the things he found out about their new city. "After a fire in 1871 that destroyed the central business district, the city grew exponentially and became America's rail center and a dominant force for manufacturing, commerce, finance, higher education,

NUMB

religion, high culture, sports and jazz." He laughed. "Have you heard this Jazz music?"

She laughed with him. "Yes from the small radios that are in the other apartments. I stopped and listened. What great music and tunes. It astonished me that I would be humming it or tapping my feet. Not like the jigs we are used to."

"We live in a different world now Catherine, and it seems like it's a much better world."

As usual, she listened to her husband, enjoying the details about their new city. The man had never failed to surprise her with his ease of understanding things. His ability to tell histories, gather facts and to know all about the world around him. Him being a teacher had been a natural choice for a career. She listened and asked a few questions, but she was more interested in something else. "Did you go to that school to ask for a job?"

"Yes, I did, but it seems like I cannot be a teacher yet. They asked me about some sort of authorization I need to have in order to teach in America. I told them I didn't have it and I asked what I have to do to get it. Catherine, I'm not sure we have enough money to live on, so I have to do what needs to be done to get that paper. The man that helped us with the home and other things suggested I should get a job as a hod-carrier."

"What kind of job is that?" Catherine asked.

"Well, a hod- carrier worker helps transporting the construction materials like, bricks, concrete blocks to the construction sites and hod-carriers make good money."

"Do you mean hard, physical work?" Stunned, Catherine now felt angry. "You're not made for it. No, you have to be a teacher, this is your job, and you trained hard for it."

Her husband sighed heavily. "Catherine, we came to America to make money, so you have to understand it will take forever to get that authorization. Do you think I'll like lifting heavy bricks and bags of concrete and who knows what else? No, I won't like doing this, but I have to get this job. I have no real choice right now."

"Okay, but you have to promise me you'll get the authorization and go back to teaching," Catherine said in desperation. She just couldn't allow him to waste such a wonderful mind. Such intelligence. He was so good at teaching children, they all loved him so much back in Ireland as he was gentle, patient and so wise..

"Come over here," Patrick said with a huge smile, hugging and kissing *his* Catherine.

The years passed by as the Murtaughs were growing into a solid, large family.

Catherine was waiting for her husband to come home from work. She had some happy news. "Patrick, we're going to have one more baby, we are so blessed," she said hugging her husband. "I so hope it is a daughter! I love our boys but I want an Irish lass."

He chuckled. "Yes, and I hope she is just a fiery as you, my Irish lass. We have to thank God that we have such healthy children. I just wish I could bring more money home than I do. So far, we're able to do well enough. The kids will have what they need and more than this is. We all love each other. It is god who has helped us and god who teaches us about love and honor."

Then months later, Anne, a beautiful baby girl, came into this world. Having a girl was like an answer to their prayers. Patrick and Catherine Murtaugh were thrilled to have a girl because they had been told by elders many times here and

NUMB

back in Ireland that a girl would always take care of their parents later on in life, boys were different as they would have their own families to support.

One day, Patrick came home after work and said, "I wish I could come home earlier to play with our children. Look at them. Thomas is getting so big he's the head of his brother's team. Michael and Patrick, I love calling him Packie, both of them are listening up to Thomas already. They ask him things that I don't have the answer for and he always shows them how to do things. Now, I understand why families have more than one child. Growing up, each brother or sister helps the younger ones. Look at how they care for Anne and protect her. it just makes me feel so proud."

Catherine listened to her husband thinking how hard he worked and she felt like she had to say what was on her mind, "I'd like to work to help you with the money Patrick, but there's so much to do at home, even now that Thomas is a big helper."

He nodded. "Oh, my sweet Irish girl, you already have a job. Many jobs here at home. Do not worry. I feel good every day, knowing you are raising our children while I work. Please feel proud of that."

She swiped her tears away and thought once again of how lucky she was to have this man as her husband and she vowed to try to make his life easier in any way that she could.

The family was finding new things to discover and each day that passed by, they were consolidating the strong bonds among them.

The neighborhood where they lived was full of Irish stores and places where people could get things they needed, parks to take their children for a nice walk to let them play and use their energy. A few of the Irish men of their community went to college and became lawyers or worked in the Justice Field and Patrick was proud to see these men going to college, to see many becoming successful Irish Americans.

One day, Catherine was in the kitchen getting dinner ready when she noticed her son, Thomas helping one of their neighbors. She peered through the kitchen window to see his actions.

Then her son made his way inside and smiled at his mother.

"Thomas, I was watching how you helped that sweet old lady and she needed help for sure. I'm proud of you and you set a good example for your brothers." She hugged her son tightly.

Thomas didn't say a word but he smiled, he was definitely proud of what he'd done. His father told him to always help his elders or those in need.

When Patrick came back from work, Catherine told him, "Our son Thomas did an amazing thing today. You know our older neighbor, Mrs. Murray, she came back from the grocery store and she was carrying heavy bags, way too heavy for her. Well, Thomas ran to help her. He took all the bags from her and brought them into her house. Even helping her to put everything we're it belonged. It made me very proud of him. Michael and Packie would do the same thing, I know. The way we raised them has started to show."

Patrick couldn't be happier. As he nodded while feeling just as proud of his wife for raising such strong children who had the same values his parents had instilled in him.

The prayer said at the dinner table that evening was a tradition with the Murtaugh family. It always brought the family closer. The couple sat and ate as they passed the serving dishes along, so they could all eat. The room filled with noise as usual but it was such a happy sound as the children sat around the table, laughing but trying to behave. However, the boys we're messing with each other like there wasn't room

NUMB

enough. Elbowing each other and making faces while sniggering.

But this evening, they were lucky, as their mother didn't pay attention or correct their bad manners like she usually did. She didn't want to say anything to ruin the feeling in the room, she was too happy. Catherine knew how much help and happiness a large family brought and often, you just needed to allow them a wee bit of mischief and shenanigans as the Irish always say.

The years went by and the Murtaughs were now a well known and respected family in their neighborhood. Their children were a good example for the other kids and they even helped many of them with their school work.

Anne was a good student and whatever her mother asked her to help with, she was more than happy to do it. "Mom, may I go to my friend's house? They invited me for dinner, and I promise I'll be home soon."

"I know Babe, let me ask your father and I'll let you know." Catherine said.

The moment Anne heard her mom calling her 'Babe' she knew she would get go to her friend's house for dinner. Almost everyone called her Babe and only people that were new to her, called her Anne.

After awhile, Catherine called her daughter to come in the kitchen where she was preparing dinner and said, "Yes, Babe, your father said you can go, but your older brother, Thomas will come and be with you on the way back home," her mom said.

"Thank you Mom. I like that Thomas will be with me. We get along well, plus it makes me feel important."

"Who else is coming there? Are they all Italians or did they start accepting friends from different families, like we did?"

"You know, it's amazing that you asked this question, because I heard my friend who is Italian, as you know, telling her mom that she has an Irish friend and if it was okay to invite me, and her parents know how well we treated their daughter, my friend. I mean, my Italian friend."

"Did her parents accept to have an Irish person in their home for dinner? I know they will like you. We enjoyed having Fiorella for dinner; did I say her name correctly?"

"Yes, you did. I love her name, it sound so romantic. Mom, I'm not sure if her parents will like me, I will ask her about this, but I'll find out when I'm there, I suppose.

"Actually, your father and I are not like the other neighbors," Catherine said. "We do not hate the other immigrants, we don't think we're better than others, but we would like to keep Irish with Irish, because that's how we had been raised with that kind of mentality, but the world seems to go in a different direction, and I'm okay with this,"

"What you just said makes me proud to have you as my parents. We are human beings; we all have to work hard for a living. We're from Ireland and others are from Italy, Germany, France, Africa and a lot more places. I'm so glad you didn't instill hate in us."

"You see, I shouldn't let you go there once I found out it would be an Italian family and not Irish, but it will be something against how I feel inside. I liked your Italian friend and she is a good girl. Anne, I have to be honest, you are a beautiful young girl and soon will start dating, and I do pray the man you date will be Irish, because I'm afraid to break the rules. It's something that was put in our brains since we were children and this makes me scared. But I love you too much to stand in your way. I'm not talking about this dinner. I'm

NUMB

talking about your future. Okay, let's get ready for your dad, he'll be home soon."

The Carones

The North side of Chicago, the Italian neighborhood was large and quite populated with hard workers, willing to make a good living for their families.

Giuseppe Carone finished working in the yard and went inside the house, cleaned up then went into the living room where his son was finishing his homework.

Ed had tried to help his father but he was sent back inside the house to study.

"Ed, soon I'll take you to meet somebody."

"Where are we going? Who is this person?" Ed asked his father.

"Do you remember my friend from Palermo, the guy that I came together with on the boat? Well, he was luckier than I was, and our padrone, Antonio, found him a job at a large printing company. He makes good money and the work is not as hard as farming or working in construction, his name is Stephanos Molineri. You love to read and I see you every day reading the newspaper."

"Yes dad, I like to know about everything. To see what's going on in the world and honestly, I would like to have more knowledge."

"Son, it's easy to see that. I'm glad I brought you to this country. I am a simple man, but I want you and your sisters to get better than me, a lot better and my heart is happy for you when I see you reading and writing."

"So, where are we going?" Ed asked again.

His father grinned at him. "Oh, I forgot to tell you, you're right. I was talking about something else. I was thinking to take you to my friend's work place and hopefully you could get a job there, what do you think?"

"I started looking for jobs already, but this sounds better than what I found it. I'm excited to go there. When are we going?" Ed asked and his eyes were full of hope.

"Let me talk to my friend, he will tell me when the best time is to talk to his boss."

"Dad, it's my turn to help you and Mom. Thank God, for my health and I think I can work anywhere. I speak perfect English, I have all my documents in order, and I don't get in trouble. I know of a few young men like me, the same age, which started to drink and gamble. Do you know that they tried to convince me to join them going to an Irish Pub? When I refused, they were angry. Since then, they don't talk to me like before, but I'm okay with this. I have other friends that I like."

His father looked up and thanked God for guiding his children's steps in life. Giuseppe was proud of his children, the kind of people they had become.

Ed's mother, Rose was baking her son's favorite cake, an all Italian cake that she learned how to make from her mother. The only place she could find the necessary ingredients was in their Italian neighborhood, nowhere else. She noticed that more and more people were coming up to their Italian stores to shop. Their Italian food started to be liked by lots and lots of people living in Chicago. Rose couldn't be more proud of her children, the way everyone loved them, proving her that she did a good job educating them, with love but being firm.

Rose never learned English, because she stayed home taking care of the house and raising up her children.

NUMB

"Mom, what is this aroma? Is this my cake?" Ed asked in Italian when he came home.

"Isn't this the one you like?" Rose asked lifting the cake up, so Ed could see it.

"Yes Mom, thank you. I love it, but I think all of us love it, because it's gone in a few minutes, every time you make it," Ed said kissing his mother.

"Your dad told me about going to find a job?" Rose asked.

"Yes, I cannot wait to work and help you with the house bills," he said.

"You don't have to help us, save money for yourself, you'll need it. Life is getting more expensive every day; the prices are getting higher and higher. It will cost you more and more to raise your children."

"I'm not even married and you talk about children." He rolled his eyes. "But all the other things you talked about, you're right about. I can see the cost increase in everything. I'm determined to make your proud of me, pray for me to get the job."

Giuseppe was ready to go with Ed to the big printing company. The streetcar took them right there and Ed liked what he saw, a large building with a prosperous look.

Giuseppe asked his friend to meet him and his son at the main gate. At 11 a.m., like his friend suggested, Ed and his father's friend met each other, shook hands, and went to the big boss' office.

"Hi, I'm Stephanos Molineri, nice to meet you. I am going to introduce you to my boss. If you've turned out to be like your father, then for sure you'll get the job. Your father is a good man and all his friends respect him. I will recommend you to the big boss."

They walked few yards and Stephanos knocked at the office door.

After being invited to come in, the man behind the large desk introduced himself, "Have a seat, my name is Mr. Geraldo."

Giuseppe's friend, Stephanos had worked for here for many years and he was sure he would be willing to hire Ed, knowing that he couldn't be friends with someone that wasn't a good person.

"So, I understand this young man is ready to work and start a new life, am I right young man?" Mr. Geraldo nodded at him.

"Yes sir," Ed answered standing up and feeling quite important to be called 'young man'.

Giuseppe was so proud of his son for showing respect to his probably future boss and he praised Rose for raising their son right, teaching him to be polite and respectful.

"What do you think? You think could you work here?" Mr. Geraldo asked.

"Sir, I'm willing to do anything you want me to do, and I cannot wait to be trained how to do things."

"Good thinking, I'll tell Stephanos what I decide. Good luck, young man," he said, shaking Ed's hand.

Sparkles were showing in Ed's eyes with hopes for his future.

Giuseppe was so happy that he shook Mr. Geraldo's hand, saying 'thank you sir'.

Before leaving the office, Ed Carone had a nice conversation with Mr. Geraldo, answering all his questions and he made a good impression on him.

"You raised a good man, be proud of yourself and congratulations to his mother," Mr. Geraldo said.

Ed, his father and their friend left the office with hopes that he would get the job.

NUMB

All the way back home, Ed was talking about how excited he was to work for such a big company.

Looking around, they could not believe how much the city grew. The Chicago River was large and impressive, as many businesses had put their buildings alongside the river.

The city attracted many people looking for better lives, for better access to education. Ed wasn't intimidated by the grandeur of the city he lived in. The suburbs were located not too far from the center, three to six miles, making the transportation bearable. Ed and his family lived in a rental home in the South side of Chicago and he loved living there.

Seeing his parents doing well, his sisters, Lillian and Cara were doing well also and always getting along with their neighbors, made him feel happy that his parents chose to come to America. Ed was grateful for his parent's decision. "Dad," he said wrapping an arm around his dad's shoulders, if I get this job, I'll save money so we can buy a large house and we can keep living together."

"Son, this would make your mom and me, really happy," Giuseppe replied. "We're getting older and will need more and more help."

"Dad, I promise you, whatever life will bring to me, I will always be there for you, my parents and for my sisters. I will protect you all... help me God to get this job."

"I know son, I know," his father said as tears filled his eyes.

When they arrived home, Rose couldn't wait to ask them how the job meeting went. "What did they say? Did you get the job?"

"Mom, no one gives you the answer that fast, but dad and I have a good feeling. The boss, I mean I think he is the boss, shook my hand and he said I was a good man. In a few days, I'll know if I got it. If I do, we have to celebrate. I know we don't drink, but we can have a fun event without alcohol. We never do more than work, work. I'll ask dad to invite Mr. Molineri, dad's friend to thank him for taking me to talk to the big boss. We can have your famous cake and something else then enjoy a few hours together, what do you think?"

"What a good idea! I'm glad you thought about this. We all need some fun, you are so right. Talk to your father and let me know when Mr. Molineri can come, so I can bake a cake the same day, to be fresh," Rose said.

"Let me go and talk to dad," Ed said, already looking for his father. He went outside. "Dad I have an idea..." Ed said, telling his father what he had told his mother.

"Oh, I never thought about a party and considering we are Italians, we should like to party! I think life changed us because we work so much, we don't realize we need a break sometimes. Okay Ed, let me talk to my friend. Oh, do you know something? I don't think it'll be a good idea to invite only him, he has a large family, and he wouldn't want to leave them at home."

"Of course, I'll be happy, the more the better!" Ed agreed with his father. "How many children does he have?"

"Well, he has two boys and a girl. The boys are older than you but the girl is about your age, I'm not sure."

"Perfect, so I'll have somebody to talk to," Ed said, happy to meet people his age or closer to his age. Ed, at his young age made him see things and potential events as bringing new people in his life, making new friends and getting more involved in the place he lived in.

He was eager to find out if his father's friend would accept the invitation.

Giuseppe didn't wait long and as soon as he finished talking with his son, he called his friend, "Stephanos, this it's me, Giuseppe. I wanted to thank you for what you did for me and my son."

NUMB

"I'm glad I could do it and I hope your son will get the job. It will be so good for him," Stephanos replied.

"I called to invite you and your family to spend a few hours at our home. The house that we rent has a large yard, so we can relax and have some fun, what do you think?" he asked.

"Let me talk to my family, do you have a date in mind?" Stephanos asked.

"No, I wanted to talk to you first but any weekend is okay. I know we work some weekends too, but we'll find a time to relax."

"You know, my family loves these kinds of things, so let's arrange it now that I have you on the phone. What about next weekend, is that too soon?"

"No, it's perfect," Giuseppe answered, happy to have something done, so he could start preparing for the get-together party. He knew he should wait to see if his son got the job, but it was nice to say thank you to his friend, for introducing Ed to the big boss. Giuseppe was sure his son was going to be hired and he would start a new life. So let's the party starts....

The Murtaughs

On the other side of town, Patrick Murtaugh came home from work, tired but happy. He looked around for his beautiful wife, spotting her as she came from the yard where she'd planted a few new plants. Catherine loved working in the yard and she was good at it. Women from her neighborhood were asking her advice most of the time because everyone could see the beauty of her place.

"Catherine, I made good money today, the company introduced new equipment and all of us could do a lot more with less physical effort. I love when someone comes up with a smart idea. It made my work a lot easier and getting older, lifting and carrying bricks is not easy on my back, but today I felt really good," Patrick said smiling.

"This is good, because I'll need your help with the party. Our neighbors will think we're rich, but it is okay, we can be rich for a day!" Catherine said, organizing her kitchen for preparing the food.

"Catherine, these days it's a luxury to have a party, but we need a little bit of fun once in a while. And we really, have a good reason to have a party. Anne finished school and we have to show her our appreciation. Anne has so many talents and she will be a hard worker, whatever she decides to do. Actually, she's learned so much from you, she can already run a family. I mean, not her family, I meant that she knows everything that needs to be done as a housewife."

"Hey, what are you talking about? She is way too young to start a family. Actually, I take it back. She has friends that have gotten married already. I don't want her to start a family yet, but it's God's decision, not mine. This weekend she will go to her friend's, Fiorella Molineri. You remember the Italian girl she became friends with, when we had that charity event at St. Basil church."

"I almost forgot about that nice girl and her family works hard like we do. I wish people wouldn't be so much against each other," he said.

"You're right, we all came here for a better life for our children and for us, we should be more respectful to each other but it is what it is. We taught our kids to do the right thing," Catherine said.

NUMB

"Okay, tell me what you want me to do. We have one more week to be ready," he said.

"I know but do you see how fast the time flies?" Catherine said, writing down things so she wouldn't forget about them.

Fiorella Molineri, Stephanos' daughter was arranging her room; she cut some fresh flowers from their garden, and put them in water, checking to be sure everything was ready. So her friend, Anne Murtaugh would feel good being there. Fiorella completely forgot what her father told her a few days ago about going to a party and she realized it was too late to cancel Anne's visit, so she asked her father. "Dad, I forgot about this weekend event we have to go to and Anne, my friend is coming to spend a couple of hours with me, if she wants, may she join us?"

"I don't see a problem, but I better ask my friend, Giuseppe," Stephanos said. He made a quick phone call and Giuseppe was more than happy to accept one more guest, when he was asked. "Thank you, we'll be there at the time you said," and Stephanos was happy to give a positive answer to his beautiful daughter.

Fiorella was waiting for the answer to be sure she could take Anne with her. When Anne arrived to her friend's house, Fiorella greeted her with hugs and kisses, and as soon as they sat down, Fiorella asked, "Anne, do you want to go with me to a party? You'll think I lost my mind to say such thing, but it happened."

"What day is the party?" Anne asked.

"Today, I completely forgot about this when we made arrangements to see each other, but it will be fun." Fiorella tried to convince her friend that was looking at her like she really lost her mind.

"I think I'm okay, but wait a minute, I'm not dressed for a party!" Anne exclaimed.

"Don't worry, we'll be outside in the yard, and we won't stay long," Fiorella said.

"If you think it's okay, why not?" Anne nodded.

Stephanos and his family, plus Anne were heading to Giuseppe's house, ready to spend some time together and it didn't take long to get there.

"Hi everybody," Stephanos said when he entered Giuseppe's house. "This is my family." He started introducing each member, adding few words about every one of them. The way he did it, it was like an ice breaker, making people feel comfortable with each other.

Giuseppe and his family were all smiling and hugged everyone, wishing them a cheerful welcome. They'd worked hard to make their party a really good one and treat their guests with the best they had to offer.

Ed Carone was behind his father, wondering who the other girl was, thinking his father forgot that probably Stephanos Molineri had two daughters, not only one, but soon his question got an answer.

"Hi," Stephanos said, "This is Anne, my daughter's best friend."

Ed's face was getting red when he was introduced to Anne. "Hi, I'm Ed Carone and these are my sisters, Lillian, Cara and Lena. I'm the oldest, nice to meet you.

"Hi, I'm Anne Murtaugh, nice to meet you, too."

Her friend, Fiorella was looking at Ed, "Actually, I think I saw you at St. Basil church at their charity event, did you have a table there?"

NUMB

"Yes, my mom bakes lots of cakes and I took all of them over there to help with selling, to raise money for church. You're right, I had a small table not too far away from yours, I saw you there, too."

"Anne is my best friend and she's Irish. We'd made arrangements to spend a few hours together and my father told me about your family's party at the last minute, so I had no time to tell my friend and reschedule our date," Fiorella said.

"I'm glad you didn't, it's good to have people my own age around," Ed said.

Everyone grabbed a lemonade cup and headed to the yard where a large table and chairs were waiting for them. Giuseppe's BBQ was so delicious that almost everyone asked for more food. The weather was just perfect too, creating a friendly atmosphere.

Ed sat between Fiorella and Anne being happy to have such beautiful girls to look at. That evening he felt so preoccupied, he couldn't eat anything, not even his mother's delicious cake.

His eyes were on Anne the entire day and he didn't seem to care that everyone noticed.

Fiorella moved closer to Ed sisters, to let Anne and Ed talk more.

Ed told Anne, "You know, I hope to get a job at that large printing company where Mr. Molineri works. I had the opportunity to talk to the boss there and I pray I'll get the job."

"Oh good, I'm happy for you. I hope you'll get the job soon. I'm looking for something to do also. I would like to be a teacher like my father was in Ireland, but I'm not sure if I can get all those papers, it cost lots of money. My dad had to make a living right away, so he couldn't pursue his dream. He is a hod-carrier now," Anne said.

"I would like to go to school too, but my parents need help, they're getting older," Ed replied.

The evening brought a nice breeze and Rose brought some scarves for the girls. She gave two of them to Ed, to give to Fiorella and Anne.

When he wrapped the scarf around Anne's shoulders, she looked up and caught a smile on his face. She liked it and her body was getting warmer, she didn't need the scarf, but she enjoyed Ed's touch.

Stephanos and his family, including Anne, thanked the Carone family for the wonderful time they had and promised to find time to be together again.

It felt good to have friends around and spend a few hours laughing and joking.

Ed couldn't be happier and as soon as everyone left, he started to clean up the table, helping his mother and his younger sisters. "Mom, thank you for your hard work, I know you did it for me," he said kissing his mom's cheek.

"Son, I have a feeling that you liked the party for more reasons than that, am I right?"

"Yes, you're right, it was such a nice surprise to see two girls instead of one and I liked it, we had so much to talk about."

"Ed, as a mother, I have to remind you that the girl you like is Irish and you know Irish people don't want anything to do with us Italians," Rose said looking deep in her son's eyes.

"I remember you told me about this, but times have changed, at least I hope it's true. I do like the girl and I want to see her again."

"You know who decides it, pray and talk to God about it, he's the only one that can make it possible, but I don't want you to have your feelings hurt, son. I never understood why this happens. We want a better life and so do they, but

NUMB

something must have happened a long, long time ago and it's still going on today," Rose said mostly to herself.

"Next week I will be going back to the printing company. Mr. Molineri told me to go and check, and I'm so happy. I think I got the job!" Ed said smiling.

"Oh, I cannot wait to find out," Rose said. "You'll learn so much about printing if you start working over there. I heard they print lots of advertising stuff for the automobile and railroad industries."

"How do you know all this? It is true, Mr. Molineri told me about what they print there. Mom, this city is growing like weeds. Every time I walk or ride the streetcars, I'm amazed at how many new things I see. There are lots of new buildings, cranes all over the city, construction sites everywhere. I love this city."

"Son, I know everything is going on around us, do you think that because I'm a housewife, I don't pay attention to what is happening with our community? I know I don't speak English, but the Italian community is so big that we can find out everything we want from just going to the grocery shop, to the doctors and all the other businesses we visit when we need something. I think if we lived in a mixed community, I mean, Irish, Germans, French and Italians, then everyone would have to speak English to be able to understand each other, but keeping separated, they all talk in their native language. I never needed to speak English, because I was able to get whatever I had to, speaking Italian language only. But for you and your sisters, it is a different story. You're young and if you want to work, you have to speak English and I'm glad you do. Look at the girl that just left, she is Irish and if you wouldn't have spoken English, you would not be able to communicate with her. I looked at her and I noticed how her eyes lit up when you talked to her."

"Mom, I really hope you're right. I didn't see what you saw but I would like to see her again."

NUMB

The Murtaughs & The Carones

"Hi young man, it seems you're going to start working here pretty soon," Mr. Geraldo greeted Ed.

"Thank you sir, I'll do my best to be a good employee," Ed Carone said, grateful he got the job.

"You'll start training so you'll learn what your job requires. There are many things you have to learn but you're a smart man, welcome to our team." Mr. Geraldo shook Ed's hand.

All the way home, Ed felt like he wanted to jump from one foot to the other, to share his happiness with everyone in the street.

"Mom, Dad! I got the job, I got the job!" Ed was shouting so even his neighbors could hear the good news.

"We're so proud of the man you have become, now. I'm okay that we came to America, now that we see you spreading your wings, we feel like we did a good job. We had made a good decision, your life will get better and better and ours, too. You see Ed, when parents see their children doing well and going in the right direction, their lives get easier, they get healthier because happiness is the best medicine," Rose said in Italian.

"I know mom, you already look younger and more beautiful than you were," Ed said hugging her.

Ed's father had no words to say, but he looked in his son's eyes with pride.

Ed hugged his father and whispered in his ear, "Thank you, Dad."

The job wasn't too far away and for Ed, it was a nice trip back and forth to work and soon, he learned what he had to do. His supervisor was pleased to see how fast his student got

NUMB

it, how good he worked with the printing equipment. The supervisor knew Ed Carone would certainly promote soon to a higher level, he could see how much Ed wanted to learn more, to do more.

One day, when Ed came back from work, he hugged his mother and said, "Mom, I heard there will be another charity event at Saint Basil church, are we going to participate? Are you going to bake more cakes?"

"Do you want me to? I know why son." She smiled at him. "And yes, I will bake lots of cakes to thank God for his help."

"Yes, please, I want to go there. I hope to see that girl again, she has such a strong and simple name, I love her name, Anne, Anne!" Ed chanted to his mother.

Ed worked all week long then was ready to go to Saint Basil church and sell his mother's cakes for raising funds to help their favorite church. He noticed more and more Irish and other Catholic people were attending the church services.

The day for charity fund rising event came and his designated table was closer to the entrance and for Ed, this was a good sign. Meaning, he would be able to see Anne when she came in. He took all the cakes his mother baked and set up his table trying to make it as beautiful as he could.

He wasn't sure her parents would be a part of the bake sale, but Anne told him that she wanted to be a part of it. She said that her parents also went to another Catholic church closer to their house, alternating their attendance for services, but she would try to convince them to come to St. Basil church for the charity fundraising.

"Ed, you did such a great job the way you set up your table!" the priest told him. "All those cakes look so good and they smell divine. Your mom must have baked for days and days before you brought them to sell here. Your family is a good family."

Ed thanked the priest his eyes were busy watching the door.

Fiorella and Anne entered the church hall, holding heavy boxes full with cookies.

As soon as Ed saw them, he rushed towards them to help them by taking as many boxes as he could from their arms.

Fiorella showed him their table and he put the boxes on it. She thanked him for his help.

Anne said, "Hi," and she went back to bring more boxes.

Ed joined her and on the way to the place where the boxes were. "I don't know if you remember I told you about me getting a job?"

"I'm so glad for you and of course I remember what we talked about. So now, you work every day," she said happy to walk with such a handsome guy next to her.

"Yes, I could work every Sunday, but this Sunday, I preferred to come here. I knew you'd be here."

Anne cheeks turned a rosy color. "How did you know I was coming?"

"I asked my father to ask his friend, Mr. Molineri, and he said that his daughter, Fiorella, was going to the charity bake sale and that she would be helped by you."

"I'm glad you asked," she said looking down.

Ed couldn't believe she said this. "I'll see you at the end of the bake sale and I can take you home, if you want?"

"I'm glad you can take me home, so Fiorella will go home with her father. He offered to take me home, but now I can go with you, thank you."

Ed was selling with so much joy that people were feeling attracted to his table. His table was emptied before anybody else's. His mom's cakes were a hit.

"Hi Ed, thank you for helping us," Fiorella said. "Hope to see you again. My dad told me that you got the job. Good for

NUMB

you, congratulations. And thank you for taking Anne home. You've saved my dad a trip."

"It's my pleasure and thank you so much for your kind words." He said goodbye to Mr. Molineri and turned to Anne. "Would you like to walk a little or are you too tired?"

"No, I'm not that tired, let's walk." Anne nodded.

"Don't worry, you won't be home late. I'll take care, so you'll be home on time."

The large avenue they were walking along was crowded more than other days, because the weather was so welcoming. Young and not so young couples were enjoying the beautiful weather. It looked like love was in the air as people were smiling to each other like they knew. Ed was walking next to Anne and words weren't necessary to express their happiness. Two very young hearts were meeting for the first time without saying much.

"I told my parents about you, that you're Italian and they seem to be okay with me seeing you at the bake sale, they knew you'll be there. How they knew, I have no idea. Maybe they checked the vendor's list at the church. My parents are smart and they know what to do to protect us," she said.

"I'm so glad you came today, Anne," Ed said.

"I am too."

When they were close to Ann's home, Ed wanted the trip to last a lot longer, to spend more time with this beautiful, blonde girl. "Unfortunately, we have to say goodbye. I hope to see you again."

"Yes, I'd like to see you again, too," Anne said, looking up in Ed's eyes.

"Are you going to your church on the south side of the city? I know there are few." Ed tried to get the name of the church that she was going to.

"Yes, we used to go to St. Michael the Archangel Catholic Church on the South Shore. Do you remember I told you that my parents used to alternate churches but they love St. Basil Catholic church? It was opened in 1909, it's absolutely majestic, but it became too Polish. I mean people were talking only in their Polish language and it made us feel uncomfortable. Why don't they speak English? Look at you, you're Italian, but you have learned English. Anyway, I don't understand it. So my family started looking for a church where they could feel at home and they could understand the service, the priest's message."

"I'm impressed. Please tell me more about this. I love God and it makes me feel good to see that you are the same way."

"You know most Irish people I know live in Bridgeport; it's a neighborhood where men, the bread winners of the house, work as bricklayers, meat packers. Do you want to know an astonishing thing?" Anne asked.

"I would." Ed nodded willing to listen to the beautiful girl next to him.

"The Great Chicago Fire from 1871 started in the barn of an Irish couple that has same first names as my parents, Patrick and Catherine, but their last name was O'Leary, thank God, not Murtaugh!" Anne told Ed, educating him about the history of the city they lived in, Chicago.

"What else did your parents tell you about our city? I learned more from you than I've learned in school," Ed said.

"You're right, my father being a teacher in Ireland, has been always fascinated by history, traditions, events, wars, and economics ups and downs, and he used to read a lot. Now, working such long hours, he doesn't have the same time like he had back in Ireland, but he still finds time to educate himself and share his knowledge with us. It amazes me to see him being a hod- carrier and to be so knowledgeable."

NUMB

Ed smiled at her in wonderment of her beauty and her knowledge.

"Let me tell my parents that I came back and, hopefully they will let me stay a little bit longer with you." Anne ran into the kitchen where she knew her mom was waiting for her. Catherine was there and she was ready to go to bed after seeing Anne home. Anne kissed her mother and in a few words told her who Ed was. She asked permission to go back to him and talk a little bit longer.

"I remember you telling me about him last time when you went with Fiorella to a party at this young man's house, right?" Catherine said.

"Oh, you have such a good memory! Mom, you're so young, smart and beautiful," Anne said.

"Are you complimenting me, so I'll let you talk to that young man, a little longer?"

"No, I know you'll let me go back." Anne laughed. "I'm telling you what I think about you, because I love you. Do you know what the subject of our conversation was? I've been telling him all that I know about our city. He knows the city but not what made the city and its history."

"Okay, go back but don't stay too long," Catherine warned.

"I promise. Love you mom," Anne said running outside.

Ed stood up when he saw her. He'd found a bench and had sat there waiting for her. "I'm happy they let you come back, I enjoy being with you."

"Me too," Anne said and a beautiful smile lighting her face.

The rule of contrast was working its magic between these two young, beautiful human beings.

"So, let's get back to talking about our church." Anne smiled. "You see because we, Irish people speak the English language, we didn't have to go through what the other immigrants went through, as you know. It was a lot easier to adapt to the rules of America. I mean it became easier to adapt, understand what the requirements were. In school, I had a couple of German girls and I could see how hard they had to work to achieve what for me was a piece of cake! Ed, I had never talked so much, let's go home and we can continue our history lessons next time when we see each other. You have to go to work, so go and get some rest."

"Are you tired? I'm asking because I don't want to leave!" Ed grinned.

Anne giggled. "I'm not tired at all but I do want to be with you again."

"Me too, when? I can only be around after church service."

"Let me see if my mom will let me come to your church. I say my mom, because my dad always says it doesn't matter what church you go to as long as you go and be with Christ."

"I kind of agree with what your father said. God is only one and he is everywhere." Ed nodded.

"This was one thing I was afraid of, I wasn't sure if Italians loved God as much as we do...well, most people do," Anne said.

"Now, it seems that it will be my turn to talk about the Italian devotion to religion, culture and freedom. You see, when I was in school, I read about my heritage. I wanted to know as much as possible, because like your father and you, I love history. I love not only my people's history, that I'm proud of but history in general. I'm fascinated by how much you can find out, things that you never thought was possible. Anne, I shouldn't say this but, I'm in love with you," Ed said, without breathing.

Anne gasped as she stared at him then ran inside her home, that's how scared she was at hearing what Ed said.

He waited a few more minutes, realizing that he shouldn't have interrupted the magic with his love statement but

NUMB

somehow, he was happy. He knew Anne had the same feelings for him.

All the way back to his house, Ed sang his favorite songs.

Rose Carone greeted her son, "I'm glad you're home. Now I can go to sleep. How was your day son?"

"Mom, I love Anne and I want to marry her," Ed answered, short and clear, but scared of what he was going to hear next.

"What did you just say? Say it again?"

"Mom, she is so beautiful and smart. We talked for more than two hours about our city history, about our love for God and about our families. I cannot believe how much she knows. Her father was a teacher in Ireland and he loves history."

"So, he's a teacher here?" Rose asked.

"No, her father is a hod- carrier now. He needed a special authorization to work as a teacher."

"Well, I am glad you like this girl. Let's go to sleep now, get a good night rest, I love you." Rose kissed her son's cheek.

Ed went to bed and for the entire night in his head, he had 'history lessons' with Anne.

Work was going well and Ed was making decent money, saving most of it and helping his parents too.

The history lessons continued and Ed was more and more in love with his lovely Irish girl. "Anne, your parents are such nice people. I feel comfortable with them. Actually, I feel good with all of you," Ed stated as they were walking towards her house.

"My parents said that I can bring you home if you want," she said.

"You're asking me if I want to? I am honored and happy to do so! Are you sure?" he asked.

"Yes, I'm sure. Ed did you know that my family calls me Babe?" Anne asked.

"You told me before I think, but I thought you were joking." Ed laughed. "I'll call you Babe on special occasions but I love calling you Anne."

"No, from now on you can call me Babe, we are family!" She laughed with him. "But you're right. It's more serious when you call me Anne."

"Babe, Anne, do you want to marry me?" Ed asked. He was afraid she would run away again.

She paused and looked deep into his eyes. "Yes, I want to marry you, but you have to ask my father first," she answered, calm and serious.

Ed's hands were shaking, he was so happy Anne said 'yes' accepting to share her life with him, to start a family. He knew he would have to look for a place to live with his wife and raise children. Ed as an Italian immigrant even if he was so young when he came to America, had lived only in his Italian neighborhood. He wanted to keep living close to his work and his family. He remembered one of the visits to the St. Rita Catholic Church.

One day when he had a school break, he decided to check as many Catholic churches as he could. He went to the first and only Italian Church in the City, built in 1886, before his father came to Chicago. It was a remarkable repository for devotional art with spectacular stained glass windows and a splendid altar. He'd liked the church so much that he wanted to live close to it. Chicago's most colorful Italian sector was on the city's North side, where his family lived. It was like an extension of Sicily as most of the people originated from the small towns surrounding Palermo, his father's city.

Ed always enjoyed the food stands, rides and games and the "flying angels." He knew that getting married represented a milestone, being an important step in his life. Growing up, he noticed there were almost no divorces and very little desertion.

NUMB

Ed wanted to keep their tradition by staying married and raising children.

Looking for a home to take his bride there, he knew he had to avoid the 'death corner' Milton and Oak streets. As the name said, there were about ten murders – usually unsolved– per year. Most of these murders, police blamed on the Mafia, but the residents were convinced that all the police were on the take and that they were only making excuses for their corruption or their incompetence.

"I'd better bring Anne with me. It'll be a lot easier to decide where we want to live. One thing I know for sure, it has to be closer to my work place," he told himself, going back home.

Next morning on his way to work, Ed couldn't wait any longer and asked her, "Anne, when do you think would be the best time for me to come and talk to your parents? I miss you."

"Let me talk to them and I give you the answer Sunday in church. Or if I see dad in a good mood, I'll ask him then, is that okay with you?"

"No, I want to come right now and marry you right there, right now!" Ed exclaimed.

"You're just crazy!" She laughed. "I want it too, but we have to do it right. Oh, and I have a surprise for you."

"Tell me, tell me," Ed urged impatiently.

"I found a seamstress for my wedding dress and I already got the fabric."

"What? You found the wedding dress and I haven't even talked to your father? Well, I'm happy you're moving so fast though."

"When dad comes home today from work, I'll ask him and mom to arrange a day for you to come and ask my parents to let me marry you. I wish it were tomorrow Ed. You've made me happy and I promise, I'll be the best wife, I love you."

"I feel the same way. You are all I think about. Okay, wait to see your dad in a good mood, like you first said. I want to be sure his answers is yes."

Sunday was approaching and Ed felt on the verge of panic, waiting for Anne's answer.

Anne saw him there in church and asked her parents to let her talk to Ed.

They agreed but she had to be quick, to not spend too much time with the man.

She would have liked to tell them he wasn't an ordinary man. That he would be her husband and the father of her kids, but she was thankful they agreed. Ann came closer to Ed and said, "Tonight at 7 p.m. can you come?"

"I'll be there. Love you, thank you," Ed said.

Anne went back to be with her parents.

Ed rushed home to change his clothes, buy flowers and a bottle of wine.

Giuseppe Carone, Ed's father, joined his son, he showed him the best wine to buy and together they showed up a few minutes before 7 p.m. at the Murtaughs.

Anne's brothers, Patrick, Thomas and Michael, all of them came together to the door, checking their guests head to toe and keeping them outside to be sure they were good people.

Giuseppe and Ed Carone looked so festive, wearing their best suits and holding wine and the flowers.

Finally, Mr. Murtaugh came to the door, shook his guest's hands, and invited them inside the house. The Murtaughs home was located in a very nice neighborhood where the Parish of St. Rita's Catholic Church and school were close by.

"Mr. Murtaugh, thank you for opening your door for my father, Giuseppe Carone and I, Ed Carone. It's an honor, thank you," Ed stated, giving Patrick Murtaugh the bottle of wine.

NUMB

Behind him was Catherine, holding up her youngest daughter.

"Mrs. Catherine, this is for you," Ed said, offering her a large, beautiful bouquet of flowers.

"Thank you so much, you're so sweet. Please come in and sorry for my boys keeping you both outside."

"Oh, don't worry, my sisters would do the same thing," Ed said letting his father enter the home before him.

The food's aroma made them feel welcomed. Mr. Murtaugh, Anne's father didn't want to have a real sit-down dinner, he wanted to look tougher, but his wife had the last word. She knew a lot more about Ed and his family than her husband knew, and she wanted to treat them right, so they had a nice sit-down dinner.

"So, I understand that you have something to ask me," Patrick Murtaugh stated, looking into Ed's eyes.

Poor Ed was sweating.

His father noticed right away and for a second, he remembered back in Palermo and Sicily in a lot poorer conditions, how he'd asked Rose's hand from her father.

It was a long tradition and his son kept it alive.

"Mr. Murtaugh," Giuseppe said. "I hope you don't mind I came with my son to enjoy seeing him asking for your beautiful daughter's hand. It's a tradition we have in our family. It is the same thing that happened when I asked for my wife's hand in marriage and I am proud for my son respecting our traditions."

"Please call me Patrick and may I call you Giuseppe?"

"Of course, thank you," Giuseppe said.

"All right, now, that's the ice is broken, let's see what this handsome man has to say," Patrick said, looking at Ed.

"Sir, I love your daughter and I came here to ask you to give us your blessings for Babe to become my wife," Ed said, without breathing.

"Let's see what she says, but first, I want to know how are you going to provide for your new family?" Patrick asked.

"Sir, I'm working for a large printing company and I want to learn as much as I can. So, later on, I would be so grateful to have my own business. I'm not afraid of work and I would do everything for my family," Ed vowed while waiting Anne, but she wasn't in the room.

"I wish you good luck. It seems like you'll really have a printing company someday," Patrick said. "I see you doing this. I saw you several times in church and you made a good impression on my wife and me. And I know for sure that our daughter loves you, she already told us. Yes, you have our blessings to marry Anne, our Babe." He stood up.

Ed and his father did the same and they shook hands.

It was the handshaking agreement of founding a family based on love and honesty.

Catherine came in the room where Anne was and just hugged her daughter with happy tears in her eyes. "Anne, your dad likes Ed, I know it. I saw it in his eyes and soon you'll get married!"

"Oh, thank God, I prayed for this all day, thank you for listening to me!" She ran into the other room where her love was.

"Babe," her father said. "Giuseppe and Ed asked for our blessings to let you be Ed's wife and we accepted. Good luck, my sweet girl, I love you."

"Dad, thank you so much, I'll never be too far from you and my family," Anne said crying.

NUMB

The dinner went well. Everyone was full of joy and laughter as the newly-engaged couple had their hands locked in love and hope for their new life.

The month of May 1914 came with cherry blooms and a nice breeze, so needed after the Chicago winter. Beautiful and simple was how Anne wanted her wedding to be. Saint Basil church had the altar decorated for Ed and Anne's wedding. Love was in the air, making everyone feel blessed to witness the young couple becoming one in God's name.

Anne's blonde hair was a lovely cascade of waves on her shoulders and her dress hugged her body graciously. She was wearing a narrow shining band on her forehead and her veil went all the way to the floor.

Ed gazed at his bride with so much love that many couples in the audience were holding hands bringing back memories of their own weddings. The church was impressive and the newly married couple knew that what had just happened under God's eyes was something that would last forever, sealed their commitment to each other.

May 26th 1914, was the day a new family united in Catholic faith, set the foundation for the fruits of their union to come in this world.

The apartment they rented was really close to Ed's work place and this made his wife, Anne, happy to see him coming home as soon as he was done with work.

"Anne, if I'd had you in my life a long time ago, I would've saved a lot more money," he said.

"What do you mean? How could you have saved more money?" Anne asked.

"Well, I'm not stopping here and there to grab something for lunch now. You send me to work with my lunch packed. Thank you, your food is so much better and I noticed how much I was spending before."

"You better save a lot, because our baby will arrive here soon," she said smiling.

"Did you say our baby? What are you talking about? If I hadn't said something about my lunch you weren't going to say anything about our baby? When did you find out?" Ed was so excited he was speaking way too fast. "Babe, I love you. Let's go and tell our families about our baby!" He grabbed her up and was dancing with his wife in his arms.

Laughing at his exuberance, Anne warned, "We should wait a little bit longer and tell them about the baby later on."

"Okay, but I don't think I can do it! Don't forget, I am Italian and I feel like a volcano inside. I just have to let everybody know how happy I am! I will just burst if I can't share it!"

She kept shaking her head at what a happy husband she had. Ed was always so upbeat. "If you cannot wait, let's go and tell our parents only but to nobody else, promise?"

"I promise. Let's go and make them happy!"

Not too long afterward, they told the parents she was expecting, her mother, Catherine Murtaugh, brought a heavy package to their apartment. She opened the box and let her daughter to unpack the beautiful gift. Patrick and Catherine had saved money to purchase gifts for their first grand baby, clothes and toys filled the room bringing a nice feeling in the room.

Mother and daughter spent time removing tags and washing the baby outfits then put the toys in order.

When Ed came home, the entire home had a new different look and he loved each detail of the new style. Giuseppe and

NUMB

Rose we're bringing fresh fruits and vegetables from their garden, to be sure Anne had the best food for her and the baby.

"Mom," she called Rose Carone, her mother-in-law. "One thing I know for sure, Italians are crazy about babies, right?" Anne asked.

Ed laughed. "Babe, you do know my mom doesn't speak English, right? But look at her eyes, she understood everything you said! I wonder how my mom and dad will talk to their grand baby, but God has a special way to show love and for sure, both of them will find a way. Hopefully our baby will teach my parents English." He kept laughing.

"I'm not even worried about this. They will talk to our son or daughter. They *will* be guided by God and their hearts. I know the baby and them will love each other.

8 Months later, Joseph Carone, a beautiful baby boy filled Anne's house with joy. Joseph was healthy and he seemed to understand his grandma's Italian language that sounded like music to his ears. Every time Rose was holding him, he was content and happy. When the new parents wanted Joseph to sleep, they put him in Rose's arms and he would fall asleep right away. A magic connection existed between Joseph and Rose.

A year later....

"Babe, our lives have changed a lot with our son's coming, I feel more responsible now. Thank God, I have work and I can provide for my family. You are a gift from God and I adore you more and more every day."

Anne so loved this tender, caring man and she knew she was the lucky one. "I know you save money so we can have our own printing company, one day. If we can achieve such a dream, our kids are going to have a much better life."

"Did you say kids? We're going to have one more baby?"

"Yes, Ed, I'm pregnant!" Her beautiful hair was covering her porcelain face.

Ed hugged her pulling her really close to him. He moved a strand of hair from her face and kissed her passionately.

Anne became still in his arms. "One more baby, we are so blessed, if we're going to have a girl, I would like to call her Rosemary to honor your mom, Rose. I think this will make her feel loved, respected and appreciated,"

"Let me ask you something, what about if we have a boy? Are we going to call him Giuseppe, like my father? I'm kidding. We live in America we should name our kids American names to blend in easier, don't you think? I don't think that my dad would be offended. He knows what it means to have a foreign name. We'll give them American names we can choose one when the time comes."

Joseph was almost 2 years old when a beautiful baby girl became his sister.

"Ed, do you remember our conversation about baby names? Do you remember when I said I'd like to name our baby Rosemary if we are lucky enough to have a baby girl?" Anne asked.

"Yes, I remember and I loved the idea. So, her name will be Rosemary? My mother will be so happy."

"Yes, I think it's a good name for her."

Joseph knew he had to take care of his sister because Anne, his mother, taught him what to do, she showed him how to be gentle and how to play with his sister.

Ed Carone kept working at the printing company where he was working, where lots of Italians and migrants were making

NUMB

a decent living. But Ed's dream needed more knowledge, more money to see it become real.

"Now, that the baby is here, I mean Rosemary, what about inviting our families and friends together and have a nice party to celebrate her coming in this world. For her baptism" Ed suggested.

"Ed, I cannot take the Italian from your blood. Every time we have a party, it was because you wanted to. All those parties cost money. We can baptize her and have a nice dinner at the house, after we come back from church. We can invite the priest. It'll be nice and our parents will love the idea. Did you forget about the printing company, our printing company?" Anne tried to convince her hardworking husband to give up the idea of a big party.

"Babe, we didn't throw a party with our first child when he was born. Now we have two kids and I want to share our happiness with everyone, but if you don't think we should, I'll agree with you. Our children's future is more important than a party," Ed said, without being upset.

"Come here, I just want to kiss you," Anne said to her sweet husband.

Ed came closer to her and he was kissed with fire and passion, his heart beating ever faster.

Spring of 1917, America decided to bring military contributions to the Allied effort by entering the World War 1, that had originated in Europe

America civilians provided extra food and fuel to the war effort. Rose and Giuseppe Carone had a victory garden, cultivating vegetables to follow the government propaganda that asked people to help the troops. The entire economy was mobilized to win the war. So, everyone helped in one way or another, even by turning the furnace off or using less electricity, even the smallest sacrifice helped the American troops. The ocean was always considered a safe border for America and being a nation of immigrants, it was difficult to pick a side, the Allies or the Central Power and their help was decisive to the Allied effort. The families had to work harder to bring home what they needed so that no one would feel the war that had spread its wings, ugly, bloody wings.

Europe was torn apart by the war that was leaving marks on people, buildings, economic situations and leaving behind tragic devastation.

Ed and Anne tried not to let the kids feel the sacrifices they were making like any other family, to help the country that helped them.

America was still the best place to live, have a business and raise a family. Rosemary was growing surrounded by the love and care of her family, with loving grandparents, a mother and father watching over her, for each step she took.

Her older brother, Joseph was her constant companion, everywhere she went and everything she did. Soon, the Carone family grew again with another baby boy, Earl Carone.

"Babe, we're growing like a good Catholic, Christian family, and nothing makes me happier than to see our home full of our kid's laughter, screams, fights, but also with love. Look how happy those kids have made us. I couldn't be happy without you, my beautiful wife."

"I know and you would like to have a party, right?" Anne teased, as she knew he was leading up to this.

"How did you know? Yes, I'm dying to have a party, but I know we have to save money for the printing company and I think our dream is getting a little closer and closer. A few

NUMB

more years then you and I will be the owners of a printing company."

The family went to bed early to be ready for the next work day. Ed went to his job where he was feeling so needed. His coworkers were asking him all the time to help them with different issues they were having. His knowledge made them ask him first before going up to their superiors. Ed became the manager of his co-worker's group and he was bringing home more money.

Things seemed to go well. Everyone was healthy, including the grandparents and the kids.

"Babe, I want to buy a nice dress for you, can we go to the big store?" Ed asked his wife. The kids can be taken care of by our parents, they'd be happy to spend time with them. You have to let me spoil you a little? You work all day, all the time, please, let me do this for you?"

"Okay, I'll let you spoil me one time, remember one time only," Anne said.

Ed and his wife arranged to have half a day for them. She chose a beautiful dress and even if Ed suggested another color, Anne liked the dress she chose. It was hugging her body, showing her beautiful curves, even if she gave birth to three children, her body didn't show it.

Ed looked at like her like he was seeing her for the first time. He didn't like the fact that the dress she'd chosen was black. The color made her look thinner, but she didn't need that, she *was* thin and beautiful. But if this was what she wanted, he agreed and paid for it.

Not too long after that beautiful half a day spent together,

Rosemary didn't feel good, having chills and body aches.

Anne got so scared that she called the doctor that took care of the children.

The doctor checked Rosemary and he asked Anne to follow him in another room, where he wanted to talk to her, so no one else could hear. "Ma'am, do you read the newspapers? I know your husband works at a printing company. We have an epidemic influenza. Rosemary is only 2 years old, I'm afraid your sweet daughter has got it.

"Doctor, from where could she get it? I know what influenza is and I do read the newspapers. In October this year, more than ten thousands people died of this in our city. Doctor, please tell me that you're wrong!" she begged.

"Mrs. Carone, I wish I was wrong. I pray to God that I am and I'll do my best to save your precious, beautiful girl, but we're dealing with things we aren't prepared for, it could be bronchitis, pneumonia but I believe it's that horrible Spanish influenza that filled our cemeteries. I shouldn't talk to you this way but I have to prepare you because there's not much I can do."

Unfortunately, he was right—their sweet baby girl soon lost her life. She became a victim of that horrible epidemic influenza, nothing the doctor and her family did could save her life. Rosemary was only two years, three month and twenty nine days old!

Ed and his wife were devastated. Poor Joseph couldn't understand what was going on, but seeing his parents crying he started crying, holding his mom's hand. The joy and beauty of their young family suddenly took a tragic turn, everything changed and Ed and Anne didn't know how to face the tragedy but one thing helped them. Joseph didn't leave his parents alone even at night time.

Anne's life as a mother became more intense, she had to

NUMB

work hard to put a smile on her face, but God blessed them with another little angel, a handsome boy. They named him Edward. His smile brightened their lives. He played with Joseph all day long and their mother could do more things around the house. He was the balm for his parent's wounds.

Every time Anne was playing with Edward, she could see Rosemary, swirling from heaven around the children. Her two boys were healthy and Ed and his wife thanked God every day for keeping them safe and healthy. When the Spanish influenza hit their family, they were sure the contagious flu would attack Joseph, their firstborn child, most of the cases being children his age.

"Anne, I will never understand why Rosemary had to be taken away from us! I find myself at work talking to her trying to play with her until I realize she is gone," Ed said with tears running down his face.

"I know it happens to me all the time but being so busy it helped me to stay normal. My heart was broken then our newly born brought us the joy of parenthood back. I feel sorry for Joseph; he looks at me with his huge innocent eyes, asking questions that only he would have. Ed, our older son misses his sister. Do you remember how wonderfully they played together? He never made her cry he was so protective, so loveable. Joseph will be a real gentle man. He will be a good husband and father, I just know it."

"I would like to ask you how you know all these things, but for some reason, I prefer to believe all the things you say. Don't lose your smile, I love you," Ed said wrapping his arms around his hurting wife.

Edward Carone was growing into a healthy boy and his parents were ready to bring another soul in their family and this is how Catherine Carone was born the month of March, 1920. Anne couldn't be happier to have another girl blessing their family.

"Anne," the doctor said. "This girl is so beautiful but she has some respiratory problems, I will do all I can to see what is going on."

"What do you mean? Will she survive? Doctor, you have to save her. Save my baby!" Anne was screaming at the top of her lungs.

Ed took the boys into another room and asked his mother, Rose to take care of them. Anne's mother, Catherine had been taking care of the newborn baby girl.

The doctor didn't leave the room, trying to make the baby breathe better. He called Ed in and told him, "Ed, this poor beautiful baby cannot make it. She can't breathe on her own. I took her to her mother to be fed and she is not doing well. I don't know how to tell your wife, this will be such a tragedy, after she already lost a girl. I called one of my colleagues and he will be here in a couple minutes, so hopefully, he can do more than I did. Ed, she isn't the only baby born like this, it is a condition that doesn't forgive. Be strong."

"Doctor, you have to save my baby girl, do everything you can and your colleague too, don't let her die," Ed said crying like never before. He looked up and talked to God, "What did we do wrong? Why can't we have a girl? We love our kids. Please don't take her away from us!"

Anne asked her mother to help her get off the bed so she could check on her Catherine, like she called her to honor her mom's name.

"Babe, you shouldn't be walking, please go back to bed," Ed said.

"How's she doing?" she asked with her eyes wide open.

"He has a another doctor coming, he's our doctor's colleague and together, they will do everything possible to save our baby. Let's pray, as that's all we can do." Ed held his

NUMB

wife that was so weak after just giving birth just that morning. They sat next to their baby girl and prayed, asking God to let their baby live. Tears and prayers were filling the space around the baby.

"Anne, let's try to feed her again, maybe she can breathe better this time," the doctor suggested.

She took the baby in her arms and started feeding her daughter, while she was crying and praying. The baby was holding her mother's finger, like saying, *"I love you mom."* The touch of that tiny finger brought hope into Anne's heart.

"Ed, this is my colleague, Dr. Walsh. When your wife is ready, he will check the baby." Dr. Johnson said.

Ed shook the doctor's hand and begged him to save his daughter's life.

A few hours after Dr. Walsh arrived to their home, Ed and Anne's hopes seemed to be lost.

Both doctors looked at each other sadly. The poor girl had only a few more hours to live. They tried everything they knew, both of them being excellent doctors, but sometimes even with their knowledge, saving lives was impossible. Tiny Catherine was one of those unfortunate cases, she took her last breath in her mother's arms, the same day she was born....

The doctors left the house, sad and so unhappy that they couldn't save that tiny, precious human being.

Rose Carone and her daughters, Ed Carone's sisters Cara, Lillian and Lena, were waiting in another room to see what the two doctors were able to do. The room became a prayer chapel.

Anne loved her sister in laws and she wanted them to be with her during this hard time. She found that she couldn't move... she was like a statue. No tears and no expression on her face, but when everyone entered the room, she exploded into tears. "I lost another girl. I want to die!" she screamed so loud that the neighbors came to see what had happened at the young family's house.

Soon, two different families from two different sides of the world became united in sorrow and suffering. Brothers and sisters, mothers and fathers became one entity pouring love over the young couple that lost another girl.

Ed Carone gathered what he needed to open his own printing company. One afternoon, he took his family for a walk and Anne noticed her husband's excitement. "Where are we going?" she asked looking around, this isn't a place to take us for a walk, the park is in the opposite direction."

"I know but I wanted all of you to be with me when I show you our future business place," Ed said, proud that his dream had a place already. "Anne, I know we are young but I am convinced we can do it."

"So where is the place?" she asked

"Do you see that building right in front of us? Doesn't it look good?" Ed asked his wife.

The boys looked too, but they were busy running after each other.

"I like it, so tell me what exactly do you have in mind? I want to help you."

"Well, the hardest thing will be to find people to work like I do, but God will send them our way. There are so many immigrants looking for jobs. Anne, it's our turn to help people like my father and your father had been helped. Our church will help us find them."

"You keep saying *we*. I don't want to be the co-owner of your business. I know I used to say our business all the time

NUMB

but, I still want to have a girl. I want to be a good mother to our children, but I will learn and I'll help you every day," she promised, kissing her husband.

The boys stopped running and they came closer to their parents, waiting to be kissed, too.

Ed looked at his sons and he swore this image would be in his mind forever. "You and you, all are my reason to succeed and I promise I will." He was determined to work hard and make his new business a success.

Later after they were home, Ed and the boys came into the kitchen where Anne was preparing dinner.

Ed grabbed his boys and spun them around them room.

Anne was slowly coming back to reality after losing Catherine, her baby girl, but it was still a struggle.

"Sweet Babe," Ed called to her. "Come and join us. We love this happy dance, look how much the boys like it."

"It's okay, I can see from here. Dinner will be ready soon," she said, and her face was missing the smile her family was used to.

Ed noticed his wife's expression, no tears, and no happiness, just a face belonging to someone that was 'not' there. He knew the only remedy for his wife's condition was time.

He was getting really busy with his new business, looking for help, workers to hire, equipment and all the things a printing company needed to function. He only hoped things would get better.

"Ed, you've made me proud of you," his father said one day in Italian.

"I promised you I'd make you proud of me. It's hard but all that I learned to run such a company, it helped more than anything, but what helped me the most was you! If you hadn't brought me to America, I wouldn't be able to have my dream achieved. Dad, I'll be grateful forever, thank you," Ed told Giuseppe, his father.

"No, be grateful to God, he did everything. I was only his tool. I love my grandkids, now you should go back to your work. You have so much to do."

Ed Carone knew where to look for good workers and sooner than he had expected, he found himself with almost everything he needed to open the doors of his printing company.

Anne decorated and furnished his office, as she was proud of her husband. "Ed, today after church service, two ladies approached me and asked about your new business, can you believe it? I'm so glad for you, you worked so hard and now, it's time to get the harvest from your efforts."

"How did they find out? Babe, you've made me happy and I would like to hear more."

"Well, it seems like you printed some phone books for one of those lady's friends. The quality and the price was a lot better than she ever had before. When I heard what she had to say, I felt so proud of you. I gave them your business information and soon, you'll have new clients."

"Thank you Babe. Yes, the company is going well and the new people I hired are smart, hard workers. If everything goes well and if God wants it, we can buy a larger home. I know this will make you so happy, right?" Ed asked his wife. Hoping that a new house would keep his wife so busy that she would think less about Rosemary and Catherine, the girls they lost. He hoped she would be more preoccupied getting the house furnished and decorated, the boys were in school and all the things she would have to take care of living in a larger new house. His heart was suffering to see how deeply it hurt and how much the pain hit his beautiful wife. He couldn't talk about his girls either. He knew they needed more children and

NUMB

especially a girl... a healthy girl that would live.

The family spent a few good hours together in order to decide which house to purchase. Ed wanted all of them to be a part of such an important decision. "Joseph, what do you think about this one?" he asked his oldest son, knowing that he'd suggested a brick house.

"I like this one. The other ones didn't have two stories," Joseph answered, making Ed proud of his son, he really paid attention and took the trip seriously.

"Babe, I cannot believe what Joseph said," Ed told his wife later.

"What did he say? I hope he liked it because I love this house," already answering Ed's next question.

"Joseph is only 6 years old and I'm really impressed with what he said. You know I thought the boys took this trip as a play trip and I didn't expect them to look at the houses we showed them. Joseph said he likes the house because it's a two story and the others were smaller, can you believe it? Smart boy! Like his father!" Ed exclaimed, hoping to make his wife smile, and she did smile. His heart was so happy to see that lost smile coming back! He looked up and thanked God. He knew the new house would become a sweet home for his family that was hit so hard by tragedy.

Lots of hopes were attached to this house, a larger family and a better life.

"Ed, I feel better now, something inside my soul is telling me we should buy this house and also, I think it God's way to bring more kids here, hopefully a girl," Anne said.

"It seems like we all love this house it is two apartment house, and the neighborhood is exactly what we want for our family. Okay, let's make an offer and I know it will be ours. Anne, you'll be on a mission to make this house a home. Your soul will be shining everywhere."

His wife smiled and the way she was holding her boys close to her made him think she was protecting her family with love and fearless, she would never let anyone hurt them, it showed in her eyes.

On the way back home, Ed was picturing his wife happy. He prayed to have her smiling like before the tragedy struck them.

"Ed, the boys cannot wait to move to the new neighborhood," Anne told him. "Joseph and Edward said they already have friends living there."

"Perfect, this makes me happy! One thing I know for sure, it's a good safe community. The schools are better than we have now and you know how I am, everything for my family," Ed said kissing his beautiful blonde wife.

"How's the business now?" she asked Ed. "Anymore clients from all those ladies from our church? Someone else asked me about you again too."

"Actually, I got a few new clients and most of them have been recommended by your ladies! Babe, you're the boss, you know how to send people my way. Do you know how much our workers love you? They said they understand the instructions a lot better from you than from me. Do you think it's my English? Do I have a thick Italian accent?" Ed said, joking. "Because coming to this country at such a young age, I consider myself almost born here."

"Don't be silly, you speak English better than me. I have an accent, not you! But I think they just want to please you, to make you feel proud that you married such a smart beautiful wife!" Anne teased.

"Oh, I don't need reminders to know how lucky I am, I love you Babe!" he said.

NUMB

Christmas of 1924 brought the Carone family an amazing gift, another baby boy on his way to join his handsome brothers. Beau Carone was born at the end of January of 1925 making his family blessed with 3 boys now.

"Ed, of course I am blessed and happy to have three handsome boys but my heart is crying for a girl. I want a girl! I know I shouldn't talk like this, when I just gave birth to our son, but I'm just telling you how I feel," she said with tears in her eyes.

"Babe, I understand and sometimes my mind is busy with the same thoughts, but I try to believe that time will come."

"You're right. There are so many people giving Novenas to our priest to pray for, because they have no children and they want to be blessed with at least one child, and look at us, we have been blessed with three boys, a business, and a nice house with good neighbors. Ed, I think maybe I committed a sin by saying what I just said? I will ask Father Greg to forgive me."

"Sweet Babe, what about if you write a Novena like other people do? Then give it to Father Gregg and St. Rita will send us her blessings. I remembered that a Novena is a series of prayers that are said for nine straight days as the Apostles and the Blessed Virgin Mary spent in prayer between Ascension Thursday and Pentecost Sunday."

Anne agreed. "My mother told me that St. Rita is the patron saint of the impossible and it seems like what I would like to have is impossible, so I'll do it. Ed, I forgot to tell you about my dream last night I had a beautiful dream, Lena your sister that died in 1921, soon after you started your business. She came into my dream and she told me that now she is in a peaceful, beautiful place. That she was happy to see how well we all are doing. She told me how sorry she was for her parents when they lost her to tuberculosis and how much she wanted to be with us, to help with the kids. Do you know what made me tell you about my dream? Lena told me to pray to Our Holy Mother, Virgin Mary at Saint Rita church, and to write the Novena! Ed, it is absolutely amazing how God tells us what to do, using different tools! Lena was one of his ways to tell us what to do. Your sister had a huge heart and we liked each other from the first moment we met. I will listen to what she told me to do. How come the both of you told me about the Novena almost at the same time? There are too many signs to not listen to."

Ed smiled sadly. "I wish she would visit me in my dreams too. I loved my sister and her death was hard on our parents. That disease had no cure. I have no idea how she contracted the virus, it was horrible. My parents thought we'd all die of tuberculosis, but it was only her. I miss my sister she would've been such a good aunt for our kids. God rest her in peace." He wiped a tear form the corner of his eye.

Anne hugged her husband and her touch made him feel better.

"We have to get ready for my sister's wedding. It will be a nice one Babe. I'm glad we're going and have some fun," Ed said.

"Lillian is such a beautiful young woman." Anne nodded.

"Yes, I love my sisters and they know it. Even if I'm the oldest, both of them tried to teach me how to behave. They think they know everything. Michael Ramon will be a good husband for my sister. I watched my mom to see if she liked him and I could see how much she agrees with him becoming her son in law. Babe, she loves you and she poured her heart for you when we went through those tough times. You see, even if she doesn't speak English you were able you

NUMB

understand her love. Love doesn't need words...it needs actions and my mom did just that. I know we're lucky to have such a large loving family."

"I need a nice dress for Lillian's wedding; everything I have in my closet doesn't fit me anymore. Those pregnancies made my body ugly, fat and big," she said looking down at her body.

"You can buy all the dresses you want but never say that again. Babe, you're beautiful, your body is curvier now, and I love the way you look. Don't you think you have to be different than you are for me, because I love you," Ed said making his wife forget about the "side effects" of having babies.

Ed didn't lie to her either. Anne had a beautiful well proportioned body where the curves were making beautiful sexy marks. It was impossible to see her walking down the street and to not turn your head and look at her a little longer! Ed was a lucky man and he knew it. His heart had deep scars but God left room enough for happiness.

"Babe, do you remember my sister Cara's wedding? I hope Lilly has as much luck as Cara had. The reason I'm asking is because you were the most beautiful woman there, very elegant and simple. I know you'll be the most beautiful lady this time too."

Anne blushed as she smiled at her sweet husband. She truly didn't think he was right about her beauty.

Ed smiled back at her and winked at her.

"Cara deserves to have a good husband." Anne kept smiling. "Steve works in a factory now, and they're doing really well. Your sisters are happy to live together, that their husbands agreed to be together and help each other with raising their children. It's good for the cousins to play together too. Our boys will have lots of cousins. Cara already had Vincent and Joanne. I don't think they're going to have more children, but we don't know for sure, time will tell."

"I know. Let's hope Lilly will have more than two kids, and then we can say we have a large family, but I think we have more family members than most of our neighbors. Don't you think?" Ed asked.

"Oh, for sure we're a large family and considering I'm going to write a Novena to Our Holy Mother at St. Rita's, soon we'll be an even larger family than we have now," Anne replied. Being sure her prayers would be answered by Virgin Mary, giving her a girl that would live. She just knew her time would come.

Beau was getting taller and stronger, making his brothers happy to teach him what they knew. It was like growing up with private teachers.

Ed's printing company was doing well, as client's recommended his work to their friends.

Anne learned a lot and she helped him anytime she had a chance and when she had to help, someone watched her younger boys. Joseph Carone was almost thirteen years old when his parent's prayers had been answered.

Holy Mother Virgin Mary listened to the meaningful Novena that Anne Carone prayed for along with the priest of St. Rita's church and many of the church goers. She was to have another baby.

August 1928, the weather was so good that people were spending a long time outside enjoying walks along the river. New buildings were framing the beautiful river. The restaurants had terraces outside, umbrellas and chairs so people could sit comfortably for their lunch, dinners and conversations.

This was the day, Dr. Johnson stopped in to check on his patient, Anne Carone who was expecting soon. Dr. Johnson

NUMB

visited other patients in the area and Anne's name wasn't on his list of patients to be visited. But something made him go to her house. After he examined her he said, "Anne, we should get you to the hospital right now. I cannot believe how God brought me here at the right moment."

Anne stood up and the baby didn't want to wait any longer to be born. The baby just rushed out eager to face the world. The Novena to the Holy Mother responded by sending a baby girl to the young Carone family. This baby girl was full of energy from the moment she came into this world.

"Ed, we prayed to our Holy Mother Mary at St. Rita's church. Our girl's name will be Mary Rita, okay?" Anne said with tears in her eyes

"I would never come up with such a logical association of names, Babe. Mary Rita Carone!" Ed exclaimed. "What a beautiful name. I feel like she will be a survivor, she will be a fighter and God sent her to us as a gift." He sat and held her in his arms as he cried with her.

"I'm so, so happy," Anne went on, "Holy Mother, keep my girl alive, don't take her away from me. Thank you for listening to my Novena. Thank you for answering my prayers," Anne talked to the 'sender' of her precious gift. She turned her head to her husband and said, "Ed, I think I'm happy with three boys and one girl, now my entire life belongs to them. I know I always did everything I could for my kids but now, it is something extra. This tiny girl that brought me happiness. Look at her, she is smiling already."

Happiness entered their home again. Anne was so happy that she asked Ed to arrange a trip to Italy with the kids. It was a way to show the children the country their father came from; to thank God for bringing him to America, where he met their mother. Anne always dreamed about this trip.

Ed agreed. "Don't worry I'll take care of this. I've already talked to one of my employees whose parent's business is a travel company. It will be the trip of our lives and the children will remember it forever. Mary Rita is too young, but she will have pictures to look at when she's older. Do you think she will be ok to travel that far? It will be a long, long trip."

"Yes, and having her three brothers playing with her will make her feel at home. I'm sure she will do better than all of us. Ed, this girl is such a fireball look at her! She knows everything that moves in this house everything we do or say, she is just eyes watching us all the time and soon she'll be the one watching over our boys." Anne was so relieved to have such a healthy energetic girl, and overall she just felt happy to have a girl.

"You're so right, Babe! I did notice how she looks at everyone and checks everything with her beautiful eyes. I am a happy father," Ed said kissing his wife. "I forgot to mention that our girl will have her Italian cousin Joanne Gramarosio to play with. Cara Gramarosio, her mother had Joanne a month before we had Mary Rita. Your sister gave us a beautiful gift, because we have so many boys in our family. Joanne and Mary Rita, are the only girls, I bet they're going to be spoiled. But it's okay, they can only be spoiled with love and I'll give them plenty."

The printing company had more work to do, more orders, more clients and Ed thanked God for taking care of the financial side of his life. "Babe, if you want we can move to a bigger house, we can do it."

"Oh no, we all love this home and the neighborhood is exactly what we need for our kids," Anne said. "The church the school, the playground, the neighborhood, the shopping, everything is close to us and we know everyone. Yesterday, the lady across the street made this big cake for us and our children. Can you believe it? No birthdays, no parties, she just

NUMB

wanted to say 'I love you' to us. Ed, we're so blessed to live here. I've never been so happy!" She put her head on Ed's shoulder, and closed her eyes like she wanted to stay there forever.

Ed kissed his wife's hair and for a few long seconds, heaven was on Earth in their home, right there.

Giuseppe Carone, Ed's father, the man that began the saga of their family, passed away. His time came to be with Jesus, the One he loved and trusted his entire life. Rose, Ed's mother, lost the love of her life, but her children, Cara, Lillian and Ed, with spouses and children, made her suffering easier.

The Italian family always lived together, so Rose was busy all the time, and this was the way, she had less time to think of the loss of her husband. Love was coming from everybody she talked to. Even from those that didn't speak her language, the Irish side of her family. Hugs and flowers, cakes and food, everyone was trying to bring comfort to the old woman that followed her husband to an unknown land.

Ed, Cara and Lillian lost and immense part of their foundation. Ed was now their father. He said, "I promise I'll be here for you anytime you need me." He was their big brother, the one that they ran to for protection, advice and for all answers to their questions. He was the head of the Italian family now. Now he had more responsibilities. He was ready to take it all on too, but something prevented this not long after his father's death.

One day, he came home from work, complaining about not feeling well. Anne made him stay in bed and gave him a warm soup but Ed couldn't eat.

The children were quiet and stayed around him, not knowing how to comfort him.

Anne told him she was going to call Dr. Johnson, he needed to come and see what's going on.

Ed was feeling so bad that he didn't even answer his wife's suggestion. He asked one of the boys to bring him some water and a cold compress.

Doctor Johnson came and examined him and he didn't rush with the diagnosis but in the end, he told Anne that her husband had tuberculosis.

"Doctor, please don't tell me this! Ed's sister died of tuberculosis and I know there is no cure for this horrible disease, even if we live in 1930 now. Do something, he's too young to die, and we have four children to take care of!" Anne cried.

"You've known me for so many years and you know I'll do everything I can to save Ed," Doctor Johnson said.

"How in the world did he get it? How come I didn't see anything? Doc, my husband's never complained about any health problems, what happened?" she asked him hysterically.

"His tuberculosis been in his body for a long time, his case is advanced. I'm going to administer the latest treatment that doctors have access to, I will be with your husband all the time but I want you to understand, Ed's days are numbered. You should take your entire family and try to enjoy a way to spend all the time he has left. I'm really sorry, Anne," Doctor Johnson said.

He left saying he would be back that afternoon to bring the newest medication he talked about. Dr. Johnson knew better than anyone what tuberculosis could do to a human being.

Anne refused to accept the verdict. She asked Dr. Johnson to tell her who was the best specialist for tuberculosis. He promised he would bring a telephone number when he came back with the medications for Ed.

NUMB

Anne went downstairs where her parents lived and talked to them. "Mom, can you come here please? I will go and get dad."

Catherine knew right away that something was wrong. She saw Dr. Johnson was here and she knew her son-in-law hadn't felt good for the last few days.

When Anne came back followed by Patrick, her father, they all sat down and discussed it.

"Doctor Johnson just left after he examined Ed and I have really bad news. Ed has an advanced case of tuberculosis."

"Oh, no!" both her parents said at the same time. They knew there was no cure for this horrible disease.

"I'm going to talk to the best specialist. I hope he will find a way to make him healthy again. I'll have to be at work more than before to take care of the business. Thank God, Ed taught me what to do. How to run the business, but Mary Rita is only 2 years old and she needs me to be around her. You'll have to spend more time with Beau and her, they are so young!" As soon as she finished talking, Anne put her head in her mom's lap and cried till her tears dried.

Catherine let her daughter weep and held her to her body.

Patrick left the room crying and he went outside to check on his grandkids. The bad news was killing him.

"Grandpa, why are you crying?" Beau asked.

"My back hurts," he replied. "But I'll play with you." Patrick grabbed his grandson's hand and let him lead him to the playground.

"I don't want you to cry, grandpa."

"Well, look I'm not crying anymore. Where is your sister?" Patrick asked.

"She is waiting for me to show her the tree house you made for us! I could play there all day long. But I'll have to come down to eat."

Patrick nodded. "I think she plays with you like a boy, am I right?" he asked his grandson.

Beau nodded. "You're right, she is tough and fast, and I like playing with her."

Patrick's health was getting worse also, but he made efforts to not show it, knowing his daughter had enough on her plate. He played with Beau and baby Mary Rita in the yard and it made him feel better. After a while, he went inside the house to look for his wife, Catherine.

She saw her husband and she asked him to follow her.

"Anne's going to need all the help in the world. Ed is not doing well and the doctor said he has very little time left to live. Patrick, when I look at my daughter and our grandchildren, I don't know what we should do first, how to help more than we do," she said while crying so much that her husband held her all the way to the chair where she had to sit to not faint.

Patrick called his grandson, Edward to check on his younger brother and his sister outside. He was such a mature grown up boy for being only 9 years old.

Edward ran outside and checked on Beau and Mary Rita. He came inside and told his grandpa that everything was okay and went back to play with his siblings.

Joseph had been busy working at the A & P factory. He didn't know how his father was until his mother told him.

Joe liked that his mother liked to call him 'you're the head of the family now'. She sat him down and told him that now he really was going to be that as her oldest son.

"What do you mean I'm the head of the family? I'm only 15 years old!" Joe exclaimed.

NUMB

"Son, I know this but your father was diagnosed with tuberculosis and he doesn't have too much time to live to be with us." His mom threw her arms around the young man that suddenly had to become the one that needed provide for his mother, brothers and sister. For a long while, no words were spoken.

"Mom, I'm so sad about dad. I wondered that Grandpa wasn't doing well, but I didn't expect my dad to be the sick one. How come you didn't tell me when this happened?"

"I didn't know either until your dad came home and he didn't feel good. I called our doctor and he told me that your dad had tuberculosis and that it was an advanced case. Joe, I'm asking a specialist, a lung doctor that knows more about tuberculosis and I pray to God, he will find a cure for your dad. I want you to go to school and study, I don't want this tragedy that happened to us, to stop you. You already work and I am so proud of you. Even Edward, our Eddie, who is only nine years old works! Do you know he is saving the money he makes from helping the Milk man? He runs to the milk delivery man and put the crème, milk bottles in the ice boxes outside our neighbors' houses. The Milkman said your brother, Edward is a good worker. Do you know that your younger brother did the same thing you did?"

"No, what did he do?"

"Do you remember when you offered me money to help with house? Well, Edward did the same thing, Anne said crying, "I'm so proud of both of you. I raised you well. Joe, I'm glad we talked, you made my waiting easier."

"Waiting for what?"

"Right now, we're waiting for the new doctor and he will be here in a couple of minutes. We have to be strong and keep your eye on your brothers and your grandparents. As soon as the doctor leaves, I will have to go and check on our business and see who can help us there. I'll tell you everything. I love you, Joe."

"I know Mom. I'll do everything I can to help you and Dad.

The younger kids were still playing in the yard when the doctors came. Doctor Johnson brought a well-known doctor to work with and try to save Ed's life.

"Let's go to the patient's room," Doctor Johnson said, after introducing his colleague to Ed's family.

Ed was lying down on the bed and he tried to get up when the doctors came in, but he couldn't.

The lung specialist examined Ed and Doctor Johnson could read the diagnosis on the doctor's face.... not too much time left. The specialist closed his bag and looked deep into Dr. Johnson's eyes, expressing agreement with his diagnosis.

Anne followed them to another room and invited both doctors to sit down but both of them refused, trying to make the painful situation shorter.

The new doctor said, "Ma'am, your husband doesn't have too much time to live. We don't have a cure or an efficient treatment for this disease. Dr. Johnson brought with him the best medication one can have at this time and we already administered the dose to him. I'll be back to check on him. By any chance, can you take your husband to maybe, Arizona? His lungs will work a lot better there. I'm not sure but if you can afford to take him there, it would be for the best." He looked over at their family doctor.

Anne noticed the disagreement on his face. After the lung doctor left, she asked Dr. Johnson what to do.

"Anne, I'm not a specialist. I'm a family doctor but with all my years of experience, I can assure you going to Arizona, it will be very stressful for your husband and the quality of air is less important at this time. I know what you're thinking right now and it makes sense if you think that if you don't take him

NUMB

to Arizona and he dies, you will feel guilty for the rest of your life. So even if I don't agree with this stressful trip, do it for you. You're like a daughter to me and I love you and your entire family. I know you'll make arrangements for Arizona. I'll be back tomorrow to give him a second dose. You see this new treatment was brought here from Europe and it does something that the other medications do not do. It helps patients with tuberculosis handle the disease easier. Unfortunately, it brings more comfort but not a cure." Dr. Johnson grabbed his case to leave.

"Doctor Johnson, thank you for everything you did all those years for our family. And yes, you know me well. I'll do as much as I can to give my husband what he deserves and all the love and care. I'll take him to Arizona like your colleague suggested."

"I knew this of course as I know you," Dr. Johnson said. "See you tomorrow."

As soon as Anne came back from the printing company they owned, she asked her parents to come and talk about this new situation. "I found a good experienced employee. One of the people Ed recommended and talked to him about what happened to us and I asked him to keep an eye on the production of the business. We're going to Arizona." Then she explained why she'd made that decision.

Catherine and Patrick were speechless and the house went quiet. There was the house, the children and so many things to consider but both of them agreed with their daughter's decision and it had to be done.

Ed's life was the main reason of their daughter's decision; it had to be done. Anne would be back and forth, so almost they would have to take care of everything.

"Patrick, we can do it," Catherine told her husband.

~ 94 ~

"I know and we have to find the best place for Ed," Patrick answered.

Anne took care of the business, and left everything the children needed. She talked to some of the doctor's and found out the best place for Ed's lung condition was Prescott, Arizona. This city had the cleanest air in the country. Prescott was located a hundred miles Southwest of Flagstaff Arizona.

After she finished all the preparations, she took her husband to the railroad station to start his healing, and a long journey. The train took them through Indiana, Missouri, then Oklahoma, New Mexico and finally arrived to Arizona. Both of them were exhausted thinking of the children and the parents.

"Babe, I'm glad Art O'Shea agreed to take care of the business. He will need more than one person to help him, he cannot do it by himself," Ed said.

"Don't worry. I will go help and be back to you. You shouldn't think about work right now, think about getting better. And our parents will take care of our children. Joe is doing really well at the factory as the company has grown so much that they keep hiring more and more people. He'll finish school and it is good that he makes some money. Eddie is working with the Milkman and he started saving up all the money he makes. Beau and Mary Rita get along great they're in love with the new tree house my dad built for them. So you have no reason to worry."

"Yes, I worry about you and the kids and I know what the doctor said... my days are numbered and I have to put all the papers in order and I have to get the will done. I will share or write down where all the documents are, so you don't have to spend hours looking for them."

Anne tried not to cry as she spoke, "Ed, if I would've known that you were going to talk about those kinds of things on our

NUMB

trip to Arizona, I would not have joined you. I should let you ride alone. I appreciate your care but we're here to help you fight tuberculosis not to make funeral arrangements."

"You're right." He smiled. "Let's look at this amazing landscape. This country is so beautiful." He gazed out through the window trying to forget about his solemn thoughts.

Soon, they arrived at a wonderful welcoming inn, where Anne found all the things she was looking for. The moment she looked at that place, she felt a wave of peace going through her veins. It was so serene, surrounded by dark green forest with a creek running on a side of the inn. Looking further, high mountains were protecting the valley where the town started to become a city. Prescott Arizona greeted the young couple with a tranquil atmosphere and good quality fresh air.

 Ed even got a dizzy for a second that's how strong the fresh air was and told his wife, "We should bring everybody to live here is so beautiful, thank you Babe."

"Maybe we will, you never know where God will take us," she answered with hope in her heart.

The owners of the inn were a friendly couple that never left their native place. They were so caring and attentive to all the patients and their families.

A week after Ed and Anne arrived in Prescott, things were going smoothly. Everyday they took a walk with deep breathing. They enjoyed good food and relaxation.

"Tomorrow, I will go back to Chicago to check on the kids, our parents, and the business. I already purchased tickets to the train. I want to bring everybody here. When I get back, we can spend a few days together. The lady who owns the inn will come and bring your food if you don't want to go to the family room. I asked her to be sure you take your medication daily and do not worry, I took care of her."

"I miss you already Babe. I feel like this was our honeymoon. I love you. I'm glad you're going to check on everyone and everything."

Anne looked at her husband and for the first time, she noticed how much he'd changed, how much thinner he looked. A dark heavy thought finally came into her mind...*my husband is dying*... she looked up and talked to Him... *'God don't let this happen, we have kids to raise, parents to take care of and a business to run'*. She tried to hide her tears.

She packed a small bag and took the train back.

All things were fine at home.

Mary Rita jumped into her mom's arms and no one could take her away from her mom.

Beau was holding her dress and it seemed like she had to walk while being 'blocked' by her youngest kids.

Joseph came home from the factory and he quietly listened to what his mother had to say. Their home had the wings of death covering everything including everyone's soul.

Anne went to the printing company and was pleasantly surprised to see how well Art O'Shea took care of the clients and the business.

On the way back home, she stopped at her church to weep and pray.

The priest saw Anne praying and let her have her time. He knew what the family was going through and he prayed for them every day.

When Anne felt her soul getting lighter, she stood up and looked for the priest to talk to him.

Father Brian welcomed her with a friendly hug.

"Father, m-my husband is dying and we have to make arrangements for—his funeral," she said trying to get her words out and to sound clear through her tears.

NUMB

"Anne, come over here," he invited her to sit down and pray together.

Those divine moments of devotion, gave piece and closure in her heart and she went home knowing what she had to do. The entire family was ready to go to Arizona to see Ed and give him strength to fight the tuberculosis, but they knew this trip was a farewell trip, saying goodbye to the man that gave them life and did everything he could to see them really happy and healthy.

Long hours with a toddler made the trip harder but the thought of the family arriving to the inn and the joy of seeing each other made them forget about the exhausting trip.

Mary Rita was holding up her mother's skirt and she did not want to go and hug her father, thinking he was a stranger so she asked loud, "Is this my daddy?"

Ed heard what his three-year-old daughter had said. And for the first time, he realized the truth. He was dying and he had changed so much that even his daughter didn't recognize him. He took Mary Rita in his arms, his weak arms and hugged her with so much love to last forever; he knew this was the last time he would ever be able to hug her.

Ed's death came fast after this, taking him away from those that loved him the most.

The trip back home was darker than any storm clouds with tears of fear for their future. Anne was now a single mother with four children and she'd lost the love of her life, the father of her children and the man that she thought she would get old with—she had lost everything.

A few days after Ed's funeral, she went to check on the business. She called Art O'Shea, the employee she trusted and said, "Art, thank you for coming to the funeral and for taking care of the business, I don't think I'll be able to run it without Ed. I have too much to do at home, as my parents are getting old and they cannot help us as much as they did before. I will do my best and I will pay you for what you've done for the business, you know," Anne said.

"Ma'am, do not worry. You are going through tough times now. I will keep doing whatever I have to in order to help you and your family. Your husband taught me everything I know and I am so grateful."

Anne thanked him with tears in her eyes and she felt better about the business.

Time went by and Mary Rita entered kindergarten while enjoying her new friends. Beau was doing well in school. Joe and Edward were working and attending school.

Church was the best place for Anne to go... the place where she could look up and talk to the man of her life. She had conversations asking him advice, telling him everything that happened in with the family.

Patrick Murtaugh, her father became so weak that he couldn't do much around the house not even for himself. When he was really ill and needed more physical help, Anne put him in a nursing home. Her and her mother went there every day to visit him and spend time together. Her brothers missed him and often brought gifts and food. Anne's brothers were already situated, they had their own families, so they were pretty busy but they visited him a lot.

One day Patrick Junior's wife, Stella called Anne and said, *help me.*

Anne, I don't know what to do," she was screaming loudly. "May I come over; I need to talk to you and Mom?" Stella said, she always called her mother-in-law mom and Catherine loved it.

NUMB

"Of course, come. I'll wait for you," Anne said.

Catherine and her daughter were supposed to go and visit Patrick in the nursing home, but they asked Michael, Anne's brother, to go instead, so both of them could be home when Anne's sister-in-law would come.

Stella and Patrick Murtaugh had a loving marriage and a beautiful family. They had two boys, 3 and 5 years old, and a baby girl, Kathy, loving each other. Everyone called Patrick with a sweet nickname, Packie and he seemed to enjoy it.

Anne loved her nephews like her own children and she couldn't wait for them to come and play with her younger kids, Beau and Mary Rita.

Catherine heard the phone conversation and rushed over, it was about her son, and she wouldn't miss it.

"Mom, you don't have to worry about this, please go back and play with your grand kids," Anne said. "I will see what's going on with Stella and come and tell you what it's about. You don't need any more stress than you have already. Dad wouldn't let me have you here."

Anne tried to send her mother away to avoid things that would upset her.

"No way, I'm not moving one inch. Give me a glass of water please," Catherine said grabbing a chair to sit on. Her love for her children was more than worrying about her health. Catherine was still a beautiful woman, her blonde hair was gray now and it framed her face with dignity. Her green eyes were full of life and she made people feel loved when she looked at them with a soft and understanding way. Neighbors and friends loved Catherine and the way she treated everyone.

"Stella, I'm glad you came. Here have a seat," Anne said inviting her sister-in-law inside the house.

"It feels good to be in your house, it's so welcoming," Stella replied.

"You two stay together. I'll be back in 2 minutes, I'll make some tea," Anne urged. "But don't start telling her about the situation until I'm back, promise?"

"Yes," Stella said getting closer to Catherine. "I promise."

Anne left the room and went in the kitchen to prepare the tea and put some cookies on a tray. She was in a hurry and didn't want to miss what Stella had to say. "Okay, help yourselves," she said putting the tray on the table between Catherine and Stella.

"Anne, I'm too nervous, I can't eat. I hope you don't mind but I'll drink the tea," Stella said. "Well, as you know, Packie drives people around, from one place to another. He takes them where they need to go and brings home good money. Yesterday, he took two men to a particular spot where he was told to wait for them to come back and not to leave. So, my Packie was waiting for his clients, taking a nap in the car. Later on, the police knocked on the car windows and asked him what he was doing there. He said he was waiting on the two men that told him to wait there till they came back. The policeman handcuffed Packie and took him to jail!" Stella exclaimed crying.

"Why did they take him to jail? And how do you know all of this?" Anne asked.

"He called me from jail and he told me that the police said that he was part of a robbery! But Packie would never do this, A person would never take a nap if they knew about a robbery. It makes no sense but now I have to find a lawyer to help us. My husband isn't guilty! He loves his kids too much to do such a thing, and I have no place to go with my kids," Stella said.

"Don't worry we know he didn't do anything wrong but the judge is the one to say if he's guilty or not," Anne said. "Now, we're going to help you move here with us till the situation with Patrick is cleared."

NUMB

"How could I do this to you? You're a widow now and you need help too," Stella said.

"Let's do it. I'll ask Joe to help us to bring the kids and the things you need here and we'll figure everything else out later."

Catherine was speechless and cried the entire time Stella talked.

Stella's kids were scared when their mom came home. As soon as they heard the door open, the boys Ray & Don hugged their mom's legs.

Even if she wanted to, she couldn't move the boys, as they were not going to let her go. Kathy was their little sweet baby sister and she smiled back to their mother. Stella looked at her boys and said, "We're going to move to Aunt Anne's house where your grandma is. I know you can't wait to play with your cousins, Mary Rita and Beau. Let's help your mom to pack. Everyone can bring his favorite toy, but only one. Beau has plenty for you guys to play with."

Anne helped her sister-in-law to pack a few necessary things and then she started packing for her niece Kathy. The baby girl was watching all the activity around her and smiled like they were playing with her.

"Mom, why are we going to Aunt Anne's House?" Ray asked while looking for his favorite wooden toy, a horse he got for his birthday from his father.

"Well, your father had to go to an important meeting out of town and he suggested we stay together with your aunt's family and your grandma. Doesn't this make you a happy?"

Ray nodded. "Yes, let's go. I want to play with Beau."

"Well, what about Mary Rita," his aunt asked, being curious what answer she would get from her nephew.

"Oh, she can play with our Kathy... girls with girls and boys with boys," he said convinced that was the rule.

A little while later, Catherine opened the door and let the large family come in. The house smelled so welcoming that both women Anne and Stella forgot their problems for a few minutes.

Grandmother Catherine knew what everyone needed the first thing, so she made room for Ray and Don to sleep in Beau's room and for the baby girl, she could have the big crib used by Mary Rita. So, there was room enough for baby Kathy.

Things were going smoothly and soon, they were able to find a lawyer to defend Stella's husband, Patrick Packie Murtaugh.

"Mary Rita, let's go for a walk with the boys and Kathy," Stella said. "I'll take the buggy and you can take turns walking, let's go and I'll show you what I mean."

The boys couldn't wait to see their aunt's new idea of walking. Stella was right, the kids were taking turns walking and riding in the buggy.

"Mom, I love going with Aunt Stella," Mary Rita said. "She made us walk and than sit in the buggy and I had fun. Can they stay with us forever?"

Her mom smiled. "She'll be with us until your Uncle Patrick comes back from his business trip, but we can see each other more often. I'm glad you like having them with us."

"Yes, I do like having them here. We love having a big family. I like to have cousins to play with," Mary Rita gushed.

When Anne went to work at the printing company, she found a pile of documents she had to take care of. She made some coffee, grabbed a chair slipped her shoes off. She then pulled her sleeves up and started to read, sort and throw away papers.

It was getting late but she knew her children were in good hands with her mother and her sister-in-law. Day by day

NUMB

though, she found out that taking care of the business, her older mother and her children had become overwhelming.

Someone knocked on the office door and Anne was considering who could be here so late. "Come in," she invited.

"It's me, Art O'Shea. I wanted to see if you needed anything before I go home," he said.

Anne smiled. "You are always there for us and there are so many things necessary to run the business."

"Ma'am, I don't know how you do it. You have so much on your plate since your husband died. I admired and respect your husband and I know that everyone here feels the same way. We admire you a lot, too," he said.

"Art, I would like to thank you for the huge help. I couldn't do this without you. Everything was on your shoulders and I know this. Maybe other people don't realize what all you do. But I do, because I have to do it now and it is getting harder and harder, especially with young children," Anne said feeling grateful for Art's help.

"Ma'am, if you ever consider selling this company, may I be the first one to know please? My parents are willing to help me start a business and this is the one I love," he said.

Anne felt like the lightning struck her. She hadn't thought of selling. She just didn't know what to think about this.

"Ma'am, did I say something wrong?" I apologize. I am so sorry," Art said.

"No, no, you didn't say anything wrong. I think God talked to me through you today. I'll get back to you in a couple of days, okay?"

"Alright," Art said. "Goodnight." He left the room full of hope.

The robbery trial process was short but tough. There was no way the judge would accept the fact that Patrick wasn't a part of the robbery. He wouldn't accept Patrick innocence, so the verdict was 'guilty.'

Money spent for Patrick's lawyer was consuming the family's accounts. The court days were also taking lots of time and nothing helped. Patrick would remain in jail for a couple of years, but with good behavior, you could finish his sentence sooner. He was grateful that his loving family was taken care of. His boys, his young baby, and his wife now had a safe place to live. Patrick couldn't be more grateful to Anne and he felt more than sorry for taking so much space and time of her and the family's lives.

Stella said, "Hopefully, this ordeal will be over soon. I'm talking about Patrick in jail not my ordeal. I love living here and the kids have never been happier. I cook less, I wash dishes less. Every day with all the children around me, I even have time to have some fun. Your neighbors are very nice and their children are well educated. My Patrick will be out and I'll talk to him about this neighborhood. It would be close to your home and it's a lot better place than where our house is now."

"I wish you could be closer." Anne nodded. "Look at my Italian relatives; they all live in the same big house helping with work, the kid's homework. I think they're even happier than we are."

The two young women grabbed their cups of tea and went to watch their children playing together.

Anne left her house later to go and check on her printing business. All the way there, she kept wondering if she should consider Art O'Shea's offer. It was so tempting. She also remembered the conversation she had last night with her

NUMB

mother, Catherine and how good it felt to hear her words of wisdom.

"Babe, you're a young widow with three boys and a girl and I'm not going to live forever," Catherine had said. "I have pains and aches every day, so it's like having five children now. Plus, you brought your sister-in-law and her three kids into your home. How long do you think you'll be able to handle all this by yourself? You have no time to do anything for yourself. Consider selling the business and getting a part time job somewhere. I can still do a little bit around the house and watch the kids. I'd like to say more but I am afraid that you'll hate me."

"Go ahead and tell me what you're thinking. I can handle it," Anne said.

"Okay, but don't say I didn't warn you! Well, I don't even think you remember how much you loved to dance, do you?" her mother asked.

Anne paused at this, as she hadn't expected to hear this question at all. "It's hard to remember that I ever danced," she answered with nostalgia in her voice.

"Yes, you used to love dancing. And every time you and Ed went out dancing, your husband was happy to have such a happy wife. You used to be a joy to be around."

"Well, I am sorry to be such a pain to be around." Anne pouted.

"You're not a pain!" Her mother laughed. "But I haven't seen you smile for a long time and this isn't good for you and your children. You need to find something or someone to make you happy again and it's not your fault that Ed died at such a young age. So yes, I am saying you need a man in your life." Catherine knew her daughter wouldn't like hearing this, but she did warn her after all.

"Sometimes, I think the same way, Mom."

Her mother looked surprised at this.

"But I don't want to have a stepfather for my kids. It has to be a man with a huge heart because he has to let my children come before the love he might feel for me. Otherwise, there will be no room for him in my heart. I know that you're right. Time is flying and my children need me happy. I think I will start working on my future by selling the business and then God will show me what the next step is. I love you so much Mom."

Mother and daughter hugged each other and Anne felt like a young girl again when she hugged her mother.

While thinking of this conversation later on, Art O'Shea entered her office.

"Ma'am, I came as fast as I could. I'm sorry to be late but it was a large order that had to go out right away and I couldn't leave but I'm here now."

"It's okay Art, take a seat. I have something to tell you."

"Did I do something wrong?" Poor Art asked.

"Oh no, it's about our last conversation." Anne smiled. "Do you still want to purchase my business?"

Art looked stunned. His knees were shaking and drops of sweat appeared on his forehead. "Ma'am, are you asking me if I want to buy the business... your business? I want to be sure that I just heard you right."

"Yes, you heard it right. So let's talk about it. I cannot do it on my own anymore, I have too many things to take care of and I think now is the best time for me to make a decision or I will hire a specialist to evaluate the business. I'll let you know as soon as I find out, but it would feel good to sell it to you because you already know everything about the printing and especially about this business. You have watched over it all this time, too. I will keep in touch with you as these progresses."

NUMB

"Oh, Ma'am, thank you! I apologize for my shock. I will take care of this business and will make you proud of me," he said before leaving the room.

"Thank you Art," Anne said.

As soon as the door closed, she put her head on the desk and started crying. It was a huge thing to sell Ed's business like this and a hard thing. But she knew he would want the best for her and the kids and this might be just that. When she felt her heart lighter, a little later, she took her purse and looked around the room.

She left and took the streetcar to the place where she wanted to be, the cemetery where her husband was buried. She saw Ed's tombstone with his name and she threw herself over it hugging it with love and tears. "Ed, I love you so much still. Why did you leave us so early? Look how much we all need you. Mary Rita was so young when you died. I show her your picture every night and we pray together over it. I want her to remember you forever. The boys need you and I miss you so much. I miss your kisses, your hugs Ed, and I still love you with all my heart," she said through tears.

A cold dark stone was the only answer to her love and crying. It was getting darker and a cold breeze made her cross her arms. She kissed the stone saying goodbye when she remembered to tell her husband about the printing company. "It has become harder and harder for me to run your business and take care of our children. I tried and I thought I was doing a good job but when I let Art stay in place for me for a couple of weeks, I realized how much better the company could be. He is still amazing at his job, so I came to talk to you about it. He would like to buy the business and I wanted you to be the first one to find out before anyone else. I know it meant so much to you. And I know you agree with me.... thank you. I'll be back and tell you how everything went. I love you," she said kissing her husband's grave stone again.

Catherine was waiting in the kitchen wondering where her daughter was at such a late hour. She knew that Anne went to check on the business and she prayed that nothing had happened. When she heard the door open, she jumped up and ran towards Anne, happy to see her safe and sound. "Why didn't you call us saying you would be late? We all were worried about you. Are you all right? Why have you cried?" Catherine asked.

"Mom, I'm sorry I should have called you but my heart was so heavy today. Let's sit down."

Catherine nodded. "I cooked your favorite meal. I'll warm it up and let you eat while you talk to me."

"Mom, thank you so much. You work so hard to prepare food for all of us but I'll eat later, thank you."

Catherine knew it wasn't the right time to insist she knew the only thing that she had to do was to listen to her daughter's heart.

Anne did just that, opening her heart. She started with her conversation with Art, and then told her mom about her 'date' with her husband.

Catherine's compassion for her daughter's suffering was more than what she could handle. Mother and daughter became one body again, like back in time when Catherine was carrying Anne.

"Mom, tomorrow I'll tell Art that I agree to sell the business to him. I feel like I'm losing a family member because that printing company was Ed's first baby." She cried.

"You'll be okay. You can't be everywhere at the same time. You will be free to have time with your own life and the family," Catherine said.

NUMB

"Thank you Mom. I don't know what I would do without you. You've been my savior."

"Go to sleep and pray harder, so that the transaction will go smoothly with no incidents. Get some rest. Goodnight."

"I'll check the kids first, and then I promise I'll go to sleep. Goodnight, Mom." Anne went to check on everyone. She made the cross sign above each of them and finally, she went to her bedroom where Mary Rita pretended she was sleeping.

When her mother entered the room, she stood up to hug her. "Mom, I was waiting for you. You know, Beau and I have to go to one of our neighbor's birthday party. We had been invited long time ago and we need a present."

"Why don't you sleep? It's too late for you. Go to the bathroom, please and brush your teeth really well and go to bed. You never upset me but today you almost did," Anne said.

"Mom, I'm sorry, I was just thinking what present to take to our neighbor's birthday, but I'm going to sleep and we can talk tomorrow."

"Don't forget to say your prayers."

"I did already few times while waiting for you," Mary Rita said kissing her mother goodnight.

Once Anne was sure she was sleeping, she stayed above the blankets thinking what a strong will her daughter had. She would do whatever she wanted to do. If she said she would go to a friend's birthday party, she would go for sure. Then poor Beau would do what his sister told him to do. Anne prayed over her daughter's bed and finally she was ready to draw a close to the day.

That night, Ed, her husband, Rosemary and Catherine, the daughters she'd lost were visiting her in her dreams of them. This made her wake up happier. The sun was up and she took care of just about everyone in the house.

Catherine wondered what happened with her daughter overnight but she felt happy to see her like this. Catherine knew this was a new beginning for her beautiful blonde, still young daughter.

Art O'Shea signed the purchase contract and now the printing company had a new owner, one who had certainly earned it over the years. "Ma'am, thank you from the bottom of my heart I feel that this was more like a gift than a purchase! Thank you!"

Anne smiled. "I am glad you were the one to have it and not someone I don't know. My husband would say the same, he is happy now for sure. God rest him in peace." She went home feeling years younger and a lot lighter spiritually.

Mary Rita and Beau Carone, her younger children were waiting for her to tell her about the birthday party they wanted to go to.

"Okay, tell me whose birthday this is."

Mary Rita answered, "Mom you remember Beau's friend Billy White, the one that lives at the beautiful home a few minutes from us? You always liked the house and you said he's a good kid. It's his birthday and we've been invited!"

"I know who he is and I do like his family but you have to find an excuse. We cannot spend any money on presents," Anne said.

"Don't worry, we'll find something Mary Rita," said. She told her brother to follow her and both came up with an idea. They had a game that looked like new, so they packed it and they headed to the party. The house was full of families that came to celebrate Billy White's birthday. There were balloons everywhere, food and games. The kids had so much fun and played together for quite some time when suddenly, Mary Rita heard a noise, a voice saying, "How could anyone give a toy that was used as a gift?" Mary Rita and her brother left soon

NUMB

after that incident and as soon as they got home, she told her mom what they did. "Mom, I didn't feel right when I heard what that lady said. I didn't know you could tell the game wasn't new, but it looked new!"

Anne shook her head. "It's called embarrassment. This is how you made me feel by doing what you did. I know it was your idea, only you could come up with such a thing. But don't ever do it again. If you cannot give a nice new gift don't do it at all, it's better to excuse yourself than to embarrass you and your family. If I don't teach you now when you're young, you will do it again later."

"I'm so sorry Mom. I promise I'll never do it again," Mary Rita said kissing her mother's cheek.

"It's not that we cannot buy a gift for someone Mary Rita, we can, but we all have to be careful how we spend the money, so we can live in our nice home for a longer time."

"I don't know what you're talking about being careful. I know I do love to buy nice things and make my friends happy and I love living in our home," Mary Rita said as she shrugged.

"Anne, I have a few minutes to talk to you after the afternoon mass, can you come?" Father Dylan, the Priest of St. Rita's church asked over the phone.

"Oh, thank you for answering my request, Father. I'll be there. May I bring my youngest children as they do love seeing you?"

"Yes, I cannot wait to see them," the Priest said.

Anne went into the kitchen to tell her mom about the call she received.

Catherine wanted to go with them. Her prayers had been answered a lot faster when she prayed in church and she could feel it deep in her heart. She wanted life to change for Anne, for the better, so badly.

They all dressed up and went to church. They waited for few minutes until the Priest opened his office door.

"God bless you all, I am happy to see you here, let's hope there's room enough for everybody. Catherine, how's your husband doing?"

"Father, you know he's in a nursing home. He has really good care but his health isn't good. Every time we go there which means almost daily, he keeps saying how grateful he is to live so long to see his grandchildren getting old enough that they would remember him."

"Hug him for me please and tell him I pray for him every time I read my prayers," the Priest said.

"I'll tell him, he'll be happy to hear this." Catherine nodded.

"Wait a second. I'd like to go with you all next time when you visit him. I always had a great respect for your husband Patrick's knowledge as a teacher and all of his sacrifice to work as a hod- carrier in order to put food on the table. I don't know too many people that would do this, Catherine. He is a man of character and I admire him," the Priest said.

Catherine and Anne had tears in their eyes and almost everyone forgot the reason they were there in the Priest's office.

The kids were looking at everyone wondering why their Mom and Grandma were crying, but they were quiet while waiting for everything to be over, so they could go home and play.

"How old are the kids now? I cannot believe how fast they grow up."

"Father, Beau is 11 years old and Mary Rita just turned eight. The older ones are working at the A & P and go to school. God blessed us with good children."

NUMB

"You are so blessed. God knew how to comfort you after losing Ed. Anne, you are now their mother and the father for your children. I checked with some people I know, so I could help you with what you asked me to do for you. I did find someone that can help you get a job at the American Can Company to pack tin cans. What do you think?" he asked unsure that this was something she would be willing to do to make money.

"Thank you Father. I am interested. I sold the printing company but the mortgage is too high and I have to find a job. I know it'll be difficult for me as a woman to get a job because men get hired first but I'll go where you send me and talk to that person and I'll let you know right away about the results.

When the family left Father Dylan's office, Mary Rita complained about being hungry and Beau jumped right into it, saying he was hungry too.

They stopped by a Street Deli; an air stream that offered good fresh food and Anne got something for everyone. They sat down on some benches near the street. It was crowded as people were coming back from work rushing to their homes for dinner to spend time with their families.

Anne was glad Mary Rita had that idea. It felt good to be outside enjoying the company and the food. Everyone was smiling and for a couple of minutes, their worries were behind them.

Beau and Mary Rita finished faster than their mom and grandma then started playing around the benches, laughing.

Anne looked at her mom and she was happy to see her smiling.

The next day, Anne got dressed like when she was going to her printing company, looking ready to work, to run the business.

Catherine wanted to tell her daughter that she looked more like a boss than a meat can packer but her admiration for her daughter's beauty was so much that she kept her mouth shut. She felt excited for her daughter, maybe now she would meet someone. She envisioned her next to a presentable handsome man that would adore her and her children. Catherine got lost in her future vision and she almost didn't hear when Anne asked *how I look* a few times. "You look beautiful you should get a better job and maybe later you will. I know you need money to keep the house. And I wish I had the money to help you but the nursing home is eating away at all of our savings."

"It's okay. I pray dad will live longer but every time I see him, I notice he isn't doing so great. We need to pray more I love my dad so much. Actually, I will pray for both of you, I want you around for as long as possible."

"Whoever said that getting older is not for sissies was more than right. I can tell you it's the truth. I do hope you get the job!" Catherine kissed her daughter's face.

Anne left the house thinking of what her mother told her and wondering if she was hiding something from her. Anne was determined to take her mother for a full medical check up to be sure she was fine.

She looked so professional that the person who met with her wasn't sure what position she applied for. For sure, she didn't look like a meat can packer, at least not like the ones he knew.

"Hi, my name is Anne Carone and I'm here for the meat can packer position and I'm ready to work."

Grant Grigolieti the foreman couldn't believe what he just heard, wondering what made such a refined lady want to work in a factory and even to be a simple worker, but he told Anne that she was hired.

NUMB

Anne got the job and started working a few days after she met with the person recommended by her Priest. Now, she knew the mortgage payment would be secured by the money she would get from the American Can Company.

Anne was worried about the way everything around her was becoming more and more expensive and on top of everything, seeing her parents health declining. Being the bread winner of her family, she had these thoughts all the time, the bills hanging heavy on her shoulders, shadowing her peace of mind.

After Anne started working, the Priest of Saint Rita Church asked her if she had room in her house to help an older woman from Ireland to live there. "This woman can watch over your younger children and help you and your mother, so she can pay for living in your house this way."

"Of course, I think it's my turn to help somebody like I was helped."

"Perfect, her name is Irene and I hope everything works out well for you," Father Dylan said.

Anne made room for one more person to live in her house thanking God, her house was large enough, and she could do it.

Irene was an older woman, presentable and decent. Catherine and Anne liked her and both of them were happy to get some extra help with the kids and the house work.

When Irene came and settled into Ann's house, she got to know everyone and she tried to help the family as much as she could. Mary Rita instantly became her favorite and Irene was saving cookies hiding them, to treat Mary Rita.

Not too far from her house, Anne had a nice friend, Mrs. Beck who also loved to dance. She was almost the same age as Anne and Mrs. Beck's husband didn't care for dancing. He didn't feel comfortable dancing in public. So when his wife told him she would go with Anne, their neighbor, to dance he was relieved.

Not too far from them, was a place where people over thirty years old were meeting for different activities, dancing being one of them. Neither of them, Anne or Mrs. Beck had the time to go places or spend time talking but one thing the women had in common was that they loved to dance.

Anne couldn't wait to go dancing, she had waited for this for a long time but now she had Irene in her house to watch her younger children and she could finally go and have fun.

Mrs. Beck called her and they had decided what day and what time they would go. Both of them decided to go at the end of the week, when Anne would finish her work week.

Mrs. Beck was happy and she told Anne, "You have no idea what this means to me! I've waited for years to convince my husband to come with me but no success."

"I know and I work five days a week and on weekends, I have to do all the things around the house especially homework and a few things for my youngest ones. I'm the one to thank you for giving me an opportunity to get this new thing in my life, see you Saturday at five. Thank you again!" Anne made plans to arrange everything at home to be sure her mother and her children had what they needed for the evening.

"I'm glad you live in my house now, Irene. You are really spoiling Mary Rita, too. She told me how you run when the ice cream truck comes to buy her ice cream and treat her. I'll pay you for everything just try to do the same thing for Beau when he is around you if you can? Edward and Joe are not here too often but sometimes Edward brings his best friends that are almost the same age and they spend time in the basement. Saturday, I'll go with Mrs. Beck to have some fun but I'll come home before midnight."

NUMB

"Oh, I will try and you're right, I love Mary Rita a lot," Irene replied. "She will be a successful woman someday. Her mind is so fast and precise. So not to worry, I'll take care of your children. I'm grateful you offered me a roof over my head, thank you,"

When Saturday arrived, Anne came down the stairs wearing the only beautiful long dress she had.

Her daughter ran to their neighbor's house to ask her friends to come and look at her mother. She never saw her mom dressed like this. She came back accompanied by two girls one little bit older than her and the other one was close to Mary Rita's age.

Anne was embarrassed at what her daughter did but she whirled around so the children could see her dress. Her natural blonde hair was wavy, falling all the way from her shoulders to the middle of her back. Her green eyes were sparkling with joy and happiness. Years and years had passed without her feeling like this.

Catherine couldn't take her eyes from her daughter, seeing herself a half a century ago but having Patrick Murtaugh, her husband next to her. Memories surrounded her. Catherine forgot for a few minutes where she was—and her pains disappeared getting lost in her daughter's joyful eyes.

Mary Rita broke into her thoughts, "Grandma, isn't she almost the most beautiful mother in the world? Even my friends said so."

"Yes, you're right. Your mother's really beautiful!" she said with tears in her eyes while imagining her daughter next to the man she was hoping for. *The time will come and my daughter will have a man for her children. I cannot leave this world till I see this happen.*

~ 118 ~

Mrs. Beck drove her car to the dancing place and it was a lot of fun, better than using the streetcar when dressing for a party.

Edward Carone invited some of his friends to come over and spend time in the basement of his house.

Irene wasn't a big fan of his friends. When she first met Anne's older children, Joe and Edward, she wasn't thrilled about them either, seemingly without a specific reason. "Why did you invite those young men here when you know your mother will be gone?" she asked Edward.

"Miss Irene, my mother knows about my friends coming over. She knows we don't do anything wrong. We will go in the basement and spend some time and play cards, so don't worry about us please?" Edward said as he could see Miss Irene's expression wasn't happy at all.

Irene went to the living room and grabbed a book. She started reading it... at least she tried to read it. After a while, she put the book back on the shelf then picked up the phone and made a call.

Police cars pulled into the driveway as neighbors were all up looking through the windows curious to see what had happened at the Carone's house. Everyone had a theory or story they attributed to the police presence there.

The police crew searched the basement and the only thing they found was Edward playing cards with his friends, no drinking, and no cigarettes even, nothing usual. They apologized to Catherine Murtaugh, Edward's grandmother, saying they received a phone call to come and check the house for illegal gambling activity.

Catherine told Edward's friends, "You boys please leave now and go to your homes. I'm sorry this happened. Someone informed the police that you were playing illegal games in the basement. I'm sorry, good night." Then she waited for each

NUMB

young man to leave. "Edward, I can see how upset you are and I would be too. Can you imagine what your mother is going to say? Do not worry. I will wait for her to come back with Mrs. Beck and tell her what happened. Go to sleep now.

"I wonder where Irene is? She must be sleeping while all our neighbors are awake," Edward hinted. He kissed his grandmother's cheek feeling a little bit better about the consequences he'd have to endure from his mother.

Catherine went to the kitchen and waited for her daughter to come home while trying to get peace in her mind. Her bones were hurting and her body was aching, but she knew how to hide all these.

Not too long after that incident, Anne got out of the car and said goodnight to her neighbor then came inside her home directly where her mother was waiting for her.

"Oh my God, are you sick? What's wrong with you Mom? You scared me being right here so late at night!"

"Thank God, you're home. I'm perfectly fine and everybody else is too," Catherine replied.

"So why are you here instead of sleeping?" Anne asked.

"Well, sit down first," Catherine said. "About an hour ago, the police came here."

"What do you mean the police? We never had the police here before. What happened?"

Catherine sighed. "I have no idea really. They showed up and showed me a paper then they went directly to the basement. Yes, now I remember ... wait a minute, isn't this odd? Why they didn't check the house first? Why did they go directly to the basement?"

"Mom, I don't understand any of this. Let me change my clothes. I'll be back in a second." She went in her bedroom where her daughter was sleeping, changed into her regular clothes and went downstairs to grab her purse. "Please go to sleep, Mom. I'll be back soon. I'm going to the police station to find out why they even came to check our house. Did they leave any papers with you?"

"No they did not even say goodnight, they said everything was in order and left. I don't want you to be out alone at midnight, it's so dangerous out there," Catherine worried.

"Don't worry, by the way where is Irene?"

"Now that you ask, I realize she didn't even come into the living room when the policemen were here. I didn't know she slept so hard."

"Okay, go to sleep, I'll be back. Mom, are you sure you're okay?" Anne asked checking her mother's face.

"Yes, I'm perfectly fine, be safe and careful."

Anne took a streetcar that was still running at that time of night and she got off in front of the police station.

When she entered, the policemen were so surprised to see a beautiful young woman wearing decent clothes and looking so presentable that they stood up in front of her like she was a high-ranked superior.

"I'm here to find out why you came to my house," Anne stated calmly.

"What is the address?" the man at the desk asked.

Anne suddenly realized she'd asked the policeman like her house was the only one in Chicago

After a short conversation with the police officers, Anne left and went directly home.

Irene was sitting in the middle of the living room with all of her stuff packed, ready to leave the house.

Anne looked directly into her eyes and asked... "Why?"

"I'm sorry I did it. Thank you for what you did for me. I was just mad at your boys," Irene said.

NUMB

Anne opened the front door and without one word... invited Irene to leave her house.

Catherine was so angry that she wanted to throw a vase at Irene but she stopped when Anne looked at her. "Why do you think she called the police? Why did she want to ruin our reputation?"

"The only thing I can come up with is that she was envious and has lots of bitterness?" Anne guessed. "But thank God, Edward and his friends we're not drinking and gambling like she told the police. No other family in our church will accept her from now on this is for sure. Mom, you look tired and pale. I'm going to make an appointment with our doctor for a physical."

"You don't have to. You have way too many things to take care of. Tomorrow, we'll go and see your father, to see how he's doing."

Anne left her mother and went to her bedroom, still wondering how people could do such horrible things.

Next day, Catherine and Anne packed fresh fruits and some sweet treats and headed to the nursing home to visit Patrick. The moment they opened the door, they both sensed something was wrong—really wrong.

"I'm so sorry, Mrs. Carone, so sorry." A nurse approached them. "Your sweet husband passed away an hour ago."

Catherine's knees bent and Anne was able to catch her before she fell. She put her mother in a chair and ran to see her father, the man she loved so much. An ashy face 'greeted' her and she knelt on the cold floor crying.

A noise made her turn her head and she saw her mother coming to say goodbye to her husband, the man she loved her entire life, the father of her children, the man she loved from the first second she saw him.

Two nurses were holding her to be sure she could stand.

Anne stood up and took care of her mom, bringing her closer to her father's death bed.

The nurses left to let mother and daughter grieve for losing the one they loved.

Catherine Murtaugh was getting weaker and weaker, especially after she lost her husband but she was still an active and hard working woman. She was there for everyone, she knew what they needed. She was the comfort and love they all needed.

After the doctor exam, she had to go to, Anne talked to the doctor who examined her mother and she was told that Catherine was suffering from broken heart, too much sorrow in her heart. She had aging signs and symptoms but the pain caused by her husband death was worse than all of her pains together. Anne knew she couldn't help with her mother's broken heart.

Time was going by and life was getting harder and harder for Anne. Stella and her kids finally moved out when Packie(Patrick Jr.) was released from prison. The Italian neighborhood they lived in had known he was falsely sentenced and so he got a job right away and finally the family could get their own house.

The day they left the house to go to their new home, Stella came to Anne who was having her evening tea. "Anne, I just want to thank you for all your kindness the last couple of years. How many women are so blessed to have such a family? You, my sweet sister in law and my mother in law didn't even blink when I called crying hysterical telling you that my Packie got arrested. Both of you reacted right away by taking me in with my three kids and miraculously, you made room for all of us, without making us feel unwelcome.

NUMB

Then in a couple of days, it felt like we'd lived here forever. My kids love being part of this amazing family and I consider myself the most blessed woman on earth. Now I understand what you and Catherine meant by 'living like the Italian side of the family.'" Stella laughed. "I'll never be able to pay you back for what you did for us. Thank you for all that you did and all that you sacrificed to take us in. It changed our lives."

Anne felt tears roll down her face to hear such a heartfelt speech. All she could do was to hug Stella.

Then life went on with Anne working and making ends meet. Despite being mostly alone, she didn't feel like getting serious with anyone. Many of the men she dealt with knew she was a widow and they did try to ask her out. To keep men at bay she found excuses like religion or work, so she spent all her time with her family and worked hard.

The economy was getting tougher and prices became higher. So one day, she came home after working all day long, and after the family had dinner, she announced, "We have to foreclose on our house. There is no way I can pay the mortgage. It's very sad as I love this house." She started crying.

Her older sons worked hard. Joe and Edward worked at the A&P and they were helping with the money but it was still not enough. Mary Rita was already in the third grade when this happened and she could feel the sadness in their home. Her mom was holding her hand when she told the family what her attorney said to the people she knew personally, the people who foreclosed on the house. Her attorney told those people, *'If you can go home knowing this woman and her family will have moving expenses and you're not giving her any help for this, I don't believe you'll be able to sleep tonight, when you could easily help.'* "Well, I couldn't believe the strong words he used and I believe it's unusual for an attorney to have such a good heart. Those people ended up giving me a thousand dollars and the attorney didn't charge me any fee for his services!"

"So now we have to move," Joe spoke up. "Mom, it's okay. We'll find a place to live."

"I know but I'm so sad," Anne said.

The family members embraced Anne with sadness. They all cried and supported each other.

Anne stood up and encouraged all of them that it would be okay. "Now we have to go find a place to move. For some reason, I know we will have another nice home," she said lifting everyone's spirits.

Like anyone moving from one place to another, the stress was heavy on her shoulders, feeling like a heavy stone, but she knew she was a fighter. She remembered how much she fought to save Ed's life. *If I was able to do what I did for Ed, for sure I can handle a foreclosure and moving to another place.* She encouraged herself.

Being pursued by time, she had to sign a six month lease in a nasty kind of apartment building, a tenement building.

"We'll have to move again after six months and I'll find a better place," she told her children.

When 6 months passed, Anne found a nice home not too far from the tenement building.

Young Edward was now in high school and worked to make some money, Beau and Mary Rita were able to take the streetcar to the St. Rita School.

"Mom, I love this house," Mary Rita said. "Look, we all have room to be together."

"You're right I like it too. It feels like our house, I mean our first home," Anne said. Memories filled her mind and nostalgia filled her soul, as her eyes were filling with tears.

NUMB

"Mary Rita, let's get some things done for Joe's wedding. Can you believe your older brother is getting married? I wish your dad could be here to see Joseph become a married man." Anne couldn't believe how fast time went; her oldest son was getting married!

"I am happy we're going to have a wedding! I love parties and I love dancing," Mary Rita said.

Anne stared at her nine-year-old daughter. *This girl is a pistol, she will be a leader. Just look at her, she is full of energy and she learns so fast. She's learned how to swim, dance and skate. She does so well at school. The Novena to our Holy Mary at Saint Rita's church gave me a real gift. I asked for a daughter that would survive. That would live and I got gifted that daughter. She is healthy and strong; her brothers can't even keep up with her. Thank you Holy Mary, thank you!* She kissed her daughter's face.

Joe Carone married his beautiful young fiancé, Sally and Anne had a wedding party in her rented home, a simple but beautiful wedding party.

"Joe, you and Sally can live with us until you save enough money to move on your own. There's room enough."

Joe embraced is his mother. "Thank you Mom, I love you. Sally is a good girl and she will help with the house. She likes to cook and she will keep everything clean and organized."

Anne nodded. "I'm glad to hear that. I liked her from the first moment you introduced her to us. A beautiful girl and she is crazy about you."

Joe grinned. "Mom, I learned that someone is crazy about you too."

"What do you mean?" she asked her son.

"A gentleman that would like to date you and you know who he is. He is handsome and the same age as you, too. This could be perfect for you, Mom. I would like to see you married again. I don't like to see you alone. I see how hard it is for you.

"Son, I would like to have that too, but this isn't as easy as you think. I need a man to love my children first and then to love me," Anne said.

"I see... well, Mom I wanted you to know about my feelings and the fact that I'll support your decisions," Joe said.

"Now do you see why I love you?" Anne kissed her son's forehead.

"I love you too, Mom." Joe hugged her.

A year later... Anne was waiting for her mom to have their ritual morning coffee together but Catherine was late. She went to check on her mother and the image she got would never leave her. Her beloved, adored mother was dead; she passed away in her sleep. Catherine died the way she lived, quiet and peaceful, trying to not bother anyone.

Anne knew something inside her would be broken forever; her love for her mother was tearing at her soul. Catherine had shared it all with her; her childhood, helping with her wedding to her beloved Ed, then all through the passing of Ed, when she took care of the children, so Anne could be in Arizona. The woman had been her rock. It shook her to the core to know she would no longer have her confidant and best friend any longer.

After a long time mourning the loss of both her parents, Anne realized she had to "wake up" and be alive for her family, for her children who needed her. She had to face the funerals and all the rituals connected with putting your loved ones to rest. It was a long and hard thing to do, while she had to take care of everything else, work, children, and the

NUMB

house... life was going on and the pain in her heart was piling higher.

One day after Catherine was gone, Mary Rita came home from school. "Mom, I'm going to be an aunt, can you believe it?" She was shouting this news at the top of her lungs.

"Come closer tell me more," Anne urged her daughter like she didn't know what Mary Rita was talking about. She knew already, she just loved to hear Mary Rita talk when she was excited.

"I heard Sally telling my brother about making plans for baby buying stuff and I didn't want to stay there and listen to their conversation, so I left. I'm so happy to have a nephew or niece at my age!"

"What do you want to have, a nephew or a niece?" Anne asked her.

"A niece of course, this is what I want," Mary Rita's answer came like a thunder.

"Me too," Anne said. "But God knows already what we're going to have and we'll be blessed either way."

"Mom, I saw you crying when we were in church last Sunday. Why did you cry so much?" Mary Rita asked.

"Come closer to me my dear. You see, you're too young to understand what I'm going to tell you really, but you want to know why, so I will try to explain it you."

Mary Rita came over and sat on her mother's lap ready to listen. It was like back in time when her mother was reading her fairy tales. Mary Rita felt so good; she didn't want these moments to end.

Anne took a deep breath then she began, "Do you remember when we lost your grandfather, Patrick Murtaugh? He had many health issues and he died in the nursing home where he spent a few years. It was so painful for me and my mother and all of us suffered. Not too long after that, we lost your grandmother, my mother Catherine. My mother was a saint, she was the glue of our family, and she took care of everything. I never realized how much she did until she was gone. My parents were the most wonderful people in the world. Catherine loved you so much; she would do the impossible to see all of us happy. I miss my parents so much. I want them to be here with us, to see Joe getting married. Catherine was always waiting for all of us, to be sure we got home safe and that nothing happened to any of us. It was an unbelievable hard day when I lost my mother. When I lost my parents; something inside me hurt more than anything has. So my heart was broken in painful pieces. I felt like I lost the only human beings who knew what was happening to me all the time, without me saying one word. If I wouldn't have had you all, I could've lost my mind. I will treasure my parents' memory forever."

Mary Rita listened quietly as tears formed in her young eyes.

"Last Sunday, it was their anniversary and I was talking to both of them. I was in their world. You see how God works... when one person dies another person is born and the new ones bring us more happiness. The new ones bring us so much joy that it makes the pain we have from losing somebody dear to us bearable. Mary Rita, this is life. Now all of us will be so happy for the newborn that will hopefully make us forget the pain and grief about the ones that passed."

Mary Rita didn't say word and she looked at her mom sadly. "I just don't like to see you crying. I'm going to wait for Beau so we can play together."

Months after the mother daughter conversation, Joe opened the living room door screaming, "We're going to the

NUMB

hospital right now! Where's my mom?" he asked Beau and Mary Rita that we're busy with their homework.

"She didn't come from work yet," Beau said. "But call us when you get to the hospital and tell us the address then as soon as she comes, I'll tell her,"

"I wish I could take you with me but you'll have to take care of Mary Rita." Joe put his wife in a taxi car and ordered the driver to take them to the hospital.

Anne called home and found out about Sally then she went directly to the hospital. She took a streetcar that left her right in front of the hospital entrance.

"I'm looking for Sally Carone. What room can I find her in?" she asked the receptionist at the hospital.

"Ma'am, she is in the delivery section," the receptionist replied, telling her how to get there.

Joe was walking up and down the corridor while biting his nails. When he saw his mother running towards him, he got to her right away.

Both were nervous but Anne tried to calm her son down. "She will be okay Joe, they have good doctors here. I know many of my friends gave birth to their children here."

"You're just saying that to ease my nervousness. I heard the nurse saying that they're going to bring one more doctor in, because the baby is huge. Sally is such a tiny woman how can she have a large baby? Mom, what can I do?"

"The doctors know what to do, Son. Let's sit down. I'll stay with you until the baby arrives, don't worry. I remember when your father did the same thing when I went to the hospital to have you. My mother and your father's mother told me how bad his reaction was. My mother stayed with your father and he was a lot better being with her and not being alone. I want you and Sally to continue to stay with us and save money so you can move to a larger apartment. I can help you with the baby too and Mary Rita is already excited to take care of her nephew or niece," Anne kept talking so Joe would worry less about his wife's delivery."

Joe tried to pay attention to what his mother was talking about but he couldn't, he was felt too concerned about what was happening in the delivery room.

Anne was looking for more subjects to keep her son's mind away from the delivery room and what was happening there. She started talking about the man who was courting her and she told Joe about Grant Grigolieti.

Poor Joe nodded and he did seem happy she had finally paid attention to the man he'd told her about a year ago.

Later on, one of the doctors came and congratulated Joe. "Congratulations, you have an 11 pound boy! He is healthy and strong we had to use full anesthesia for your wife so we could deliver the baby. Mr. Carone, your son is the biggest boy I have ever delivered and I've delivered thousands." The doctor shook Joe's hand.

Later on, Joe found out it was Dr. Hess, a very well-known doctor.

Anne was so happy to be there to hear such amazing news and hold her son so he wouldn't faint and land on the hospital floor.

A while later, both of them were allowed to go in the room.

Sally was still asleep and next to her in a crib was a huge baby that looked like a 3 month old baby already. Anne never saw such a big baby. She moved closer to him and said a prayer full of gratitude.

Joe kept going from Sally's bed to his son's crib, not being able to talk to either of them, but he had to be sure they were okay.

"Son, I am going home now and I will be back after work to see them again. Take care, I love you," Anne whispered.

NUMB

"Mom, I don't know what I would do without your help to keep me in my right mind. I feel so much better now. Thank you for everything," Joe said taking his mother to the hospital exit.

When Anne arrived at home, she ran into the living room, giving the news to her children Edward, Beau and Mary Rita. "We have an eleven pound baby boy!"

Everyone was happy that night... they had dreams full of happy faces, smiles and big babies.

The next morning, Mary Rita woke up a lot earlier than usual and went into the kitchen to talk to her mother. "Mom, I miss being with you. I wish you would stay home like other mothers do but I understand why." She hugged her mother.

"We have to be grateful for what we have. Mary Rita, we're doing well considering your dad is gone we have to thank God for everything. She tried to make her daughter understand how much harder it was for their family to pay for all the overhead. "Joe and Edward help with money but life is getting tougher and tougher. Mary Rita, your new Nun Sister Licoria told me that the training and the teaching you received at St. Rita's was so good that you are number one in your class. I'm really proud of you, smart young lady."

"Mom, I'm glad you have time to talk to me. When I was at St. Rita School, I thought it was a really small Catholic school; it had two and sometimes three rooms to each grade. Do you remember my favorite nun, Sister Helen? I loved her. I didn't mind wearing uniforms. I had a dream last night about a boy, Tommy who I was competing with. Both of us were the top two students in our class and we always got the reward pins that we traded. I remembered how much I liked St. Rita Catholic School had a lunch room for those students who were not able to go home for lunch. Now, the new school "Our Lady of Souls" is a lot smaller, attached to the church and it has four rooms on the left side for the first to the fourth grade and on the right side rooms for the fifth, sixth, seventh and eighth grade. This means I can attend the same school all the way to the eighth grade."

"Why did you wake up so early? I tried to ask you but you already started telling me things."

"Mom, I miss being with you, like I said." Mary Rita beamed at her. "Oh, I forgot to tell you that I am tutoring a student who really needs extra help. I'm working with him every day and Sister Licoria is pleased to see the progress he's made."

"This makes me so proud to have such a bright daughter. God will reward you for helping that boy."

"I know you have to leave now, otherwise you'll be late to work and we need the money," Mary Rita said laughing.

"Yes, we need the money, soon you'll need fancy dresses to go dancing like I did," Ann added.

When Anne got to work, she saw the man she'd dated a few times. He was always smiling at her, his eyes full of warmth.

"Hi Anne, I am so glad see you today, Grant said. "One of my daughters is having a few young ladies coming over and she would like for you and Mary Rita to join us."

Anne liked Grant Gregolieti and the fact that he was getting closer to her family every day. "Yes. When is this happening?"

"In a few days, I thought you might like to come."

Grant was a handsome man whose wife passed away a few years ago leaving him with two daughters to take care of. She'd known him since she took the job at the factory. She

NUMB

had gone out with him a few times and he was so sweet, nice company to have.

Her children really liked him and he had played with them a few afternoons as well. He would show up on the weekends off and bring flowers, bringing candy for the kids too.

He showed up in front of Anne's home three days later to pick them up with a huge bouquet of fresh cut flowers. "Hello, Anne, these flowers are for you. I'm so glad to see you."

"You always bring me such beautiful flowers thank you. Let me arrange them in a vase. Oh, they smell so nice. I wish we had your garden over here at my house."

"You can have it any day you want it. Anne, I want to marry you. I love you. My house can be yours. You always say that 89th Street is such a good area."

"We had this conversation so many times already. I'll marry you, I promise but only when your beautiful daughters get married, then we can have our own wedding."

"I can't wait for the moment to come," he replied with a beaming smile. For us to get married Anne. Your children are smart and lovable, so I never felt like a stranger to them. I know for sure I'll be a good father and grandfather for them. I heard that Mary Rita jumped a class too, how is that possible?"

"Well, when the time came for her to pass the 5th grade and go to the next grade Sister Licoria recommended her to go to the next grade. For her to skip the 6th grade by going to summer school for 3 weeks and she passed the test and went directly to the seventh grade. I thought you knew about it, we've been dating for quite some time now."

"I wasn't sure that she already started the seventh grade. I remember when I first met your children for the first time. Mary Rita came right to me and hugged me like she knew me for a long time. She made me feel so welcome and I could feel how much she missed her father. It was an unforgettable touching moment. We both clicked to each other instantly. The boys were polite but a little bit distant and this was normal to be that way, but Mary Rita was exceptionally warm. I love her and I know I told you before and I'm telling you again, I will be a good father to your children and a good husband to you."

Anne kissed Grant with so much love that he thought he won the battle, but he knew he had to wait till his daughters were married in order to marry the woman he loved.

Grant had loved her for a couple of years already and he refused to give up on having her as his wife.

Faster than he thought, the time came when Anne would have no more reasons to delay her own wedding. "Let me see what you're going to say now that I'm free as a bird and both of my daughters are married and out of the house. You promised that we would get married as soon as this happened. So will you marry me?" Grant said with a shaking voice as he knelt on one knee with a ring in his hand.

"Yes, I will!" Anne finally agreed happily to marry the man that had waited patiently for years. Anne's house became a place for celebration and the good news spread in their neighborhood. Soon after that, the couple was invited for family parties.

"Grant, I'd like to go to my parents' cemetery, I want them to see us married, and how happy we are."

"You see why I love you so much? How many women freshly wed would think of their parents who passed away? I knew my dear wife; I just knew how different and special you are. I love you."

"As soon as I find a break in my schedule, we'll go," Anne said happy to go and 'talk' to her parents.

NUMB

Anne finally decided the day of the wedding. It was simple but elegant, exactly the way she wanted. People said that the wedding was like Anne, simple and beautiful. The priest married them in the priest's quarters.

Lillian Carone, her sister-in-law from her first marriage, Ed Carone's sister, accompanied by an Italian cousin stood up as witnesses.

"I like that you didn't have a big wedding and I want you to know that I truly believe you married the right man. My brother would be pleased to see you happy. He's blessing you from Heaven," Lily said with tears in her eyes. She remembered how much her brother Ed, loved his Irish wife and how happy he was to have a large family.

"Thank you Lily, I know he sent his blessings for me. I know he wants me to have someone to take care of my children. Thank you for accompanying to be my maid of honor. I had many 'conversations' with Ed before I decided to marry Grant, as he will always be the father of my children, the man I loved with all my heart."

Mary Rita had just graduated the eighth grade and she couldn't be happier to see her mother married to such a good man. She was close to Lily and she loved her aunt. She had spent all the time at the wedding with her. "

"You look so pretty Mary Rita. I'm so proud of you. You already graduated the eighth grade and you're a young lady, just look at you. That dress is so elegant. You should keep it for dancing," Lily said.

"Aunt Lily, you still remember how much I love dancing! Do you want to go together? There are so many places where we can dance," Mary Rita said.

"Okay, I'd like to watch you having a fun, let me talk to your mom and we'll do something. I am impressed that you kept in touch with your Italian side of the family. When we get together, you know how we Italians like to always talk about you and your brothers. Your mother was present for all of our family events, weddings, baptisms, communions and funerals. She is a part of our family and she will always be."

Mary Rita beamed at her. "I want you to come with all my Italian family for my confirmation. It will be at the same church I had my first communion, at St. Rita Church."

"Oh, I promise, we all will be there, I can't wait to see how beautiful you'll be," Lily said.

"I'm so happy you're close to us, Aunt Lily. I'll see you at my confirmation."

Grant Gregolieti came home one day from his attorney's office and told Anne, "Let's celebrate. I bought some champagne. Bring everyone that's home and I'll share this good news." He arranged glasses around the champagne bottle.

Anne stared at him. "What news?"

He smiled. "Bring everyone and I will tell you all at the same time. We are all one family, remember?" He gave her a wink.

Anne went and got fresh lemonade for Mary Rita and Beau. Eddie, her son at was at work but she expected him home soon, so she put a glass out for him to.

Mary Rita was the first one to hug her *dad*, as she liked to call him because she didn't like the word stepdad. "Say it. Say it, Dad. Don't make us wait!" Mary Rita urged.

Her mother kept smiling at how impatient her daughter was. *My God, this girl will want to have everything and not only everything, but it has to be right away, too. She wants instant success. I hope this is a good thing.*

NUMB

"Guys, I sold the house and now your mom can choose a house for all of us, a home that she will love," he said, gazing into his wife's eyes.

Beau and Mary Rita were more than happy to have a larger home even though they never complained about their mom's home.

"Don't worry, I'll take Mary Rita with me when she has some free time and we're going to choose the best, the most beautiful house for the money we have," Anne said to her husband.

The champagne was bubbling up in the flute glasses and the kids had their lemonade with a few drops of champagne in them. The celebration brought smiles to everyone.

It didn't take long time for Anne to choose the home of her dreams. The place had two bedrooms downstairs and three rooms upstairs in the attic. It still had a lot of vacant space in the attic as well. "I will make this house a home for all of us. Edward and Beau can have two bedrooms in the attic. Then our Mary Rita can have the other bedroom up there in that extra space. We will have our bedroom on the first floor." She tried to find positive things coming from this big change.

Anne felt a lot better before, knowing her youngest children were going together to school but life had its own way. Her son Beau would start Lindbloom High School in September, so Beau and Mary Rita would be saddened to not attend the same school. "My kids aren't children anymore; they've grown up so much. Soon, they would do what their older brother did, get married and leave the nest.

Beau called to his sister from the living room as she came downstairs.

Mary Rita stared at her brother.

His eyes had sparkles in them. She came closer to her brother wondering what was happening. "Ok Beau, I'm here, why are you hiding? Did you take another fall like the one in the park?"

She remembered the day he'd ditched school and went to the nearby park. Everywhere, there were signs to not slide down on a certain slope, similar to a tube, but he didn't pay attention to any of those signs. He did slide and injured his ankle really bad. Beau tried to hide the truth about how he injured his ankle but the doctor knew he was lying. In the end, he had to tell the truth. The doctor fixed his foot and no one gave him any pity.

Mary Rita studied her brother to see where he was hurting but there were no signs of pain. Quite opposite, Beau's eyes were sparkling.

"Mary Rita, promise me you can keep a secret for twelve hours okay? Promise me you're not going to tell anybody what I'm going to tell you."

"Now you've made me curious," she replied with her brows raised. "Why don't you want the family to know, not even our mom?"

"No, I don't want anyone to know, especially our mom. I'm in love. Her name is Betty Lou and I love her. I've loved her from first sight. She is the love of my life."

Mary Rita's eyes rounded. "Are you crazy? You're only 16 years old, not even 16!"

"I know and this is our problem. Betty Lou and I, we want to get married as soon as possible but we can't do it here in Chicago. You have to be at least 18 years old in order to get married. We have to find a place in the South where we can get married officially. If I tell Mom the truth, she won't let me do it and that's why I asked you to keep it a secret until

NUMB

tomorrow. Actually, after midnight but I know you have to go to bed and sleep."

"Are they going to marry you both without your parents' consent?" she asked her brother while feeling shocked.

"How did you know about the consent thing? Are you in love too?" He laughed.

"Oh no, not yet but there are quite a few handsome young men where I go to skating and dancing," she answered smiling.

"Don't you dare to do what I am about to do! You have to wait a few more years! You are a baby, *my* baby sister. It would kill our mom. It's just that I love Betty Lou so much I don't want to lose her. I will work and support my family. Okay, I have to leave. One more time, do you promise to keep the secret until midnight?"

"I promise I will," Mary Rita said, feeling proud and excited to keep such a big secret.

The next day, Anne was wondering where her son Beau was. "Mary Rita, did you see Beau this morning? Did he already leave for school?"

Mary Rita decided to just tell her the truth. "Mom, I need to tell you something. Come over here," she said inviting her mom to sit next to her. "Beau is in love with a girl named Betty Lou and they left last night to find a place in the South to get married, you know because of their age. Are you angry?"

Anne was upset, of course. "Why didn't you tell me right away?"

"He asked me to keep it a secret until midnight Mom. The whole thing is just so romantic!"

"What do you know about romantic? You're only thirteen! Go and get ready for school," Anne told her daughter.

Mary Rita lowered head, he exuberance gone now and she headed to her bedroom to get ready to leave the house.

Her mother called to her, "Mary Rita, come back please."

When her daughter came closer, Anne sighed. "Of course, I'm mad but at the same time I know what love is. I fell in love with your father at a very young age. We didn't do what your brother did. We had our parents' consent but I would have preferred for him to tell me, instead of running from the house. I wish them love and happiness. But just now, let's talk about you. You should've come and talked to me, but you didn't. There are two sides of this: one is, for not telling me about what your brother was going to do and secondly, I admire you for keeping the secret. You're going to be a reliable person and people will trust you with everything. So despite how it turned out, I am proud of you."

In just a couple of minutes, Mary Rita's confidence and self-esteem hit the roof. "Mom, I love you." And that's what she said, thanking her mother in a very simple way. She prepared all she needed for school and went downstairs to kiss her mom goodbye.

A week later, Anne was sitting by the windows looking at her garden where the flowers were blooming. She sniffed back tears.

"Mom, why are you crying?" Mary Rita asked as she put her book bag down on the floor.

"Eddie went to fight in the war, helping his country. Joe and Sally moved out with Joey, my grandson and your brother Beau ran from the house to get married. Mary Rita, the nest is getting empty and it made me very sad.

"I know you're proud of Eddie. He's only 21 years old but he's so brave. I have a few classmates whose brothers went to the war and only one of them is younger than Eddie. We have a teacher that tells us every day what's going on with

NUMB

the war she told us why America entered the war, the largest armed conflict in human history."

"You know more than I do, Mary Rita, but it's good to know that you have such a teacher, your nun must be a patriot. We need to pray for your brother and all the soldiers to return home safe. I'll come one day and thank her for teaching you what it means to be an American. You better go to school now or you'll be really late."

"When I come back, I'll tell you more about it. She's a good teacher," Mary Rita said.

"Yes, your school has the best nuns. Now go, or you'll be late."

Later that day, a wire came from her son and her heart was beating faster when she read it. Her first thought was that her son had been injured on the battlefield. Then she was happy after she understood what it was all about. Her brave son could come home on a leave if he had the money to do so. She ran to her husband, Grant. "Look what we got from Eddie! He can come home for a few days if he has the money."

"I know, I read the wire before you came from work," he said.

"I wish we had that kind of money, so I could bring him home with us. I miss him so much." Anne's eyes were full of tears.

"So do you want him to come home? Well, I thought this was what you would want, so I've already wired him the money. He'll be with us soon." He grinned at her.

Anne hugged her husband and kissed him, still crying. "Grant, facts talk more than words. I don't have enough words to thank you for what you did. My children have a real loving father. Thank you."

"I love your children like I love my daughters," Grant replied. "They're all my children and the way I love you, I have never loved before. I waited a long time for you to become my wife but it was worth every second."

Anne couldn't fathom having another warm, giving husband after Ed passed. She was the luckiest woman in the world, really.

Coming from the war, Anne was grateful her son was alive. The newspapers talked about thousands of soldiers dying daily. She didn't want her son to go back to the war. She wanted him to stay home, get a job and start a family but she knew he had a duty to accomplish to fight for his country. "He looked so amazing when he arrived!"

Mary Rita laughed at her mom's exuberance. "Mom, you're so right, when I saw him coming up the walk in his uniform, so handsome! The girls will go crazy. They all want to marry him already."

"How do you know?" Anne asked her.

"Well, do you remember how many times you told me that it's not nice to listen to somebody's conversations? A day or two after Edward came home, I heard him talking to a girl telling her how much he missed her and that he wanted to meet with her. I was sitting on the sofa and I guess he didn't see me. As soon as he finished talking to that girl, he made another phone call and he talked to another girl saying that exact same thing, only with another arrangement for another time. Mom, I don't think he should be doing this. I feel sorry for those girls."

"I agree with you but I think it's just because he's not in love yet," Anne said.

"I know and he is sort of wild when it comes to girls. Oh, I forgot to tell you about my studies. I used my study periods for fun all month, so now, I can play badminton. I'm a leader

NUMB

in gym activities and I love it when we have school dances. We have boys we can dance with. I just have the most fun when I can dance."

"I thought your favorite was roller skating? Did you change your mind?"

"I love them all!" Mary Rita said as she laughed.

"Remember when I insisted to the principal of St. Rita School that I pay for your last year's tuition even if I didn't have the money? I was taught to pay my dues and I hope this was a lesson for you like it was for me. The nun didn't want to accept my money saying that your father printed so much material for the school without money, for free and she wanted to return the favor to us. I ended up paying but I was impressed at how much the school and church appreciated what your father did for them. Mary Rita, Ed Carone, your father was a good Catholic man with a love for God. The way you pray and the way you study the word of God makes me feel that you are following in his steps and this makes me happy. God gave me one girl that survived and she is a good one. I cannot thank Him enough."

High school was bringing more fun for Mary Rita than she ever expected and she enjoyed it.

Meanwhile, her brother Eddie made most of his 'vacation' by making three or four girlfriends very happy. They were waiting for him to come home for good.

The war ended, and soon afterward, he went back to Germany, where the troops he belonged to were stationed. He had a powerful reason to stay longer time there, as he explained in a long letter to his family, *I'm in love. I have met a girl that I am in love with her name is Hannah. I never felt this way before. You and Mary Rita will love her. She was married with a German officer that was killed in action before he got to see his baby born.* Anne was reading his letter to her family.

Mother and daughter had tears in their eyes. Anne continued reading, *"The baby's name is Doris. I'm not supposed to marry a German girl according to our military rule but I'm determined. I'm writing to you so you all know why I chose to stay longer here. I want to marry Hannah and be a good father to baby Doris. It will take a few years maybe to get the papers in order but I will keep sending you my love often. Tell my dad, Grant that now I understand how much he loves mom and his stepchildren that he considers as being his own children. What a role model he has been to me. I love you all and miss each of you each day with all my heart. Hannah and Doris say hi."*

Anne folded the letter and cried holding it up to her chest.

"Mom, he will be okay. He's going to send us letters he promised," Mary Rita said hugging her mother.

Anne kissed her back and went into the living room to talk to the father of her children the man she loved her entire life, Ed Carone. She shared with him all the things going on in their children's lives, she knew he wanted to hear everything.

As she spoke upwards, Anne realized suddenly, that a man who loved her more than himself was waiting patiently for her even now, here in the house.

She went in search of him then embraced Grant and felt that finally, happiness was hers with another man. It was right. She never really let go of Ed completely and it wasn't fair to this man, who was so wonderful and giving.

Things were going well at Anne and Grant's home. Love made a deep mark in their hearts and Anne couldn't be happier.

NUMB

"Mom, I'm going to the skating rink as soon as I finish my homework and I promise I'll be home when you said." Mary Rita left her house and arrived at the skating rink. The skating rink wasn't far from their house and she enjoyed going there. She occupied her favorite spot rinkside where she could see who was entering the skating rink.

"Mary Rita, why do you always stay in this spot?" a girl she skated with asked.

"I want to be sure I skate next to someone who knows how to do it, not a beginner."

"And do you have a particular person in mind? I like almost everybody, but you're right, some of them need a test gate and they keep holding the bar alongside the rink, it takes time to learn but some are really awesome like Bob Wish! He's a lot older than us but he looks so handsome," her friend gushed.

Mary Rita became quiet as yes, she had seen this Bob Wish a few times here at the rink. She didn't continue the conversation with her friend but as soon as she saw the skater, her friend mentioned she got ready to hit the rink at the same moment he was getting closer to her. She started skating next him and after a while, he asked, "What school do you go to?"

"Lindbloom," Mary Rita answered.

"Oh? What grade are you in?" he asked.

"My last year," she said knowing this wasn't true. But she didn't want him to think she was a kid and for some reason, he believed her.

They skated around together and laughed.

"Where do you live?" Bob kept asking questions.

Mary Rita enjoyed the conversation. "On the Southside, not too far from here."

"Me too, I live in the same direction only a little bit further away than you. If you want, I can drop you in front of your house. That is, if you don't have somebody else coming to pick you up?"

Mary Rita felt excited. "Okay, you can take me to my house. How old are you, by the way?" she asked.

"I'll be 21, soon," Bob replied.

Mary Rita hid her surprise as he was quite a few years older than her, but she shrugged it away. So what? They could be skating friends and there was no harm in that.

The time to leave came and the two of them had no idea how fast the time had flown by.

Bob then drove her home. "Good night, I'll see you again at the rink. Are you coming tomorrow?" he asked.

"No I have to study. I love getting the best grades ever but I'll be there the day after."

"Perfect, so I'll see you soon." Bob nodded. "I like skating next to you, you're a good skater and talking to you makes the time so pleasant."

"Good night and thank you for the ride home." She smiled at him.

Once inside, Mary Rita was all smiles on the way to the kitchen where her mother was waiting for her.

Anne studied her daughter's face and noticed her huge smile. "Did you have fun tonight?"

"Oh, yes, lots of fun. I'm skating next to a boy I like and his name is Bob Wish, actually its Robert but it's a lot easier to call him Bob. He just now dropped me off. He was so kind of offer me a ride home."

"I'm glad you liked him. Maybe you'll skate together again," Anne said.

NUMB

"Maybe? Oh no, for sure, we'll skate together again! He already asked me if I'd be there tomorrow but do you know what I did? Mom, I can't believe what I said. I normally go skating everyday but for some reason, I wanted him to wait for me, to miss me, so I said that I had to study for school!" Mary Rita felt wonder at her own behavior.

Anne was puzzled as she couldn't believe what she just heard. Her baby girl had become a young woman attracted to the opposite sex. *How come I didn't see it before? My own daughter is a flower ready to bloom. I'll go to the skating rink to see this boy, as he seems to like her too.* "Mary Rita, it's okay. My mother always told me that... we, the women have to let them chase us. You just let your instincts lead you. Be careful though, you're far too young to get into a serious relationship. School is what you should participate in. It is your priority right now."

"I think I like this boy a lot Mom, but I promise school is my priority," Mary Rita vowed.

Grant Gregolieti came home from the meeting he had with his lifetime friends. Once a week they got together, had lunch together, played golf and talked about politics. It was impossible to miss one of their meetings.

"Anne, I'm glad you're home, I'd like to take you for a walk. The trees are blooming and the sun is making me smile more than usual. Would you like to go with me?"

"Of course, let me be sure I leave all things in order, so the kids have what they need. I'll be done in a second." She went to the kitchen and arranged the food so Mary Rita and Beau could find it. She grabbed her purse and was ready to join her husband.

They had a lovely day. As a couple just by themselves. It was a good ending to a long week.

The following week, Grant wanted to take Anne to a fancy restaurant that had a wonderful view of the river to give her a needed break from work.

Anne knew she could quit working anytime, Grant had asked her to give it up many times, but she honestly liked to work. The kids were all almost grown and she needed to keep busy.

The restaurant Grant took her to wasn't too far from their house and the landscape was absolutely incredible. The river was so wide, surrounded by buildings that showed the economic power of the city.

Both of them were quiet and enjoying their time together and the wonderful view. Anne was facing the sun and she pushed her head back to let the sunlight warm her face. It was a real pleasure to be there. To sit and enjoy a meal without thinking about children, work, and problems. When she sighed and opened her eyes, she noticed her husband's face was red and he couldn't breathe, gasping for air.

Anne jumped from her chair and yelled for help. The waiter thought Grant was choking, but he realized they had no food at the table, only lemonade. He ran and called the ambulance, while Anne was trying to find a comfortable position for Grant.

Grant gasped. "Anne, I want you to know—"

Anne stopped him right away. "You shouldn't talk now, you need to rest, and we'll talk later."

"Anne, what if there is no *later*?" Grant asked.

"Grant, don't make my life harder than it is already. I love you and you just have to be quiet."

"I want you to know that I never loved a woman like I loved you and your children were like my own children," he

NUMB

insisted saying what was in his mind and heart. "I'll stop talking now."

Anne had tears in her eyes knowing how true everything Grant said was. She was so attached to the man in front of her, the man who made her love for him grow everyday with all the small things he did, proving his love. She put her hands on his cheeks and kissed him with tenderness and care.

Anne tried to help him as much as she could but her husband was getting weaker and weaker. Grant's body had a tremor and his forehead was sweating. He said he had tremendous pain in his arms and pressure on his chest, feeling almost like he was burning.

Grant smiled sadly. "I wish I had the family here, sons and daughters, my granddaughter, everyone. I'll always love you all. Anne, what am I going to tell you now will sound like too much but I never loved another woman like I loved you, my dear Irish, beautiful wife. I know I told you this many times. This time though, I know it will be the last. I did my best to be a good father for your children and forgive me if I ever did something wrong and if I did, it was unintentional. I love you so much."

Anne was weeping now, feeling helpless as the color and warmth of the day all turned to a cold, black and white. She came closer and kissed her husband's face knowing she would lose him too, but praying to God that she was wrong.

When the ambulance arrived, they said Grant was having a massive heart attack and they took him to the nearest hospital. Anne went with them and she didn't leave Grant's side but when he was rushed into the surgery room, she went in the hospital lobby and made all the necessary calls to be sure everyone was informed. Those calls were hard for her to make. It made all this real. She choked through tears as she told his daughters and her children over the phone this terrifying event that she hoped and prayed would turn out better than what she feared. He was a strong man, always had been. She never even knew he'd been ill in any way.

After an hour of waiting, the doctor who operated on Grant came and introduced himself, "Ma'am, your husband suffered a massive heart attack, a full artery blockage and we had to do an open heart surgery, trying to save his life. Ma'am, I'm really sorry. Our team did the best we could to save his life; your husband had been suffering from heart disease for a long time, without knowing it. I'm so sorry," the doctor said and left.

Anne sat down hard in the chair, she was speechless. She was numb and felt so cold. Everything in her world stopped. Time stood still as she stared blankly at the painting on the lobby wall. The colors that were there moments ago were now stark lines of ashes and gray as her mind tried to grip this terrible news. Tears rolled down her face without her being aware of, it. Her pain was endless. One minute they were together in the afternoon sun....Then the next, her Grant was just—gone?

A nurse came and comforted her. She sat down next to Anne for quite sometime.

Anne thanked her and asked what she needed to do next. She had no idea what would be needed, what to do, where to turn. The nurse took her into a room where she asked Anne to sign some papers. Anne was signing those documents without having any idea what she was doing.

When she left the hospital, the first thing she did was call Grant's daughters to let them know about their father's death. It came right on the heels of the news that he was even ill, now she had to tell them he was gone, before they even got to the hospital. She had a hard time making those two phone calls; she knew how much Grant was loved by his daughters.

NUMB

Once she got home, she gathered every one and told them what had happened. For her, the color around her just never came back. She even grabbed a blanket before she sat down so she could feel warm again. But really, she couldn't feel anything.

Grant's death was received with lots of sadness because he left a deep mark in every one's heart with his love and care for them.

Anne was only 50 years old and was already a widow twice.

MARY RITA WISH

NUMB

CHAPTER ONE

"Mom, I miss my brothers and I want to spend more time with Joey, my nephew," Mary Rita said. "I know we have a large family and it's hard to keep up with everybody. I just woke up this morning, thinking of all of them. I know my dad wasn't my biological father but I loved him so much that I just never knew the difference. I will love him forever. Do you know that sometimes he talks to me from Heaven? When this happens, my days are better than other days. I wish he would come in my dreams every night."

"I know sweet girl. But you have your life to think of. And yes, Grant will be there always."

"Mary Rita nodded. "Now I have to leave to see if Bob waited for me. We have been seeing each other there for a couple of weeks now."

"It seems like you cannot wait to get there, right?" Anne asked her daughter as she smiled, knowing this feeling.

"Yes, I think you're right." Mary Rita smiled and ran through the door.

Yes, he had been waiting for his skating partner. His face lit up when Mary Rita showed up close to him, ready to enjoy the fairy tale. Their skating sessions became something that both of them looked forward to.

"Mary Rita, may I take you home?" Bob asked.

"Let me think," she replied as she turned her eyes upward. "No, I'm kidding of course you can. I enjoy the ride while sitting next to you. We talk so much about everything."

When the skating session ended, they got into the car and started driving home. Bob's car was so clean and everyone could see how much pride he had for it. he loved cars and spoke of that often to her. Suddenly, when they were on Bowie Street, a car pulled up on a side of the street coming at them fast. If Bob wouldn't have hit the brakes hard, the car could have hit them and a horrible accident could have happened.

Mary Rita fell forward and Bob fell forward too, his face hit the steering wheel really hard. Both of them were scared but happy nothing major happened and they were both alive. As soon as they both realized there were no major consequences, Bob looked at Mary Rita to be sure she was okay, He knew he at least had a front tooth cracked. "Are you okay?" was Bob's first question, being concerned about Mary Rita.

"I have a bit of a headache, but yes I'm okay, I think? What about you?"

"Well, I think I'll need a dentist," Bob said smiling. "We should continue driving, so your mom won't wonder where you are. I like that your mother is like that, she really cares about her kids like my mother."

"Let me wipe my wound, otherwise my mom will see blood on my face." Mary Rita found some tissues and wiped her forehead. She knew if her mother saw her bleeding, she would end up in the hospital and she didn't want her mom to be scared.

Bob kept waiting for her while he was checking his tooth and he was happy that it didn't hurt, yet. Once he pulled his car into Mary Rita's driveway, he held her with his arm around her shoulders and kissed her. It was a loving, tender

NUMB

kiss that pulled the both of them from reality. Love was weaving its way over the young couple.

Mary Rita ran inside her home, directly to the bathroom to look at her bleeding forehead. The cut wasn't really deep and she decided not to talk about it since her mom would only worry. She cleaned the cut and went to sleep with a happy smile on her face."

The next day, her mom greeted her, "I saw you coming home last night but it's seemed that you were so tired that you went to sleep right away."

"I'm sorry. I didn't talk to you like I always do. Yes, we stayed longer and I was tired but happy."

"I'm happy that you're happy, but tell me more," her mom urged.

"Do you remember that you asked me if I liked this guy? Now I have an answer. I love him. I love Bob Wish and I cannot wait to see him and be with him!" she gushed happily.

"Oh, I'm so happy for you. Do you remember about your brother, when he told three or four girlfriends how much he loved each of them? Be sure Bob doesn't have other girlfriends besides you."

"Bob isn't anything like my brother, he's five years older than me and I've had time to figure out if he flirts with other girls. I was amazed at how serious he was, not even skating or joking with any other girls. You will like him I'm sure."

"Don't forget how important your school is. What does Bob do for a living?" her mother asked.

"He's a carpenter and his family has a gas station."

"I asked because I need to know who he is. I will call him Bob from now on. Does he have siblings too?"

"Yes, a brother and a sister, Richard and Dorothy. His sister is a really good seamstress and she taught herself how to make clothes. I haven't met her yet or Richard."

As soon as Mary Rita got to the skating rink, the first person she noticed was Bob, the boy that kissed her the night before.

He smiled at her. They started skating and he invited Mary Rita to see a movie.

"Oh I can't wait, let me call my mother to make sure she won't be worried about me." She really liked to be with Bob even if she was so much younger than him.

They spent a lot of time together enjoying the small neighborhood close to Bob's home where they often had ice cream or went to the sandwich shops in a neighborhood where they felt comfortable and was friendly.

"I like spending time with you," Bob said one day. "But soon, I'll join the Merchant Marines."

"Merchant Marines, what is that? I've never heard of it," Mary Rita said.

"They transport cargo and passengers during practice time and during war, they can deliver military personnel and goods for the military at least this is what I understand from the recruiter. It's not a dangerous job and I promise I'll be back."

"Are you going to miss me because I know I will miss you," she said with tears in her eyes.

"Please don't cry. It's not dangerous and I won't be there for more than a year," Bob said.

"I hope you'll find time to write me," she said, still crying.

"I promise, I'll write you every day! If there is a way to mail the letters but I'm sure they figured that out by now."

NUMB

"I was happy but now I feel like everything is gone," Mary Rita it put her head on Bob's shoulder and cried.

"My buddies will have a nice going away party for me and you're invited, okay?" Bob said as he tried to make her feel better.

"Thank you, I'll come. How much time do I have till the party? So I can have a dress made."

"Let me find out and I'll let you know but any dress you wear won't change the way I see you. You're my beautiful girlfriend and I love you," Bob said holding her close to his body.

Mary Rita's eyes rounded. He just said he loved her! She wasn't sure if she would or could actually say it back yet. She still was so young and didn't know about this kind of love, the only thing she knew was that she loved being with him, kissed by him and being closer to his body.

"You know I took sewing classes in school and I can make my own dress. I remember Dorothy does a good job too. One day, we can help each other, who knows?"

Bob's buddies got together and threw an amazing party for their friend Bob Wish. Mary Rita looked beautiful and she made an effort to look older than she was. Bob's friends knew how old she was but none of them said anything on this subject. If Bob loved her, his friends loved her too.

"It's very hard for me to say goodbye. I know you will still go to the skating rink and I want you to go but don't find someone else because I'll be back. I'll miss you." Bob held Mary Rita tightly like he was afraid to lose her.

"I'll wait for you because I love you too," she finally said.

The following week, Bob left and as soon as he was on the ship, he pulled the stationary kit he brought with him and started writing his girlfriend, like he was talking to her. His letters spread the love without being love letters.

They could be read by any member of the family and Mary Rita couldn't have been happier whenever she received them.

After reading one of Bob's letters, Mary Rita remembered an event that she would never forget. Bob invited her on a date for dinner and a movie with Bob's best friend David and his fiancée, Laura. Mary Rita remembered going to a restaurant in downtown Chicago and how impressed she was to see all white table cloths and candles along with the elegant decor. She remembered how impressed Bob looked when he saw her wearing a beautiful red dress. Laura, Bob's friend David's fiancée, complimented her the entire evening and she whispered in David's ears that she wanted a dress like Mary Rita's. "Mom, do you still have a credit account at the ladies dress shop? I know you pay a small amount each month," Mary Rita asked.

"Yes, I do. Do you need a new dress?" Anne asked.

"I know how hard you work for your money but I can pay with the money I saved working at the soda fountain when I was 14 years old. I still have it."

"Did I ask you about the money? You didn't answer my question," her mother said.

"Yes, I saw a dress in the shop window and while I stood in front of the window a few good minutes, I could imagine wearing that dress when having a date with Bob. I loved that dress."

"Tell me more," her mother urged Mary Rita to describe the dress she wanted.

"Well, it was red..." Then she started describing it in detail, "With a very small ruffle around the neck that is low but not too low and the sleeves are just above my elbows. It has only a little flare and so it is even more complimentary for me having such a tiny waist. I like how it looked and I can

NUMB

imagine how it would feel when I walk around in it." It was like the dress she wore when they'd double dated.

"You described this dress like a designer!" her mom gushed. "I've never heard you talking like this with so much passion. Okay, I'll add it to my account and I'll make you happy, my little princess."

"Oh no, I'll pay for it. I have the money from when I worked, remember?"

"I do remember but you should save your money. I'll pay for the red dress. I'm as excited as you are. I can't wait to see you wearing it," Anne said.

"Mom, you are the best mother in the world and not because you're paying for my dress it has nothing to do with that. I love you for who you are and I thank you. When you are older, I'll take care of you Mommy."

Mary Rita received a letter from Bob letting her know that he'd be home for good. "Mom, Bob will be with me all the time! He will be like my Christmas present, don't you think?"

"What a beautiful gift. I'm so happy for both of you Mary Rita. It is so nice to be young and in love."

Then entire family got together to welcome Bob home.

"Bob, I can't believe how much you changed in less than a year!" Mary Rita exclaimed.

"What do you mean? What's wrong?" Bob looked confused.

"Nothing's wrong, quite opposite," she answered wrapping her tiny arms around his now very muscular body.

He smiled down at her. "This will be the best Christmas ever for both of us, I just know it."

The Christmas tree was as high as the living room ceiling just about while decorated with family memories that the grandparents, parents and kids had made over time. Each ornament was a treasure they hung and it had a story of love happiness, marriages and babies. Ornaments made by Catherine and Patrick senior. One from Anne's beloved Ed and even Grant's hung there. Then the ones Anne made as a child, along with her own kid's creations.

The house had the scent of fresh baked pies and cookies as cinnamon floated through the air. Presents filled the floor under the tree.

A group of children were singing Carols outside as Mary Rita pushed the door open and let the divine sound come into the house. Everyone stopped what they were doing and listened to the Carols.

When the children left, Mary Rita and Bob found a quiet corner where they could be alone.

Bob looked at the girl he was so in love with, searching her beautiful face for a sign of affection. He didn't have to search for long because her eyes were full of love for the young man standing in front of her.

Bob knelt down and pulled out a small box.

Mary Rita cried and laughed at the same time. She started jumping up and down ready to scream her answer. *Yes, I do!* But she had to wait until Bob finished asking her if she wanted to be his wife. "I love, love, love you Bob Wish and I want to be Mrs. Wish. But only after I graduate high school," she said.

"It is a good plan and I agree. I'm just so, *so* happy you said yes, that's all I wanted. You were all I was thinking of, all the time I was away. I knew we loved each other," Bob said.

NUMB

"Let's go and let everyone know they need to get ready for a wedding after the school year ends and tomorrow, we'll go to your family and do the same," she said.

"It will be hard for me to wait till tomorrow. I want everyone to know how happy I am but I'll still wait," Bob said.

The evening was full of laughter, joy, food, music and Anne was so happy to find out about her daughter getting engaged that she almost forgot to bring the next dish to the table.

"Mom, I see you running. Is something wrong?" Mary Rita asked.

"Oh no, my dear, my mind is busy with thinking of your wedding. Your father and Grant are sending their blessings from heaven."

"I know I'd like to have something small of theirs to carry when I walk down the aisle."

Both mother and daughter had a sweet moment crying together. "I will find something for you, okay?"

Mary Rita nodded and went back to the main room.

Anne looked upwards talking to Ed in heaven, "Your sweet baby girl got engaged and she will get married soon. I wanted so much for you to be here to walk her down the aisle but you will be with her in her heart." When her tears dried up she prayed like she always did but this time a new hope sprouted from her soul." "Then Grant you are up there too, watching. You always loved Mary Rita so much. She loved you like the father she missed as a child. I hope you know she and I miss you so much." *God, you gave me a girl that I prayed for with my novena prayer to our Holy Mother after I lost two daughters. You listened to my prayers and now my girl is getting married. Protect her and her future family.*

There were still a couple of months left until graduation and time enough to get things done for the wedding. Mary

Rita knew to be careful as she could be when spending money for the wedding. "Bob, do you remember when we stood up for your good friend's wedding, what a beautiful wedding they had. It was an expensive Polish wedding though, as his mother in law wanted to keep the Polish tradition but boy, it cost a fortune. Everyone knew they had to open the gifts to pay the couple's cost of the wedding. I don't want this to happen to us, so we'll have a small wedding."

"What do you think small is?" Bob asked.

"Almost a hundred maybe one-hundred and fifty people maximum," she answered.

"That isn't small sweet girl but let me see if we can get some kind of reception room and make a reservation."

"Good idea, time is flying and the longer we wait, the harder will be to find something affordable," she said.

The country was still recovering from the Second World War but people's spirits made everything look merrier than it really was. People had to work harder to put food on the table and take care of their families. For Mary Rita, making the preparations for a wedding was almost impossible to have the money for all the necessary things. She had a special sense of getting the stuff she wanted by knowing where and how to shop and she would even redo some things to make them look prettier.

"Mary Rita, if you find the material for the wedding dress, I'll pay for it," her sweet brother Edward said. "You're my only sister and I love you."

"Are you sure?" she asked. "Even if I do find something affordable, it'll still be expensive?"

"Go ahead and find it, I'll pay for it," Edward replied.

She knew a local seamstress, Susan for the dress and once she got the material, the lady did an amazing job. Mary Rita

NUMB

told her, "I love how it turned out. I know you were tired and you put many hours into making my wedding dress but you've made me so happy! I'm more than satisfied thank you. I hope you accept my invitation, I want you to attend my wedding."

"Oh, thank you!" Susan gushed. "I've made lots of wedding dresses but I was invited only to a few of the weddings. I'll be there to see you happy!"

Mary Rita crossed off a very important item from her list: The wedding dress.

The next step was to find a nice room to hold her guests. In her neighborhood, it was a local bar with a huge room attached to the bar with separate meeting room or hall. It also had a large kitchen with kitchen supplies. One more thing crossed off from the wedding preparations list!

"Bob, I think God is telling me where to go, what to do, and how to do things, don't you think? I'm almost done and the graduation is getting closer. The dress is ready and the room for the wedding party is booked. We just have to make the reservation for a place to stay after the wedding. What about if we go and try to find a place this weekend?"

"Let's go, I love going with you anywhere you want, You have so much life in you, so much energy. You are so positive. I'm enjoying each second I spend with you. Do you know that after I leave you to go to work or home, I have a smile on my face all day? You make me happy Mary Rita, I love you."

"Oh well..." She smiled. "I talk about the wedding preparations and you make love declarations?" she teased. "I love it! Keep going!" She kissed him with passion and her request made them want the wedding to get here sooner.

The charming, small inn they found had a fresh look. It was lovely and had special flair. Mary Rita and Bob looked at each other and it seemed both of them liked it. "

They went inside in the small lobby and the clerk greeted them from behind the desk. "How can I help you two?"

"Hi, we would like to make a reservation for July 20th," Bob said.

"This year?" the owner of the inn joked.

"Yes, 1946," Bob answered with a grin, playing his game.

"Oh, you don't need any reservations, just show up and I'll give you the key."

"Okay, it'll be our wedding night, so we want to be sure to have a room," Bob insisted.

"I understand but like I said, you don't need a reservation, just show up," the owner repeated with a grin.

"Okay, I consider that we have a room now," Bob said.

Mary Rita crossed another major thing from her wedding list.

"Today is the day!" Mary Rita started the day spinning around her bedroom. "A few more hours and I'll be *Mrs. Mary Rita Wish*. Thank you God, I even get to have my wedding at the same church where my parents were married, St. Basil. Yes, God, I'm talking to you. I will be your servant till the end of my life and I will help others like you helped me and my family. I know it sounds like a commitment and it is. I'll help the needy, this is the promise I make on my wedding day and I'll keep my promise."

The wedding was far better than anyone even dreamed it could be and far more fun than all the guests probably expected. The music made people dance all night long, with Mary Rita and Bob being in the middle of it, all the time. Their family and friends were all happy to be touched by the newlywed's love.

~ 165 ~

NUMB

"Your dress is just amazing! You look beautiful!" Dorothy, Bob's sister said with admiration.

"Thank you Dorothy, coming from you, a specialist, it's a real compliment," Mary Rita said, knowing what a top notch seamstress Dorothy was.

"I am happy you are my sister and law," Dorothy said.

Mary Rita thought Dorothy didn't care much about her and she was surprised to hear this but it made her feel better about being accepted into Bob's family. "Me too!"

A few hours later, Mary Rita said to Bob, "I cannot wait until everyone goes home so we can be alone." She stood really close to her new husband.

He didn't expect to hear such words coming from this tiny beautiful woman, as she was so young all that they had done was kiss and hug during their courtship. So he was full of love and desire to hold her in his arms. Love was calling.

When they finally got to the charming inn where they'd made arrangements for a room at, the owner was absolutely puzzled seeing the newlywed couple dressed in wedding clothes. "Oh, I thought you were just looking for some fun. I didn't believe you were getting married for real!" he said.

Bob stared at him. "What does that mean? We don't have a room reserved?"

"Oh, don't worry about it. I have a room for you. Just follow me and I'll show you."

Mary Rita's mouth dropped open in shock when she saw where she was going to spend her first night as Mrs. Wish. A small bedroom and no bathroom! There were two steps out to the bathroom and they would have to share it with other people. It was way too late for them to find another place. "Bob what are we going to do? We cannot spend our first night like this and I don't think we can find another hotel around here."

Bob shook his head. "Let's find another place. I don't see you sleeping in that bedroom."

"You're right but it's so late, yes the room is small and the bathroom has to be for a bunch of people to use. I never thought things like this existed." She smiled at him. "But we're not here to sleep," she said as she smile shyly, putting gasoline on the fire, as in Bob was already on fire.

"Okay, we'll take the room," Bob said to the owner when they got back to the office.

"Well, the good news is, nobody is next to you, so you don't have to share the bathroom with anybody else. And another thing is that a woman who cleans my inn does the best job. The room isn't perfect but it is *perfectly* clean. I mean spotless." The inn owner grinned at the couple.

The newlywed couple had the time of their lives making their first night together a memorable one. Something they were going to remember for years to come.

NUMB

CHAPTER TWO

"Mary Rita, I have to find a new job," Bob said. "You know three weeks ago, right before our wedding, my father decided to sell his gas station where I worked and my mother decided to move her beauty shop downstairs in their home."

"Don't worry about this now, let's do this after our honeymoon is over. You're so good at building stuff and can easily find a good job. Plus, I can help too," she said.

Bob smiled at her. "I think it's a good idea to worry about the job after we get back home. Wait...what do you mean you're going to help too?"

"Do you know how many useful things I learned when I was in school? I know how to make clothes, I learned steno, you know the short writing, and you know I can be a waitress, anything to help with our family expenses."

"I like how that sounds... *'Our family'*, I love you." Bob kissed her forehead.

"I love you too," she said.

"No, I'll find a good job and I know you're right, I can build anything. Plus, I know how to be a good carpenter."

"Do you remember Jesus was a carpenter?" Mary Rita beamed at him.

"I know and I am blessed to be married to you. We both love Him and we both love going to church. I want you to stay home and raise our children, though."

"Hey, wait a minute! I'll turn 18 next month. Don't you think we should wait a little bit before we have kids? I want to spend my time with you, Mr. Wish," she said.

He laughed as he nodded. "I agree, Mrs. Wish. Do you remember my high school friend that lived in the same neighborhood I grew up in? Well, he moved to Wisconsin. Now, his family has a very large dairy farm and they love it there."

"Do you want to move to Wisconsin?" Mary Rita asked having fun teasing him.

"No, I don't, but why not go there now? I thought we could spend our honeymoon there. We can rent a cabin on the lake, only 5 miles from the city where they live and we can spend our time by ourselves in the wilderness."

"Have you ever been there?" she asked.

"No, I've never been there but Pep, my friend keeps telling me how much he loves living up there. The lake is large, surrounded by forest and there are a few cabins. I can also go fishing. He told me there are lots of largemouth bass, pinfish and Northern Pike, so we can save some money with my fishing. If you want, we can get together a few hours with my friend and his girlfriend, but only a few hours because I want to be with you, my little skater girl." He kissed her.

"Okay, let's see if we can go there. It sounds really fun. I would like to be in a cabin far away from the city. I've never been to other places but Chicago. No, I take that back. I did go to Arizona when my mom decided to do whatever she could to save my dad from tuberculosis even our doctor told her it would be impossible. Bob, my mother is a saint, she went back and forth from Chicago to Prescott Arizona and one time, she even took me with her to see my dad. It was the last time I saw him. I remember him looking so sick, so thin and pale that I asked if he was my father. It must have

NUMB

hurt his feelings so bad. I didn't know. I was only three years old. I wish I wouldn't have said it but that's what I said." Mary Rita had tears running down her beautiful face.

"Please don't cry. I understand and he knows... he loves you." Bob hugged his wife.

"You're right, sometimes I'm lucky and I have dreams with my father, I know he loves and watches over me from Heaven. Do you know, at our wedding I had a small handkerchief that belonged to him and I wore it with me. He and Grant was with me in our wedding and I had their blessings," Mary Rita said through tears.

"Come closer, let's sit down, and relax a few minutes," Bob urged, taking his wife to a quiet place in their house.

It felt so good to her for him to hold her and comfort her. So this is what it was like to have a husband who loved you. Mary Rita thought as she fell asleep on Bob's shoulder.

The next day, Bob said, "I am sure that we will love the place, so let's pack and go. We need more of a honeymoon." Wisconsin was so different than the places the Wish's came from. The clean, breathable air, everything was green and fresh and it made them think they're in a different world. The neighbors were miles way and the place was so peaceful. Being far north of Chicago, the temperatures were cooler than in Chicago but the summers were absolutely beautiful. There were cabins, cottages, farms, lots to choose from. Bob's friend who lived there, found a tiny cabin in the woods, on a lake, Rib Lake in Taylor County.

"I want to move here," Mary Rita said. "We can go and visit the small town not too far but far enough. So we can go have lunch or dinner and come back to Heaven. I am so grateful to Pep and for finding us this place."

"I'll take care of them when they'll come for business in Chicago, I mean, *we* will. Now I'll have to get used to saying 'we and us' from now on." Bob chuckled.

"Oh, I know how to spend fun time and to make your friend's fiancée love our city, but I'm sure she loves living here in Wisconsin. Now, I'd like to live half and half, live home and live here, six months there and six months here."

The week they spent in Wisconsin was a week to remember. Bob and Mary Rita's love bloomed into a sold relationship. They were closer than ever before.

They came back to Chicago and their home city was ready to offer the newlyweds a new life. Mary Rita and Bob Wish couldn't be happier, eager to start a family.

Not long after the couple came back to Chicago, Mary Rita stood close to her husband. "Bob, I applied for a job as a salesperson at Sears. I know they need me. I'm good with clothes and dresses and I know what to tell people about clothing. I'm so excited!"

Bob shook his head, though he smiled. "Oh, there's no way you'll stay home. Only a baby could make that happen. Your energy is contagious. I got a job too, it's kind of far from home, but I will be working at a Lumber Company.

"Bob, if you don't like it, quit and you can find something else I'm sure. You're good, like I told you, at building stuff or as a carpenter."

"We need the money and its okay for now, but I'll start looking for something else. Mary Rita, I will always remember our little, short but sweet honeymoon. It was a *real* honeymoon. I couldn't wait to go back to our cabin from everywhere we went. Every time we're going places my mind was only thinking of how to get back to the cabin so I could

NUMB

hold you in my arms... you little, tricky, beautiful wife of mine."

"What do you mean tricky?" She winked at him. "What did I do wrong?" Mary Rita said knowing exactly what Bob was referring to.

"How old did you say you were when I first asked you out?" He kept her close to his body.

"Oh, that's when I had to lie; otherwise you would never date me. I think it was the best thing I ever lied about so far!" Mary Rita laughed as she grabbed Bob's hands and spun around the room.

"Yes, I think the same way and I thank God, you tricked me. I want to have lots of kids, to hear lots of kid's voices around us, but at the same time, I would like to be only the two of us, you and I. Life is getting so complicated and you cannot have everything but God will give us what we need and when we need it."

"Bob, your voice is so soft when you talk like this. It makes me have goose bumps." She giggled. "And you love God so much that I think you could be a really good role model and a good teacher for all the children who have no one to look up to or to listen to. They would listen to you. Even when you get old and grey, I think they would listen. They would think that Heaven sent one of its Saints here on Earth. Your face shows nothing but happiness and everyone can see the goodness in you."

"Mary Rita, I am only five years older than you and you've already made me an old, gray haired man, with all your energy," he teased.

"Yes, ha-ha! This is my way of telling you that I will love you even when you are that old man, Bob Wish. I cannot see my life away from you or without you. So you'd better get another job closer to home but most importantly, a job that you will like."

He grinned as he shook his head. "You have to be happy around someone as sweet as you, my dear. We have a long journey ahead of us. You might have never thought of it this way, but we will have years and years together. And I cannot wait."

"Let me hug you my dear Mr. Wish. You're big hearted. A good and kind man. And I have something to tell you. Bob, I think we're getting closer to hearing kid's voices around us," she whispered, "Just like you said."

"What do you mean? Wait a second, are you pregnant?"

Mary Rita nodded.

Bob was happy with tears in his eyes. He picked up his wife spinning in circles all over the room with her.

Mary Rita looked up at him. "Do you remember when you told me that God will give us what we need when we need it? Well, the time came."

"Mary Rita, I knew I was a lucky man to marry you but I'm adding more reasons to the list everyday. You do make me really happy."

"You'll have to find another job to be closer. And I have a question for you, do you remember Dr. Hess? Do you remember when I told you about my sister-in-law, Sally giving birth to our eleven pound nephew, Joey? Well, I want that doctor to be my doctor, not that I'm having an eleven pound baby, but just in case." She laughed.

His eyes got wide, and then he laughed.

She grinned at him. "I'll start looking for him and asking my neighbors to find out where he is now."

Bob nodded. "Yes, it is a good idea and I'll start taking care of the things we're going to need for the baby's room. I mean

NUMB

"Mom, I can rock the baby's cradle with my left foot and my right could run my sewing machine and I can make some money," Mary Rita said.

"The daughter like the mother," Anne said kissing her cheek.

"Yes Mom, you were the best role model. I've learned so much from you, I love you Mom," Mary Rita said.

So the 'work' started to come to the small apartment in the attic. The month of November was a beautiful month in Chicago, people were busy with the Thanksgiving preparations while Mary Rita and Bob were busy with other kinds of preparations, the coming of their first baby into this world.

"I feel safe knowing that Dr. Hess will be here with me," Mary Rita told her husband as she lay in a hospital bed.

"I know but you're already three weeks late. I want it done and see the baby... my baby," Bob replied.

"Me too, I wish it were that simple, but look I have no pain and I should by now. Okay leave now, the nurse is coming and it will be okay."

Bob kissed his wife as he looked worried and left the hospital room. He went to wait inside the waiting room. He knew the baby wasn't turned and it would be breach. This birth made him nervous.

Mary Rita spoke up when the door opened, "Nurse, I look around me and those women are screaming in pain. What's wrong with me? Why doesn't my baby come?

"Don't worry you'll give birth, don't worry!" the nurse said.

The doctor came in, accompanied by three other men wearing white jackets. They were in training and Mary Rita was a good case to learn from with a breach pregnancy. Even when the doctor did what he was supposed to do, trying to daughter while I make some money to help with our overhead."

"I can't believe we're having this conversation few hours after you gave birth! You know how much I love you and we already made plans to have a large family, but it seems like you forgot about it."

"You see, this is not the right time either to talk about our growing family, she was a breached baby. I could've died or both of us could have died. God took care of us."

"I'm so sorry, you're right. Whatever is there for us, it will happen as it is written in His book," Bob said looking up, being sure God witnessed what he said.

"Now we can talk!" Mary Rita laughed. "I like what you said though. We will see what He has planned for us. We'll go home and we'll see.... "

Several weeks later, the family had an appointment with Dr. Hess for a routine baby exam.

At the end of his examination, the doctor said, "Mary Rita, your baby girl is doing excellent, growing perfectly. I'll see her again in a few weeks."

"What's wrong with her?"

"Nothing, everything is ok, but what I want to say has nothing to do with Kathleen. I want you to wait at least a year before getting pregnant again and more importantly, to plan to have the baby in July."

Mary Rita thought Dr. Hess had lost his mind. "Why July, may I ask?"

"July is the month when I come back from my vacation and I want to be sure I'm here when the time to have your second baby comes. The procedure I performed on you is

NUMB

usually performed for the second child, too. The percentage of probability is overwhelming. Don't worry, your babies will be healthy, I promise."

"Thank you for all you did for my baby and me. I knew I was a problem case the moment you brought a bunch of students in with you. I'm glad I could help them learn and they will help other women if they have similar situations."

"I remembered when I helped your sister-in-law to deliver her eleven pound baby, but your case was more difficult than hers; please consider my advice," Dr. Hess said.

Bob Wish came and took his' girls' home, singing all the way home.

Mary Rita and Bob invited their family to see the baby and when they got home, brothers, sisters, nephews, nieces, aunts, uncles, cousins, everyone was there to congratulate the new parents and to see the beautiful baby girl.

The Italian family unity was welcoming Bob, Mary Rita and Kathleen with love and affection and it seemed the Irish side of their family, had been 'contaminated' by the noisy Italian side, too. The family had a great time together, being happy to see each other and to keep the traditions.

Anne, couldn't wait to play and spend time with her granddaughter, taking her to church and teaching her things that she had taught her own children. "Mary Rita, do you remember how many times I told you the story about my novena, the nine day prayers to Our Holy Mother, to give me a girl that would live? Losing two girls made me want so much to have at least one girl, and she gave me you! When I hold Kathleen in my arms, I feel something that not many people could understand. I feel this enormous gratitude for what I have. I'm so happy."

"I know mom, I feel the same way. Especially, after what Kathleen and I went through."

Her mother nodded. "Also, I need to tell you what one of our neighbors asked me today. She aske if you could do some alterations for her dresses and I wasn't sure if you wanted to do it, but I remembered the conversation we had not too long ago about when you expressed the desire to do this."

Mary Rita smiled. "It's exactly what Bob and I talked about... something I could do at home. Yes, I want to do it, thank you for bringing it up."

"Perfect, I'll let my friend know and put you both in touch," Anne said.

It worked out that Mary Rita got lots of alteration jobs after this.

She did alterations for few months and after that, she wanted to do something new. The attic apartment was just so small to be able to work that well there.

"Do you know something?" She said to Bob. "I think I'll start looking for a waitress job at a small restaurant to learn how to wait tables and after that, I'll look for a better job at a larger restaurant. I think I can make good money."

"You already know my answer; you do what you want to do as long as everything at home is okay, the baby and everything else. You also need to be happy, so make sure it is something you can enjoy too."

"You always support me, Bob. I love you so much for it too. I know you want me happy and home, but I can do both, trust me."

Few days later, she came home and told her mother, "Mom, I got the job! I'll be a waitress at the pizza restaurant, the one close to us. They have a Juke box and the music is great."

"Does Bob know?" Anne asked.

NUMB

"Not yet. I'll tell him when he comes home from work. Why? Do you think we don't need the money? Who doesn't?"

"I know what you're saying, but he is the head of the family."

"Mom, times are tough, women have to work and help their families. I'm determined to do it. I always wanted to work."

"Oh, this I know! The soda stand, the can company, steno job, you have always worked. I'd known this from the moment I gave birth to you and now, nothing and no one can stop you, not even Bob, or your baby girl. I wonder if you would be the same, doing the same things if I lived in a separate apartment, not with you? " Anne said with a sad tone in her voice.

Anne prayed to God that her daughter's marriage would last; knowing that men were feeling insulted to see their wives working outside their homes nowadays. People were looking down on them; society wasn't ready to accept such behaviors. *Let's hope I'm old fashioned when comes to this sensitive subject.* Anne tried to convince herself, but she had a feeling that her son in law wouldn't be too excited to hear the 'good news' Mary Rita was going to tell him.

Bob came home from work and he knew his wife was up to something, but he wanted to have dinner first.

Mary Rita knew the rule, food first, then talking. So she let him eat and when he was done she said, "Bob, I'm going to start working as a waitress at the pizza place. I would like to at least try it and see if it works out?"

"I know," he said.

"How did you know? I just got the job."

"Well, I stopped there to bring you and your mother some pizza because I know how much you both like it. Pete, the owner told me the 'news.' I had to pretend I knew already. Try it and if you don't like it, you know what to do, quit the job."

She stopped cleaning the dinner table and kissed her husband, thanking him for being so open minded and letting her do what she wanted to do. "Bob, I know you don't want me to work outside the house. That people might think you cannot afford to cover all our family expenses like men are supposed to do, but don't you think times have changed a lot? My sister in law, Betty Lou works and she is doing okay and my brother, Beau finds it helpful; the only thing is the late hours."

"Try to finish before dark, ask for that kind of schedule, can you?" Bob asked.

"I know, but that's the time when people go out to eat, after work. Well, we'll see, what's important is that we love each other."

Mary Rita started the waitress job but after several work evenings, things became more than she thought 'work' would be.

"Mom, you were right. I have to find something else, another job that will let me come home earlier. Bob will have something to say for sure, he isn't too happy about that."

"You shouldn't wait for Bob to say something, just find another job if you insist on working," Anne suggested.

Once Mary Rita decided what she wanted, it didn't take long to find another job at a very nice restaurant, closer to home. "Bob, I found a much better job, closer to home. I applied for the job and I was happy to be accepted."

"There is no way I'll say it makes me happy."

NUMB

"I have to wear a white uniform and I'll start at the counter part, first!"

"Well, good luck," Bob said with no enthusiasm in his voice.

"Thank you. I'll get home earlier, I promise."

After starting the new job, she realized she needed training to learn how to 'call' an order for the chef, because every time she called the order he was cussing!

The chef helper gave Mary Rita a manual to study and after awhile, she was able to call the orders right.

"Mom, I like working there. I'm making good money, but look, Kathleen is almost three years old and do you know what she said a few days ago? She said, 'son of a mitch, hurry up!' I know I have learned how to call orders; how to make clients happy, but at the same time I learned how to say bad words like the chef does all the time. I didn't realize I swore so much until I heard my little girl cussing. What a shame. I go to church, I pray to God every day and I cuss like a sailor."

Anne nodded. "Yes, you don't talk like a lady and your vocabulary is full of bad words. Your daughter looks up to you, learning how to behave and at this moment; you're not a good role model to follow." Anne gave her a gentle smile.

"Yes, she picked up the phrase, I shouldn't say this, but she was so cute when she said it. I have to be more careful what I say in front of her, but that's all I'm hearing all day long, cussing!"

"Okay, so what are you going to do about your job?"

"Today, I'll give my two weeks notice."

"Good, I'm glad to hear this but at the same time I know something else will come up. Like I said several times already, there's no way someone or something can stop you."

"Mom, we want to purchase a new car and we saved enough for the down payment."

"Perfect, so you can pay the rest in payments. I'm so proud of you two. You saved the money without being overly frugal and we have everything we need. I mean just look, my granddaughter is well dressed and so are you!"

"You're right but don't forget how much you spoil her."

"It's my job to buy her nice dresses and spoil her, like you just said. It makes me happy to see her dressed in the most beautiful dresses when we go to church on Sundays."

"I'll talk to Bob about the new car idea; he loves cars. That's all he's been talking about recently. A few days ago, he said that when he has enough money, he would like to buy old cars, make them look new then take them to the car shows."

Kathleen was running toward her mother to hug her; Mary Rita's face was glowing when she saw her daughter coming, it made her so happy.

"Mom," Kathleen said, "I want you home with me. I don't want you to go back to work."

Mary Rita picked Kathleen up into her arms and danced with her slowly, thinking how much better her child's life was with her being home, how much mother and daughter would enjoy their time together.

When Bob arrived home from work and saw his 'girls' playing, his face had a large smile on it. He stopped and looked at them. "Mary Rita, I love seeing you and Kathleen when I come home from work, this is how our life should be."

"I love spending time with her and you're right, it feels so good to see you happy too. Also, honey, I think is about time to buy a new car. We need a bigger car now. We can put a nice down payment and make payments, what do you think?"

NUMB

He nodded. "Let's do it and this way, you'll have to learn how to drive. Your brother, Beau has offered to take care of this. I think he feels like it's his duty being older than you, even if both of you are married now. He thinks it is a brother thing and I'm so grateful he will take the time to go with you to the park."

The following week after they bought the car, Beau took his sister to the park where she could practice driving. After driving around the park, Beau asked her, "Mary Rita, where would you like to drive from here?'

"Let's go and get the test, so I can drive alone," she said.

"But you didn't practice enough, no parking, no backing up. Sis... I really believe you aren't ready for the test."

"Let me try it, I want to drive!"

"Ok, let's go but don't say I didn't warn you," Beau said.

Once they got to the driving range, the instructor asked Mary Rita to back around the corners, to park, back up and few more other routine procedures.

The instructor advised her just like her older brother had...more practice! "You didn't pass, you have to practice more."

Mary Rita started crying, she felt like her entire world was falling apart. "I can't get someone to take me to the park to practice. My husband works all day long and my brothers too. If I had the license, I could practice more, just closer to home where there is less traffic."

The instructor pulled Beau to the side. "You have to promise me that you're going to watch her closely and help her in backing up and parking. If you promise me, I'll pass her."

Beau thanked the instructor and promised to help his sister to get better with her driving.

"Beau, I'm so grateful. Without you, he wouldn't have passed me. I promise I'll practice. I don't want to be in an accident, and I'll be a good driver. Thank you brother, thank you," she said hugging Beau.

Once she got home, she called out, "Bob, mom, Kathleen come here please. I have something to tell you."

All of them came right away; they knew it must be something important.

"You are looking at a new driver! But I want you to know that I have to practice. Without Beau, the instructor would not have passed me. So be ready to go with me, I have to drive a lot."

"Congratulations honey, we'll be with you, let us know when you want to start," Bob said.

"What do you mean, we? Kathleen will stay home with my mom till I get more experience," Mary Rita said with a firm voice.

"Ok, you're right. Even if I trust you, the only thing I'm afraid of is your energy! I don't want you to use it as speed," he warned. "You have to watch your speed. You're too fast in whatever you do. Sometimes I even get tired watching you working around the house."

"I think you're right." She laughed. "I do like speed. It makes me feel like I can do anything I want to do."

"What do you mean?"

"I mean, going to work or finding a job where I can be home with Kathleen and mom, when she comes from work. But to find that job, I have to drive places."

Bob's joy was gone the moment he heard his wife say she was looking for a job, again. *Maybe I have to understand her, she is so energetic, and she can do lots of things at the same time. I can't even really keep up with her. She's not only tiny and beautiful but she does all the things in the house faster*

NUMB

than anyone I know. This is a gift from God no one can even be lazy around her. Thank God, I work hard and provide for my family. Otherwise, she would pass me up, my pistol of a wife! "Mary Rita, if you're looking for something new to do, just be sure you don't spend too much time away from us, from home. We want you with us, we need you, promise?"

"I know you work hard and I know you take good care of us. Yes, I promise I won't accept any job that will require full time or coming home late at night. I won't do that again. Bob, I like how I feel when I work. I feel useful, and when I get the money for my work, it feels even better," she said smiling.

"Okay, but don't forget we have a deal," Bob reminded her cautiously.

CHAPTER FOUR

Five years later....

Bob and Mary Rita had purchased a lot located at Lake Eliza in Porter County and wanted to build a small cottage there. After few months, the place was calling their names.

"Bob, what about we start building the cottage, like you talked about when we bought the lot? It could be such an amazing retreat for us. We can go there on weekends and it's only two hours drive from our home in Chicago."

Bob agreed. "I already talked to my brother, Eric, and he is going to help me with the construction. I think I can do it by myself, but it would take a lot longer. Plus, I'll get a chance to spend time with him. We both work long hours so this will good for us."

"So glad to hear this, Eric is a good man. I had no idea you were missing your brother so much though. We should spend more time together as a family."

"Yes, I agree. So soon, you'll be able to spend some time there. It is such a wonderful place. Did you know that the name of the lake was changed after 1841, from Fish Lake to Lake Eliza?"

"How do you know all of this?"

"I know it because I'm smart." He grinned at her. "No, I'm just kidding. I read about it when we purchased the lot. I love that the lake is surrounded by oak groves and the landscape

NUMB

reminds me of those catalogs advertising beautiful places to live in. We couldn't find a better place for our cottage."

Soon, the construction started and Bob was so excited to work with his brother. "Sometimes, I wish we could work together all the time but life took us in two different directions. But we can still find our way to spend time together doing something positive, right?"

Eric smiled as he agreed. "Bob, you really seem to be happy now. I can see that being married has done wonders for you."

"Yes, we really are happy, but Mary Rita is on her own too much. I mean she's always on the go. She's constantly finding something new to do. I just have to allow her to get rid of all that energy. We also want more kids." He laughed.

Eric smiled at him. "Well seems to are doing well enough to now be building another home. I'm happy for you."

When the cottage was almost done, the family took a trip to spend the weekend there. Anne and Mary Rita packed all the things needed and once they arrived, Mary Rita couldn't stop admiring it.

Anne was speechless and she wanted to move there right away.

Mary Rita hugged her husband. "I love how you built that small brick area with fireplace and the stove is just so helpful. We can roast hamburgers, marshmallows and still have fun, even if the cottage is not completely finished. You're the best husband in the world. You know how to do so many things. Bob Wish. I'm a lucky wife," she said kissing Bob on the cheek.

Bob knew his reward would come later on, when everyone went asleep for the night. He smiled.

Mary Rita, Anne and little Kathleen couldn't wait for another weekend at their cottage on Lake Eliza.

Then the night before they were to leave, out of nowhere, Mary Rita woke up with an excruciating pain in her shoulder. She shook Bob awake. "I'm so sorry to wake you up, but we have to wake everyone up and leave. I've never had such pain, never."

"What happened?" Bob asked getting dressed.
"I have no idea. I didn't fall or hit anything, but I woke up with this terrible pain. You know I don't like going to the doctors but I have to this time."

They got into the car in the middle of the night and stopped at the first urgent care they saw. The doctor said she had a case of acute bursitis.... inflammation of the shoulder joint, something with a liquid sack. After she took some of the medicine that was prescribed to her, the pain vanished, but so had the weekend.

"I'm so sorry I spoiled your weekend, but the pain was bigger than being sorry for all of you," she joked, hugging them one by one.

Few more months passed, the weather was getting cooler and the family spent a lot more time home, in Chicago, especially with the holidays approaching.

The family was waiting for the spring to come and more importantly, for the second baby to come into this world.

The holidays, Thanksgiving and Christmas were so huge for their family.

"It would be so nice to spend the holidays at our cottage at Lake Eliza, but I'm so heavy now, that I don't think I would enjoy it." Mary Rita sighed. "The first few months I thought I

NUMB

was just tired but when I went to the doctor I found out why!"

"You look so good when you're pregnant," Bob said hugging his wife.

They were waiting for their new baby to come and Kathleen was happy to be able to have a brother or a sister to play with. She was kissing her mother's belly and talking to the little human being inside, they already had a close relationship.

The month of February brought a beautiful girl into Wish's family, named Christina. Mary Rita's doctor was in town and he was more worried about her delivery than she was! The doctor was prepared for the worst, but things went smoothly with no problems unlike the first time, when Kathleen was born.

Now, Kathleen would have a sister to play with and to take care of. Things were going smoothly and everyone was happy but not even six months after Christina was born, Mary Rita saw an article in a newspaper. The baby was sleeping, so she sat in a chair and started reading that article.

When she finished reading, she looked at the statue of Holy Mother holding her son, Jesus Chris, and asked, "Is this the answer to all my prayers? Since I got married, I wanted to help my family financially even if my Bob brings enough money for us to live comfortably. Why do I have this thought in my mind? Why do I have to work? You gave me so much positive energy and I have such a huge desire to help people. Holy Mother, tell me this is it, please?" Mary Rita asked the Virgin Mary located on the special prayer corner that her husband built for her, the place of her morning devotions. "I have no idea what this article is all about but I like the fact that is about women working as many hours as they want, selling something through parties and making money, if this can be true. If I can be with my children and take care of them, I think I can go for few hours to those meetings; they called them 'parties.' My mother and Bob can watch the kids while I'm gone, so I will have peace of mind. I will ask Bob and I think I will do it," she kept talking to Holy Mother.

Christina was already six months old and the family was having fun playing with her.

Her older sister was protecting her baby sister like the most precious toy she had and this was bringing joy to her parents. She was a good older sister.

"Bob," Mary Rita said when her husband came home from his carpenter work. "Let's have dinner and then I have something to ask you."

She brought the newspaper from the living room and after Bob finished eating, she started reading the article. Bob didn't really pay attention but when he saw his wife acting so enthusiastic, he started listening.

"So, what do you think?"

"What do I think about what?" Bob asked.

"About enrolling in this program I just read to you. I love what it says and if it is true, I think it will be the best thing for me to do."

"Do whatever makes you happy. I always told you that, right?"

"Yes, you did. I'll call tomorrow and check the details. It sounds too good to be true."

Next day, Mary Rita was on her mission to find out about the business. Someone explained to her how the company worked and what product they were selling. She wanted to be sure the business was something she wanted to do. So she went to Sears, the big store everyone knew about, to check on things made of plastic, containers and all kind of things.

NUMB

Plastic was something new and no one seemed aware of the products made with it.

Mary Rita touched some of them and realized there was a big difference between the ones she touched at the big store and the ones she touched at the interview she had with the person in charge with recruiting new sales persons. The quality was so much better at the Tupperware Company. This was a big plus in her decision.

Once she made up her mind, Mary Rita knew she had to have parties to be able to demonstrate how the Tupperware containers worked and to enroll more women.

"Mom, please invite some of your friends for a party. I'll call some of our relatives they will be interested. The more people we have, the better. These containers are so useful. I know it is something new and it will take time for women to figure out how good is to have them in the kitchen, but I'm determined to convince them how good they work. But I need your help, I need lots of women. What's hard is that there are no catalogs to choose your product from, no order forms, like other companies have, but I will do it."

Anne, Mary Rita's mother, always knew how much her daughter wanted to do something to help her family and was sure she got that extra energy from her and she had to use it. Anne talked to all her friends and relatives then invited them to come to her home for a gathering.

Meanwhile, Mary Rita purchased the starter kit, baked some cookies and was ready to hold her first Tupperware party.

"I'm so glad to have Betty Lou with us. I always loved my brother's wife. Beau was lucky to marry such a good woman. Do you remember when they ran away to get married? I'm glad it worked out," Mary Rita shared her thoughts with her mother.

"Of course I remember it! How can I forget it? I felt scared while not knowing where my son was going!"

"How many women do you think will come?" Mary Rita asked, to be sure she had enough cookies, coffee....

"I invited all women from our family and few friends. Let's hope they come. Be sure we have enough cookies for all," Anne said, almost reading her daughter's mind.

"Don't worry, we have more cookies than we'll need, but you're right, you never know." Mary Rita was excited, so happy to start a new thing, hoping to bring some extra income to help with the family expenses. At least, she liked to believe she was doing it for the family.

Of course, her family would benefit from whatever money she would bring home, but she knew she was doing it mostly for her, to be the person she was meant to be a leader.

Mary Rita had the words "helping others" deeply implanted in her mind.

"Mom, pray this will work because I want to have more kids, at least four and this will cost us some extra money!"

"What? You never told me you wanted so many kids!"

"I want to follow your example, mom. I love you so much," Mary Rita said hugging her mother and for few seconds they could feel the warmth of their love.

The day came for the first Tupperware party and Mary Rita had never been more excited.

She had all the products lined up, served cookies and coffee. Then the way she demonstrated how the products worked, she convinced some of the women to purchase the plastic containers. She sold enough to pay for the kit she purchased and that made her feel confident that she could do the job. She could recruit women to sell and she would become a successful distributor. Betty Lou arranged two "date parties" for her sister in law, Mary Rita to sell the

NUMB

plastic containers and more important than the selling was to recruit sale people.

What a blessing to have such wonderful relatives, Mary Rita couldn't be more grateful.

A few weeks after her first steps into the Tupperware business, Mary Rita saw the woman she admired the most, after her mother, the hostess she worked with at her last job, at the fine restaurant. That hostess was so confident while ushering people to their tables, and she seemed as poised as Miss America!

This is how Mary Rita saw the woman in her mind.

So, when she saw that woman on her way to a date party, how the company called the Tupperware parties, she said, "Would you like to sell Tupperware, plastic containers? It's easy and profitable."

The woman agreed and signed on.

Mary Rita got everyone she knew involved. She was always looking up a name or someone she knew that would like to make extra income.

The parties Mary Rita held started to bring more women that were buying more and more containers and most of the ladies signed up for membership. The parties became popular but they were scheduled too close to each other, time wise and it started to take too much time from her family. "Bob, I need your help and I'm not sure if you want to help me."

"I will help you, but you have to understand we had a deal, do you remember?" Bob asked.

"Yes, I do. I promised to not be away from home for too long and I have to admit, I love the money I make. In order to make that kind of money, I have to attend more date parties but you're right, it takes too much time away from all of you."

"Okay, at least you remembered what we have talked about. So what about only two date parties a week? How do you feel about this?" How could you expect to have five parties in one week?" Bob asked.

"I promise only two date parties a week and I will give three of those five parties away," she said.

"Oh no, now that you already have them lined up, do it but after that, you have to keep your promise."

Mary Rita jumped up and down and kissed her husband for accepting to drive her from one party to another, but she knew to not do something that would hurt her family time, the love of her life and her beautiful daughters.

Kathleen Wish was getting ready to start first grade at Catholic school and she couldn't be happier. Her parents believed she would be an excellent student.

"Bob, our Kathleen will be a very successful business woman, I just know it," Mary Rita said.

"I think you're right, she gets it from her dad!" Bob dared to say.

"What about her executive mama?" Mary Rita asked being proud of her recent achievements.

"I have to admit, you're a damned good recruiter. How do you convince women to sign up?" Bob smiled at her.

"It's not so difficult. I tell them, 'do you want to make money selling a product that sells itself, have time for your family, and get a gift each time you host a party, meet wonderful people and have lots of fun?' And the answer is always, 'yes, I do.' This is how I got so many distributors. Bob, I don't feel like this is work for me. It's more fun than work. It's only the time I'm concerned about."

NUMB

"Perfect, but don't forget, money isn't everything, but sometimes I feel like this concept is one everyone knows about, but it isn't applicable to you." He laughed.

The only person living in the South Eastern suburb of Chicago selling Tupperware products was Mary Rita Wish, followed by her recruiters and she was unstoppable.

"Bob, can you believe we sold a thousand dollars at one of the parties? That's a lot of money for the times we live in," she said.

Bob nodded. "I agree, it is a lot, anyway it is a lot more than I make at my woodshop! It seems like soon we will be able to buy a larger home."

Mary Rita didn't say more than this. She didn't want to make her husband think of all the time she put into making this money, so she pretended like she didn't hear his comment.

Bob was right; soon they bought their first brick home, a three bedroom house, so beautiful that the entire family fell in love with it. The event brought much joy to the family.

Anne couldn't have been happier to see her daughter being so productive.

"Do you know what I think? We kind of stopped using our cottage in Indiana at Lake Eliza, right?" Mary Rita asked.

"Yes, I noticed that too," Bob agreed. "We're so busy with our lives and this isn't a good thing. We have to enjoy life, Mary Rita. We're still young and we have to spend more time as a family; money isn't everything. I keep saying this more and more, but at the same time we get more and more money."

"We should sell the cottage, what do you think?" she asked.

"Let's do it, we can buy another one when the time comes. We have been so blessed the moment you decided to give a this Tupperware of yours a try. Yes, it was a good thing and it's making you happy. You're glowing every time I pick you up from those parties."

"Because what I'm doing really does gives me joy! To help women have a better life, it does make me feel good. Bob, if the things keep going this good, I will start helping charity organizations. You know... the ones that help underprivileged women, those that struggle to make ends meet to raise their children. I have this call in my heart and our Catholic church will guide me in my mission."

"I know you'll do it, you're such a godly woman and that's why God helps you, He must have to have a plan for us, because I feel the same way about helping others," Bob agreed.

At the end of one of the Tupperware parties, Mary Rita went home and she was surrounded by her loving daughters and her mother.

Anne had the food ready and all of them were waiting for Bob to come home from work.

A call came to the house and Mary Rita answered the phone,

"Ma'am, your husband had an accident and he is in the hospital," the voice at the other end said.

"What? Is he alive, what kind of accident?" she asked.

The person who called gave Mary Rita the name of the hospital located somewhere in a suburbs of Chicago.

Mary Rita grabbed a chair to sit down; she dropped the phone from her hand. "Mom, Bob had an accident and he's in the hospital. I have to go right now. I'm desperate. The guy didn't say more than this. God, please let him be with us for a long time, we all love him," she said leaving her home, as soon as Anne assured her that everything would be okay with her daughters and her.

NUMB

She was wondering about how bad the accident was, what part of his body was hurt, if he would be ever back to normal, all those things were going crazy in her mind, during the drive there. Just last year in 1964, she'd received a similar phone call that her brother, Joseph, the firefighter, lost his life in a horrible building fire that everyone heard about as it was burning down, falling from the third floor all the way to the basement, a flooded basement. Most of his colleagues escaped the fire with minor injuries, but Joe couldn't be saved. She'd felt so bad for Sally and the kids and she mourned the loss of her sweet brother Joe. He helped to raise her and he'd always been her hero. He was a hero and he died as one.

She knew that carpenters could have lots of accidents because of the nature of their work, but her Bob was always calm and careful.

Mary Rita arrived at the hospital and was directed to the room where Bob was lying down. His ankle, foot and entire leg was wrapped in white bandages and his leg was on the top of the bed sheet.

Seeing her husband like this, Mary Rita almost fainted into the chair.

The doctor that took care of him came in the room and told her that Bob broke his ankle in a way that would require surgery and a very long recovery time.

"Bob, how did you break your ankle, tell me please?"

"Well, a young guy that I work with was supposed to hold the ladder I was on at the place I was working, and when a young girl walked by, he forgot about me and here I am! It destroyed me, I have to work, and I have a family to take care of!"

"Bob, this should be the last thing you should worry about. We can live on what I make with Tupperware, don't worry, please. Your job is to get better and be healthy like before. You wouldn't believe what a beautiful, young girl can do to a man's focus. You might have done the same thing he did." She tried to make her husband smile.

The recovery took such a long time and it was so hard that Bob was debating on whether to give up his job as a carpenter at the woodshop he'd managed. He couldn't do much anyway; at least not strenuous physical activity and he had no idea how long it would take to get on his feet again, without hurting. He'd had 2 operations and lots of physical therapy to make sure his ankle would heal correctly. "I can help you when you're jammed, I can answer the phone. It's better than doing nothing,"

When the women had questions about the parties, about the products, asking how to do the demonstrations, Bob was answering their questions with a professional aplomb, full of confidence. Soon, the ladies enjoyed talking to Bob, feeling like he helped them a lot and they received the same help they would get from Mary Rita.

Day after day, helping the Tupperware women became a real job for him. Bob was so good at doing it that he quit his carpenter job and became his wife's team partner. And what a good job they did together! Working became fun for Bob. He never knew he could enjoy sales, any kind of sales, but he did. "Mary Rita, after helping you answer the phone and talking to your sale ladies, I realized how often I said, 'this is what Mary Rita says, this is what Mary Rita would do!' And they trust me and everyone thanks me for helping them. I never had such a good feeling that makes me feel so useful. I think I had the accident for a reason, I broke my ankle so I could work with you."

"You could never say more loving words than what you just said, not even when you said that you loved me all those

NUMB

years ago!" Mary Rita replied with a laugh. "Now that you said what you think about the accident, I might start to believe it, but we could have become a team and work together without you breaking your ankle."

Bob nodded. "Our daughters have a good future, they are healthy and beautiful. They can have whatever they need, but we have to teach them what hard work is. Nothing was given to us, we never inherited anything. My parents gave everything to my sister, Dorothy, because they lived with her and it was the right thing to do. Your parents worked hard to have what you and your brothers had, and look, your mom is still working. I admire her so much. If we buy another house, she should live with us, because it is not easy getting older and she will need us. We're going to do for her what she does for us, she's a strong Irish woman."

"You're such a wonderful husband, thank you for all that you do for us, for the fact that you see all the things my mother does, all the love and how much she cares about our daughters. I love you so much, Bob Wish."

Five years later, the sales were growing like weeds and the money started to follow even more. The company was happy to have such loyal people, such a productive, strong family with record high sales.

One day, Mary Rita came home and announced, "I have a surprise for you. Do you remember the money I saved working as a waitress? You told me to save that, because you were the one providing for our family. Well, with all the interest it accrued, we can pay off our new Ford."

"Oh, I thought you spent it on clothes? I know how much you like nice outfits." Bob laughed.

"Honey, with two daughters, I take a break from shopping, once in a while!" she joked.

The couple sat down for dinner and they talked about their family's issues.

"How's Kathleen doing in school? She seems so bright." Bob grinned at her.

"St. Beads School is a good school and I'm glad she goes there, she likes it," Mary Rita said proud of her older daughter.

"What about our Christina?" Bob asked.

"Bob, you ask me all these questions like you don't live in this house, why?" she asked with a smile on her face.

"I know all the answers but I like to drive you nuts!" he said, laughing.

"Ok..." Mary Rita rolled her eyes. "She still has to attend kindergarten but overall, she will do well in school. She will need one on one tutoring, to keep up with the other kids. Don't worry. I already talked to her nun. This nun is kind of young and I hope she knows what she's doing...You know the nuns that teach our girls are very educated and I'm glad we chose that school, not all of our friends have such luck."

More happy years went by and the girls were ready to become what each of them wanted to be, such bright young ladies with the same genes as Catherine their great grandmother and Rose their other great grandmother. They had a bright future waiting.

Mary Rita and Bob were having a relaxing time after dinner, enjoying a glass of wine as the light breeze drifted in bringing fresh air into their home.

NUMB

Suddenly, Mary Rita broke the silence, "I don't know why this memory came to my mind, but I enjoyed it, it made me feel closer to my kids. Do you remember how one day, when you insisted Kathleen had to eat all her carrots? It was one of those days when we had lunch somewhere at a restaurant."

"Of course, it was so funny. I loved having kids. I always wanted more, but I'm happy with our two daughters."

Mary Rita laughed. "You told Kathleen, 'If you eat your carrots, you'll grow hair on your chest like your daddy' then she looked at you and answered, 'I don't want hair on my chest, I want boobies like my mommy!' I thought it was hilarious. I mean wow Bob, time is flying way too fast. It seems like just yesterday, our children started kindergarten and now, they are two beautiful young ladies."

"I agree, but look at us! If you say that time is flying, what about us?" Bob raised a brow at her.

"Bob, our strong faith in Jesus Christ kept us together and loving each other. I'll never forget what I promised, we'll build a church. That church will have a special soul; people will feel the love of the one that died on a cross for us, for all of us. He is so present in everything we do. Look at those people I meet every day. The way I talk to them, my passion, and my enthusiasm is so contagious, that everyone turns into a sale person. Show me another manager, I mean, a top manager that can do what I do! Once they become managers, they kind of slow down and rely on their sales people. But not me, I keep recruiting like crazy. It comes to me so naturally, I don't force myself to be the way I am and women like my style, they don't feel pushed to sign up."

"I know, everyone is talking about your 'style' and even the big bosses are asking you, how you do it. It must feel good," Bob said.

She smiled. "You have to have the same feelings I do because look at what you do. Look how many of those sale persons have been convinced by you! That's why I promised what I promised. We will have to purchase land and build a warehouse, because the way we were able to help my brother Beau and his wife, Betty Lou, to make good money, we can help a lot more people. Now, we have a bigger ranch home, what do we want more than this? I know is not all about the money, but it is the life we have now. I wish my mother would stop working, but I think she will never even consider it. It keeps her active. I want to be like her at her age, sharp and strong. So far, I have her work ethic, I love seeing the results of my work."

Bob agreed. "We started talking about our kids and look where we got. I forgot to mention how grateful I am also. You know better than anyone, how much I love old, antique cars. I enjoy working on them, transforming those cars into real jewels and taking them to cars shows. When I see people's eyes while they're looking at my work, my love, my baby, to put it this way....Well, my heart is so full. This is one thing I wanted to be able to do. It gives me so much satisfaction."

"I know and you have been able to actually pursue that dream too, since we have been so successful. Then there's something else, don't you think is time to buy a larger house? We sold the cottage and we can afford to get a bigger home," Mary Rita suggested.

"If this is what you want, why not? If it makes you happy, let's find a house that we all like, like we did when the kids were really young. Now the girls are older and they will need more room."

"We also need to plan our parties, and soon we will get our own distributorship. Bob, this will be the milestone of our business. Looking back from the moment I became a sales

NUMB

person for Tupperware, I think I was the only woman selling their products, and I was only twenty four years old. Someone told me back then, that there was another woman selling Tupperware but she was a lot older. I believe I was at the right moment in the right place. We're growing fast and we can afford things that we never dreamed of. We started with few people and now we count them by hundreds, how blessed we are. One day, we'll build a church to thank God for what he did for all of us."

"What a good idea. Yes, we'll build a church as soon as we retire."

The evening found them enjoying the breeze and thinking of the church, they were going to build, to thank God for all the blessings in their lives.

CHAPTER FIVE

Baton Rouge Louisiana...
A beautiful city on the Mississippi river, Baton Rouge with amazing antebellum landmarks, little castles, a city full of a French flare, only one hour away from New Orleans.

History says that back in 1699, when French explorers noted a red cypress tree stripped of its bark that marked the boundary between Houma and Bayogoula tribal hunting grounds, they called the tree "Le baton rouge" or the red stick.

There was an abundance of churches and locals never thought there enough of them either. The locals also thought that there weren't enough of the red cypress trees.

Somewhere in Baton Rouge, Louisiana, the heavy doors of St. Bernadette Catholic Church opened and the sun's rays slanted a dark orange light in that covered the last oak pews and created a heavenly atmosphere in the quiet, celestial place of worship. The windows filtered the light and it seemed to be Heaven on Earth. The fragrance of the incense burning in the altar was soothing the parishioners' heart. The background incantations penetrated their souls while venerating Jesus Christ and His Holy Mother, Virgin Mary.

A dark female shadow walked across the reflection of Heaven, without looking right or left. She seemed to be confident and sure of herself.

NUMB

She had chosen a pew and sat down. Then in the following minutes, she knelt with her hands together, looking completely immersed in prayers.

Few young mothers grabbed their children and moved closer to the altar, others moved closer to the woman that was deeply praying.

The woman seemed so absorbed into her talk to Jesus Christ that it seemed like she didn't even notice what people did. She kept still, but through her fingers, she could see everything happening around her. Later on, she stood up, went to kiss one of the saints' statues, and lit a candle.

The moment she touched the statue, she looked inseparable with the statue, one body.

Some of the church goers almost forgot why they were there, they forgot they were in church; the church became a place to wonder what was going on, what the woman was doing there....

The priest lifted his eyes to see what created the wave that he could feel in his back—that woman again!

Years and years of theological seminaries, years of being God's loyal servant didn't help to feel the way this woman made him feel with her eyes.

He knew it wasn't her eyes, but it was something she transmitted through those eyes. Like dark waves were floating over pews and most of the parishioners were mesmerized while being touched by those waves, it was something no one could explain. She made them feel numb.

The young mothers holding their children's hands felt like drowning under those imaginary waves, wanting to leave the service sooner than they planned to.

The woman finished her tour of statues and looked deep in someone's eyes.

The man she looked at stood up and followed her out of the church.

"Paul, we have to be more active, our Charity foundation is getting low on funds. Did you notice any changes today?" Eve Garner asked her husband, Paul Garner as they both strode out of St. Bernadette's.

She went directly to the main subject, money, without any introduction. Her husband was following her everywhere and doing whatever she wanted him to do. It was something she had that made people listen to her. Her eyes looked closed, you would think she didn't see anything around her, but in reality, she could see a lot better than everyone around her. It was like she had more than one pair of eyes, she had powerful eyes... seeing into people's souls.

"Yes, I noticed more and more women are trying to escape your circle and others want to be closer to you," he said without being helpful.

"Maybe they're afraid of my visions?" Eve pondered. "It does seem harder for the young ones to understand my prophecies, my premonitions. The older women and even the older men believe me, even some priests believe me. But let's get organized and make plans how to get more funds for our charity. Though this wasn't my question; did you find out who's really ill, who will be put in the nursing home, people that have no family?"

"Do you plan to help them?' he asked. "Next time, I will pay more attention, I promise. I also think Father Mathew will help us. He knows everything," Paul said.

"Not exactly everything," Eve answered closing her eyes for a second.

"What do you mean?" her husband looked puzzled.

"You should know what I'm talking about," she reminded him. "I'm not interested in old poor men or women. I'm

NUMB

looking for those that can provide for the organization. I'm looking for their donations. How do you want me to help those women that didn't plan to get pregnant, or the priests that are going to retire and have no funds? We need donations to flow daily into our charity and we don't have the time to chase them."

"You're right." Paul nodded. "I'll be on my mission to get you the information about those men and women. There are more women than men, and some of them are really wealthy. I don't think it will be too hard to get them to donate to us, because they have a strong faith in God and a huge desire to help the underprivileged. Some of them are looking to find ways to make those donations in the name of God. You were so smart to start this non-profit organization, to help people and the fact that we give the donors a tax deductible form makes them come to you easily. But we have to let them know who we are."

"Ok, it will be your job to let them know. Wait a minute, Arthur must start moving his, *you know what,* and get closer to those wealthy widows, don't you think? He looks healthy and quite handsome and he can do it. Actually, he should do it, it's his job," Eve hinted.

"I'm going to have a meeting with him and tell him what to do." Paul nodded.

"Be sure you'll tell him only what to do, not how to do it, because you are kind of knowledgeable when comes to attractive women," his wife stated.

"Are you insinuating that I go after women?" her husband asked.

Eve Garner raised a brow at him. "I'm not insinuating anything, but how come it wasn't too hard for me to divorce you from your wife of thirty years of marriage? I did in a heartbeat honey. You can think whatever you want. I need donations, and I need them fast,"

This conversation didn't seem to be a godly people conversation, it sounded more like it was coming from hell.

"Cynthia, our friend-secretary, knows many people, in many cities. I'll talk to her, too, and her daughters," Paul suggested.

"Yes, this is a good idea and it seems like you have some work to do. Now we finally have a plan, let's execute it," Eve said with a serious voice, and on the way to their office building, she told her husband, "Cynthia's mother was one of the most beneficial donors for our charity. When she passed away and I was informed that her gift for me was a few hundred thousand dollars, I almost fainted! What a generous gift...Her daughters got pennies in comparison to me. I cannot believe they're still members of our charity organization, but I'm glad they still are."

Husband and wife entered the building across from the church, opened the door of their office, and started making plans for their mission.

Eve Garner was brought to America by adoption, being one of the children that survived the Hiroshima bombing; at least this is what people knew about her origins.

A reputable journalist, a famous American reporter visited Japan after the nuclear bombing. The devastation, the consequences of the bombing, made him start a huge campaign of guilt. He convinced the American people to go and adopt children from Japan to get rid of the guilt they felt and many of them did it. Some Americans tried to compensate for the tragedy that hit Hiroshima by adopting Japanese babies left behind from the devastation.

The couple that adopted Eve gave her the best education they could and the young girl grew into a smart, educated

NUMB

woman with special religious beliefs. Sometimes, the story of her birth place, the story about her ancestors changed, depending on her audience.

People knew something wasn't always right with her but the fear of the unknown would freeze their rational thoughts and beliefs, so no one ever questioned her statements. Parishioners going to St. Bernadette Catholic Church accepted her presence without wanting to know more, being satisfied with what she wanted them to know about her past.

Eve was petite woman with dark, curly hair and her appearance was common, she looked like an ordinary woman until she looked into your eyes. This is how her spiritual power made people feel numb and annihilated. The moment she looked into their eyes, that person would most likely lose her or his will power, then they would obediently do what she told them to do. Some parishioners insisted that she was hypnotizing them and ordered them to make donations, while others weren't able to describe what they were feeling, but for sure, no one could explain the reality of it.

Eve Garner went outside the office to arrange some brochures in a container situated at the door and when she finished, she entered the office where her husband waited for her. She sat down in her chair. "We need more religious books to give to those people that come and knock at our doors. Yesterday, we had two pregnant young women that came here to be helped. I sent them to the place that helps these women. I do as much as I can."

Paul stared at her. "Eve, founding this charity was the best thing you ever did, like I said before! Even priests are blessing us for helping those in need. People follow you and listen to what you have to say. Sometimes, I can see a sign of doubt in their eyes, but once you start telling them about things that you 'saw' before they happened, their confidence becomes real."

"I think so too, I know when someone will become our charity member and when there is nothing I can do to convince that person." Eve nodded. "I want to have a worship room, separate from the office and I have to find some money for this. Let me put my mind to work so I can have the room built. I'm not sure how long it will take, but it will be done."

"Eve, it's getting late and our secretary, Cynthia, has to go home," Paul reminded her.

"You're right. I am tired and we have to have dinner." Eve opened the office door and went to her secretary's desk. "Cynthia, you can leave, see you tomorrow. We have to print more pamphlets and give them to people. I really appreciate all the work you do. Say hello to your daughters from me, good night."

Eve's voice sounded so considerate, so soft when she talked to her secretary that it made Cynthia Faulkner think something was wrong with Eve or that something really important would follow. She was used to Eve by now, working with her for more than twenty years and she knew all her moves. Cynthia was Eve's confidant and she helped the charity organization without being paid. "Good night, see you tomorrow, we had a good day, and the service was wonderful," Cynthia said.

Exiting the building, she got into her car and remembered she had to make a short stop to buy few things for her daughter, Irene Floyd.

NUMB

Irene just had her first baby and she called her mom to bring her some groceries, her husband being on a business trip.

Cynthia spent her time between two residences' Ponce de Leon, Florida and Baton Rouge, Louisiana. Her activities were simple and basic, going to Church to help the St. John Charity, doing secretarial work for the leader of the charity and looking after her family. She adored her daughters and her grandchildren, spending all her free time with them.

Something on her drive made Cynthia think of Eve Garner, her friend and boss. Old memories became so clear suddenly, and being a lifetime follower of the woman that occupied her mind with her 'visions' and her 'prophecies,' she started wondering what exactly was real and what wasn't. Her mind tried to follow a logical path but her spiritual beliefs were a lot stronger than her mind.

"Why do I never question her actions, her intentions, why do I do everything she tells me to do? Why is that my mother, daughters, sons in laws, everyone I know, accepts her 'orders' with no questions? I just need to do what she tells me to do and stop wondering."

Feeling guilty of questioning her strong beliefs in Eve, now she was afraid that something bad would happen. Cynthia tried to get rid of her inquiring thoughts. She needed to be humble and listen to her boss's orders.

This woman, the leader of the charity organization, had her own way of carrying her revenge through sickness, poverty, death, separation of spouses and other things. Cynthia quelled her mind to stop thinking of Eve, not to mention analyzing her actions. But deep in her soul, she knew she'd wasted the best years of her life following a myth, a dark angel, a person coming from the dark side of Earth.

"Why did it take you so long to get here, Mom?" Irene asked as she'd worried about her. "Usually, you drive faster, but I'm glad you're here. You can go and play with your grandbaby till I finish cooking and thank you for bringing all the goodies; it is so helpful to have you."

"Sorry, you're right, I drove slower, I needed to unwind," Cynthia said, looking through the windows, seemingly not in any hurry to play with her grandson.

Irene noticed right away that something wasn't okay with her mother. "Are you ok? You seem preoccupied, do you feel sick?"

"No, I'm not sick. I'm perfectly fine, I was just thinking of Eve Garner. I shouldn't tell you but because you asked me how I feel, So I'm telling you.

"What about her? Is she ok? What else she did she do lately?" Irene asked looking rather fearful.

"Yes, they all seem to be doing well but I feel like something new is coming over us, she looks at us like we should be the ones bringing in all the money for St. John Charity. I just paid five hundred dollars from my pension. I cannot give money all the time and I work full time hours for St. Johns, so they don't have to pay for a secretary. I think I'm getting tired of this entire situation."

"Mom, don't talk like this, this woman is a saint and people believe in her visions, even Friar Mathew consults her, even if he never said that her vision come from God. I wonder why he asks her all the time about her prophecies?" Irene asked her mother.

"Oh, let's talk about something else," Cynthia quickly changed the subject of their conversation, being afraid of consequences coming from the one that keeps everyone under her spell. Cynthia felt too scared that her precious daughter would start having the same doubts she felt. She

NUMB

was really afraid something bad would happen soon. Better to stop talking and let things go their way.

Mother and daughter stopped talking about St. John Charity and they had a good time together. Cynthia left her daughter's home happy that she got to see and play with her grandson.

Before starting the car, she said to herself, "Drive, and pray... that's all you can do. My fear is stronger than my mind, than my logical thinking. Of course, I know the truth but I'm too scared to let the truth out, I better pray and drive." And that's what she did.

Two days later, Cynthia went back to St. John Charity and entered her office, getting ready for another day of working for free. But she was getting older, so her mind and her body needed some rest. She was afraid to ask for a break, afraid of consequences of Eve's revenge.

She made coffee and leaned against the chair savoring the aroma coming from the coffee when the phone rang. Cynthia saw the red button and she knew Eve Garner was calling and for few seconds, Cynthia didn't want to answer the phone but she did anyway. The same fear didn't let her even enjoy her coffee.

"Cynthia, good morning, we had a meeting yesterday and we missed you," Eve said.

"I worked all day long, I was here. I could have come if I would've known."

"I know you're right, but the meeting was late in the evening and you were gone already. I want you to know what we decided to do for our charity, so we can get more money, come into my office, please."

Cynthia wanted to finish her coffee but she knew she had to go when her boss asked her to go so she left the cup full of coffee to get cold on her desk.

The moment she entered Eve's office, she knew her boss had major changes in mind.

Her face looked animated if you could call it that. Her hands were waving in the air as she spoke, "We have to have a special room here for me to pray and this room costs money. We have to get the funds to build it and we all have to look for wealthy men and women. I know there are plenty around us, we only have to find and convince them."

"I've done this for such a long time," Cynthia replied in a soft n voice. "And I'll keep looking for opportunities to get more money for our group, I kind of like more calling our charity organization, a group. We're only a few people and we can do so much, like we already have."

"Call it what you want, I need the money," Eve Garner repeated.

"I heard that one of our parishioners lost his wife recently, let me search the situation and I'll let you know if he can be a potential donor for us. You see, not all people that go to church are willing to give a lot for charity, some have their preferred charities established through the years, like St. Jude Hospital, the hospital for children, in Memphis. I would like to know how they get all those donations, but at the same time I know how much they do for children, how much they care and they never send out... hospital bills," Cynthia stated as her words slowed down, already regretting what she said.

"What do you mean? We don't do anything for those that ask for help?" Eve asked as her eyes became smaller, looking furious.

"On no, this is not my point, we cannot compare with them, and we do help a lot, I know that."

"You better think before you talk. If other people were here with us, right at this moment, what do you think they would understand from you just said? That we do not help,

NUMB

we only get the money for our own use. Cynthia, be more careful of the way you talk about our 'group' as you like to call it. You can leave now."

Cynthia left the office with a bitter taste in her mouth, her day hadn't started right. She went back to her office, grabbed a chair and opened a drawer of her desk. She touched the Bible laying there and kept her hand on the cover as she started saying the Lord's Prayer. The moment she finished, she shook her head, stood up, and warmed up her coffee then all the worries vanished. She felt more invincible.

I won't let her mood alter my day. I have God protecting me and my family. They need me smiling and happy and this is how I'll be. But she knew that as soon as she finished her coffee, she would start checking on the parishioner who'd recently lost his wife, to see how much money he could donate to St. John Charity.

A few days after that inquiring debate and the conversation she had with her boss in her office, she received a phone call from an old friend from church, asking if she knew about anyone selling old cars. That friend was one she met when going to her Catholic church in Florida. Cynthia loved that church very much, feeling a lot better there than in Baton Rouge. She was happy to hear her friend's voice.

"Let me talk to my daughter, she might know. I'll call you back, I'm glad you called," Cynthia said and they continued their conversation talking about grandkids and the weather.

That afternoon, many people gathered at the main location of St. John Charity to listen to what their leader had to tell them. They were members of the group and they had been called to attend the meeting. The charity building was located not too far from the beautiful St. Bernadette Catholic Church, surrounded by red cypress trees, creating a serene, peaceful landscape.

Not too long afterward, without anyone hearing the doors open, a dark haired Eve started walking to the main table where Paul was sitting.

When he saw her coming, he stood up right away, offering her a chair.

Eve didn't greet anyone and she grabbed the chair without thanking him. She sat down and Paul was still standing.

Another man, tall, middle aged was waiting for her signal for him to sit down or stand, depending on the situation. An outside person would say that what was taking place was likened to 'royal protocol' and not an ordinary meeting, somewhere in Baton Rouge, Louisiana, in a building that had nothing royal about it at all.

The room was quiet, people were not communicating with each other, and they looked like lifeless statues. Not looking at the right or left and it looked like everyone was holding their breath.

The silence was broken by Eve, "I have to let you know that the Bishop asked me to go to the Diocese next week. His Eminence needs me to share my daily visions with him. He must have found out about my prophecies," she said without any human emotion in her voice. She spoke like she was reading from a script.

If anyone had questions they certainly didn't ask, nor did any of them think about asking this dark haired leader anything.

Everyone knew her name but to call her Eve, sounded too earthly, almost impolite, and too friendly. She didn't need friends...she only needed their donations.

NUMB

She wanted them to feel that way, at least she wanted all of them believe she was the one who could make them live or die. They all truly believed she had the power to do all this.

"We need a new building for the priests to come here, like a retreat. We have to make them feel welcomed, to provide for them fresh, good food. I heard that one of our Charity members received a large inheritance and I don't see him here today. Do you see what's happened when you take your eyes from God's purpose? He should be here and offer to help with our projects; how can we help those in need if we don't help ourselves? I know some of you know this person very well, you better go and talk to him and tell him what I said. Any negative response attracts a negative reaction on him and all of his family members, most of you know this better than anyone else."

The room became a storm of worries, everyone looking at each other, not knowing what she was talking about or who the person was that she talked about, but they all knew how dangerous it was to say anything.

"We have finally received a donation, enough to print more books for those that need the books to learn, but look around you... who is paying for the electricity, the water bill, the insurance for the building, the landscape, the maintenance and a lot more? Hmm? Who? We're a non-profit organization but we have bills to pay."

"But we just received fifty thousands dollars donation from Mrs. McHenry, is it not enough for now?" an old woman from the back row said.

That moment, a hurricane couldn't do what the dark hair woman did! Eve stood up and went all the way to the back of the room, where the poor woman sat.

Mrs. Berth suddenly became a shadow, that's how scared she was. The room became darker and it felt like a storm had invaded the building. No one even had the courage to look at each other.

"Come with me, Mrs. Berth," Eve said.

The old woman stood up and followed her spiritual advisor. They entered a small room where there were few chairs and a table. Without an invite to the woman that followed her, Eve grabbed a chair and sat down her dark eyes penetrating Mrs. Berth's eyes.

Mrs. Berth's body started shaking and it seemed to become smaller, a lot smaller. True fear was paralyzing her soul and her mind.

"What did you just say in front of everyone?" Eve asked with a voice that sounded like thunder.

Silence, the old lady wasn't able to say a word; she could not open her mouth.

"Mrs. Berth, do you need a reminder of why are you here? Or maybe, you want your membership fee back. Five thousands dollars is nothing for me and my organization. The money you paid will help the poor and it will help you find out in advance what was going to happen with your family or the world, so you can take action. Kings and presidents of powerful countries would like to know me, to be able to ask me about their future and their countries' future. And you, you dared to say something? You are a small granule of sand, you mean nothing to me, and I can wipe you out from this Earth in a heartbeat. Is your old husband still ill? Well, that depends how much money you donate today, he can be alive when you go home or he can be dead, it is your

NUMB

choice. Do I have to remind you about all the other similar situations? Do I have to remind you about a few things that happened to your dear friends, our members?"

"No, ma'am, I'm sorry. I'll never ask again," Mrs. Berth said, wondering how was she able to talk, how any sound came out of her mouth.

"Perfect, you're free to go but not before I let you know that your beloved husband has been taken to the hospital. We all have to pay for our mistakes, you'll see what happened when you'll get home," Eve, the mystic said.

Poor Mrs. Berth went directly home to find out that her husband had indeed been taken to the hospital, minutes ago. She stood in the middle of the room, unable to move. She had been punished for saying what was in her mind. She never believed in this woman's prophecies, her power to know things before they happened, but now...It was too much for her comprehension, too hard to understand how things worked with Eve. How could she do what she did, how did she know about her husband, the ambulance, the hospital, when she was talking to her in the meeting room, how was it even possible?

She knew where the hospital was and she drove there to see her husband, and when she finally found him, she asked what happened.

"I have no idea," he replied. "I was feeling good when you left the house, but no more than an hour ago, a terrible weakness made me feel like I was going to pass out. The lady that takes care of me called the ambulance right away. Now, I'm a lot better, sorry I scared you," he said.

"No, I'm sorry, you'll be ok, now," Mrs. Berth said, kissing her husband, knowing she would indeed 'donate' a fat check to the St. John Charity, she wouldn't even wait till their next meeting, she would drive right back to Eve Garner's office and pay her dues.

She told the nurse in charge at the hospital that she was prepared to take her husband home if the doctors let him go home. The doctor who treated him agreed and Mrs. Berth was happy to go home with her beloved husband, but not before stopping at St. John Charity office.

"Where are going?" Mr. Berth asked.

"Oh, I have to drop something at the office, it won't take more than a minute, do not worry," she said with a huge relief in her voice, but at the same time with a deep hole in her checking account.

The dark haired woman came back into the room where everyone was waiting to hear the news, to see what happened with Mrs. Berth.

"Okay, let's go back to money." Eve nodded. "It is all I need to know. Before we start our agenda, I wish to inform you that all of us should save enough funds, so we can go and visit St. Faustina's birth place in Krakow, Poland. I know it means large expenses but we all have to see the place from where my spiritual power comes from. She was a poor girl, born in a village close to Krakow in Poland, Europe. Her father was a carpenter, like our Jesus Christ, and her family was dedicated to the Roman Catholic Church, but when she wanted to become a nun, her parents would not give her permission to do so. Do you want to know more or do you prefer to find out by yourself in Poland?" she asked the members of her charity organization.

"Please tell us more," most of them said.

NUMB

"Actually, I enjoy telling you about such an amazing saint that was recognized by John Paul II. She had daily conversations with Jesus and she is the one that ordered the 'Divine Mercy painting' to be finished. She had visited the Dark side, the Hell and she saw all the pain, the burning; the tortures of those who did not believe in God and did bad things on Earth. Jesus pulled her back to life and since then, her predictions were kept in a dairy where she wrote all the orders Jesus gave her. She was proclaimed a saint after a long process of gathering all the testimonies. It was a long process that took almost thirty years. I believe that somehow, I am related to her, I have the same visions and I want to help those in need as all of you know."

When she finished her dissertation, rumors started among the attendees. You could see how fear was holding them together, fear of the unknown and the fear of being on this woman's bad side.

People left, keeping quiet as they went to find their cars in the parking lot to drive home. Most of them were doing these things automatically. Like robots, they walked like being under a spell, her spell—Eve Garner's spell.

"I heard that one of your brothers donated few houses for St. John Charity," one of the members asked another member while walking to the parking lot, being almost afraid to be seen talking to another member of the group.

"Yes, Eve convinced him it would be a lot better to sell it to the organization for less and get the papers for the taxes," the man called Nicolas, said. "I don't think he got a good advice, but if he didn't do it, he would suffer some horrible consequences. Day by day, I wonder what I'm doing here in this group. Why I don't donate to my church, like everyone else does. Do you know something? This woman has a spell, it is something I cannot put my finger on, but I feel it. Why doesn't anyone leave her, why do we listen to her, to each word she says? Why? Because, look at me. I'm still relatively young. I inherited a significant fortune from my parents. I have a beautiful family, but the fear of something bad to happening to any of us, stops any actions I want to take, to free myself from her spell. You have to recognize, she has a spell on us."

"I have the same feelings you do, but I do not even dare to admit it," the other man confessed.

"What is your name? We attend the same meetings and yet, we don't know each other. I think this is also her strategy, don't you think?" Nicolas said.

"My name is Gregg, Gregg Martin. You're so right, it is her strategy that we don't get to know each other and share our thoughts. A few years ago, my mother came home, crying and when I asked her what had happened, she couldn't say anything, that's how hard she cried. I was patient and after a while, she calmed down told me, 'Gregg, I have met a woman, she is a saint! I want to help her in her mission. She founded an organization called St. John Charity and she helps pregnant women who didn't want to become pregnant or cannot afford to have a baby, old priests that have to retire and families in need. I was so impressed by the way she talked, that I already gave her my money I had in my personal checking account, two thousands dollars. I feel so good to know that I could help.' So, of course I was mad, I was sure my mother had been a victim of a scam, a fake organization, but then I had a meeting with this woman...you know who, and she came accompanied by few other people. The way she was asking those people about her visions and her prophecies, it made them answer what she wanted me to hear. I'll give you an example; she asked them, 'Did I say that we're going to have two popes? Did I say that New Orleans

NUMB

would be under water? Did I say that a huge hurricane would destroy the Gulf Coast? Did I say that one of our priest's brother would drown in the lake, did I say the name of the horse that won the Kentucky Derby, did I say who was going to win the lottery and the ticket would never be cashed?' How do you think those people answered? 'Yes, you did, ma'am, yes, you did say all this.' So, I started to not be as sure as I was when I first met her. My faith was shaken, my fear of her prophecies started to become real in my mind, but mostly of her revenge. I'm a successful business man, I studied in college, I believe in God. I have never done something to be ashamed of and look at me now, look straight into my eyes and tell me honestly, what do you see? In front of you stands a weak man, a man that is scared to run and scream loudly about what I went through, what we all went through. I don't recognize myself. Yes, I'm scared of the consequences of my non obedience. She has us all in her hands, connected by fear."

"I'm glad I had a chance to talk to you, we'll see what the future will bring," Nicolas said. "I'm praying day and night to God to protect my family from that woman's revenge. Gregg, she is Satan and I know I'm right, but I keep coming back to meetings and donations, isn't this weird? I should complain to the police, but ask me why I don't do it, for the same reason as all of us. We're weak, even if our faith in God is so strong, I'm ashamed to be alive, we need to pray more and trust more in the One and only One that can keep us focused on Him. I remember the story when Peter started walking on the water, going towards Jesus. How he was able to do it, but the moment he took his eyes from Jesus because he was scared, he started to sink. That's it, the only thing that can save us is looking after Jesus and to not see or listen to anything or anyone else."

"Well said, easier to say than do, but you did say it very explicitly and intelligently. I wish I could follow your advice."

"Me too, and isn't this weird that I'm the one who said all this? Then I cannot seem to follow my own logical advice? Let me tell you, something is really wrong with us, being trapped under her spell, in her donations scam, she is evil. Oh no, I just said something I shouldn't and I'm already scared of what next hour will bring to me! I think I'm lost."

The two men looked around. Both of them looking fearful as they parted quietly and got into their cars to speed away as if they were escaping a crime scene or perhaps feeling in fear for their lives.

NUMB

CHAPTER SIX

"Soon, we have to leave for Mexico," Mary Rita said. "For the Tupperware conference and we'll take Christina with us, she can go but Kathleen has to be in school the entire week, she cannot miss school. I planned this trip a lot better than I did the others. I want Christina to enjoy her first Disney World trip. So, we are going to spend two days there and after that, we'll fly to Mexico, aren't you excited? I know I am, I cannot wait to have some fun."

Bob laughed. "You always have fun when we go somewhere, this is great. For me it's okay but seeing you so happy, it contaminates me and makes me feel like you do. I hope our youngest daughter will enjoy the Disney World. Isn't she blessed that she can go there, other children can't do this."

"I know it and this is another reason I'm grateful for, I mean to be able to do that kind of things for our children and for us, so grateful, I love my God more and more. Do not think I love Him for the money, no. I love Him for everything, the way we are, for our health and for our love, having this, the rest just followed."

"Yep, you're always right, even when you're totally wrong," Bob joked with his wife.

Disney World was crowded with families that came from all over the country, even from all over the world.

"Bob," Mary Rita said after a few hours she spent on rides and splashes. "I think I had more fun than our daughter, but maybe next year she will enjoy it more, hopefully."

Coming back to Chicago, the Wish High Sales team was full of so much energy; they had so many good ideas about how to make their sale persons be more productive. The couple became more and more successful, so they started buying land, properties and all their investments turned into gold. Mary Rita's sense of business and Bob's knowledge for buildings, was working to make them productive and full of initiative, she knew what to buy, where and when. This was another gift she got from the one who she loved, her God.

"Bob, look around us, all the sale persons we have on our team, are doing so well," Mary Rita said. "They have good homes, their kids go to private schools, and they still have time to spend with their families. What a blessed moment when God put that ad in my hands! We make many donations but like I said many times, I cannot wait to see my dream come true, to build a church with the money God gave us."

More years passed by and all things were going well for the Wish's, things were going smooth and their life was a reflection of their deep faith.

"I don't think anyone can measure faith or love for God but looking around us, I can see how our girls are really growing," Bob said to his wife. "Disney was like an event that just happened yesterday and now we're getting ready for Kathleen's graduation. Well, not too far in the future and all this seem to be a reward for our faith, at least this is how I look at all our accomplishments."

NUMB

She nodded. "I see this every day. I cannot imagine my girls married and leaving the house even if I am conscious about it. You're right and I never thought that all we achieved were gifts from God. My mind was too busy thinking about how to grow our business, but in the back of my mind, I know I believed exactly like you do. I remember now, when we got married, we kept living with my mother, even if we could leave the house and have our own place."

"It was a smart thing that we stayed together with your mother. It made a big difference for her and for us. We had so much help with raising our children, with things around the house, but above all, the love she surrounded all of us with. It is something priceless. I'll always be grateful for her love and for her being with us."

Mary Rita smiled at this. "You know, first I was hesitant, as not all young couples want to live with someone else even if it is a relative, everybody wants to have the 'freedom', but I think we had it even though we lived together. I enjoyed each minute of our life together and you, being a good man, made this possible."

Bob gave her that warm smile of his. "You know, now that we started talking about memories, I have one I can't seem to erase from my mind."

"What is it?" she asked.

"I remember the day when we received that phone call that your brother, Joseph, the firefighter, lost his life in that horrible building fire. And I will never forget how many firefighters attended his funerals, how many people came to pay their respects. I still remember his firefighter's number, 5801. Mary Rita, this was a day I will remember always, it touched me to see his four children left without a father. I promised to God to take care of these kids and his wife,

Sally," Bob said with a sad voice because of his brother in law's death.

"I know and it was such a sad day. My mother was devastated and her entire life seemed to collapse once she found out. She's suffered so much loss in her life. She did lose two baby daughters when she was really young. Then my father, Ed then Grant and finally Joe. I don't know how she survived so much heartbreak. Bob, that day I thought I lost my brother, that's how much she'd suffered through the years. No one could comfort her and her pain was spreading over all of us. I loved my older brother so much that I felt like something inside me broke forever. But having to return to the daily duties, my mind was getting back to normal after a very long time, but my mother never recovered her beautiful and sweet smile. Only her grandkids were able to make her smile, what a tragedy we had to face, especially Joe's family. Do you remember my dream?" she asked. "The dream when Joe came into my dream and he said he was well, but he asked me to help his wife?"

"Oh, I do remember that one, because it didn't seem like his wife, Sally needed help," Bob said.

"So true, but losing your husband, the father of your children must have left some serious wounds in her heart and in her mind. I did the best I could and God knows how much I helped her. I hope my brother is content where he is now, in Heaven, seeing all our efforts to help her get better."

"I'm sure he is, you took her to all the doctors she had to go to and helped her get her treatments right. I remembered what you did for your sister in law and for your nephews. I miss him. We could have had so many good times together if he was still around, but one day we'll be together again." Bob sighed.

NUMB

Kathleen Wish was getting ready to graduate high school and her boyfriend, Mike was waiting for that moment to come faster.

Michael Petrovich, a strong, young man, in love with the beautiful blonde girl and he wanted to be her husband. So as soon as Kathleen finished school, they got married. He knew he had to go back to finish his college degree, but for now, he decide to enroll in the service to serve his country.

Mike and Kathleen became a couple full of hopes with beautiful dreams for their future.

When Mike was stationed in Fort Walton Beach, Florida Kathleen went there to be with her husband, to be able to see him more often. Soon, they had friends and neighbors willing to start a lifetime friendship, attracting good people like a magnet, everybody loved being with them.

They rented a mobile home because it was only for less than a year till they would return to Chicago, their home city and where their families live.

Coming from their neck of the woods, they never saw such beauty, the ocean waters and the amazing, pristine white sand.

Fort Walton Beach was a beautiful town located alongside of the Emerald coast of the Gulf of Mexico; a town with a great future. The military bases were close to the town being more accessible for the military families.

The white dunes looked like small mountains covered in snow. The sand was so white that almost looked like sugar or pure snow.

Kathleen found out not too long after she moved down there, that those dunes had been protected by law being a phenomenon of nature. Long, delicate sea oats were growing on the dunes creating an amazing view. The color of the water was something she had never seen, emerald and blue, with sandbars in between that were giving the water a specific tint of yellow- green that made for a color like she'd never seen.

Not even one person that had seen this area could say that they didn't fall in love with it. Kathleen and Mike were the same way and more and more, they were enjoying the place.

"Kathleen, we should live here once I finish my term and my college," Mike said.

"I agree, it is absolutely beautiful, looks like a paradise. I am going to invite my parents to come and visit us. It will be the highlight of their life; we never thought that there was such beauty. Chicago is a huge city of course, with all the useful things for an easier life, but this place is so special. Don't you think they should consider having a vacation home here?" she asked.

"Of course, they should. Later on, when they get a little older, it would be nice to have a beautiful place for them to call home. I want a place here too."

"Don't worry, I love this place so much that I want to live here as well," Kathleen said.

Not too long after their conversation, Mike and Kathleen went back home to Chicago where family welcomed them with open arms.

Mary Rita was very close to her older daughter and she tried to be the same with her youngest one, but Christina decided to be less visible, less active, showing her love for her family in her own way. She had her own kind of satisfactions, like riding the horses and enjoying a quiet life.

Sometimes, Mary Rita envied Christina for living in a different world, a world of her own. Christina was a beautiful

NUMB

girl and many young men were attracted to her. Mary Rita knew that a person who loved animals like her daughter did, had to have a deep understanding and love not only for animals, but for people, too.

Mike Petrovich went back to college to get his electrical engineer degree, making his family proud of him. He was determined to become a successful man and whatever he was doing, it showed his commitment for his future.

"Mom, Mike will graduate soon and we have to see where life will take us," Kathleen said.

"What do you mean?" Mary Rita asked.

"He will have to accept a job offer, anywhere in America, because he will need to get experience in order to get a higher paid job later on."

"Of course, I'm so proud of him," Mary Rita said.

"Me too, I'm like you, continuously working, even when I stop to talk to God, or I should say, when I stop to listen to God for guidance. I love going to church, like you do, I think I became another Mary Rita. People admire you so much, you pulled some women out poverty, and you can say that you did save few marriages by getting the husbands involved with the Tupperware business. Mom, you didn't do just business, you created a family with members that helped each other. I will try to see if I can do what you do, but I am attracted to houses. I dream of making beautiful homes from ruined ones, something like fixer uppers. What do you think?"

"Oh, wait a minute, too many ideas at one time. Yes, it's true what you said about business, not so sure about saving marriages but if you say so, I'd like to believe it. At least, I wanted to do it and if I succeeded, it sounds even better, but what do you mean by being attracted by houses?"

"I feel like this is my calling, to renovate houses and sell then for a profit. Give families a beautiful place to live. But I'd like to try to see if I can do what you and dad do, we'll see." Kathleen smiled.

"It would be amazing to work with houses! I can see you doing this. You have good taste and you're very practical. Plus no one can tell you what to do. This is another thing you took from your mother, but if you would like to start doing the Tupperware business, why not, try it? And see which one makes you happier." Mary Rita felt pleased to see her daughter so full of initiative.

The time came when Mike accepted a good offer to work in Pensacola, Florida, running a large electrical company. Kathleen and Mike Petrovich moved there and soon they purchased a nice brick home and they had the time of their lives. The weather was so welcoming, the salt air, the ocean, sunny days, the vacation atmosphere making them feel like they were on vacation every day, even if they were busy working.

"Mom, bring Dad, and come to visit us," Kathleen invited her parents to Pensacola.

"We'll come, don't worry," Mary Rita said.

The Tupperware business was doing so great for Mary Rita and Bob Wish and they were helping their members become successful.

The huge warehouse they built was the packing, storage and shipping place and they hired numerous employees to help with the orders coming from all over the world.

"Bob, we have to go to another international conference, but this is how we open more doors of distribution, helping more people to sell our products. It feels amazing when you see people that do not speak English, how hard they try to learn and do what we do. The entire planet needs our storage containers, they can be so helpful."

NUMB

Bob laughed. "You sound like an ad for the Tupperware Company but I know how much truth is in what you said. I can see myself when I started and I wasn't a poor man, I was the boss of a company but now I'm doing so much better."

"We are in the top twenty five in the nation, and this means something. We traveled from Europe to Hawaii, look at the silver Mark IV Lincoln Continental with rose interior and your initials on the doors. My full length mink coat, mink stole and I can say that not too many women have my extensive wardrobe of long dresses. But really, these are only 'things' all what we have is God's work. This is the reason that I keep telling you about my desire to do charity work, to help those that haven't had such an opportunity in their lives. I will do it and somehow, I am doing it but not to the level, I'd like to. It's hard to explain what I feel deep inside, but in a way, God is preparing me for this. Our girls are well situated, our family is doing well, and I feel it's time to help others."

"As long as we keep our eyes open and have a good sense of discernment, we will be able to choose the right charity organization and thank God, the Catholic churches have plenty of those," Bob said, being sure that he planted a healthy seed in his wife's mind.

"I know you're trying to protect our money that we worked so hard for and I want to do the same thing, especially thinking that soon we're going to have grandchildren. Christina is married, Kathleen is married, our nest is getting smaller, I'm so grateful my mother is still living with us," Mary Rita said.

"We should sell our large home," Bob said.

"And move where?" Mary Rita asked.

"We can rent something till we'd know what we want to do. We're not ready to retire yet, but we can explore our options. I really would like to have a cabin in Wisconsin; do you remember our honeymoon?" Bob said and his voice became softer and full of love.

"Not only do I remember every second of it Bob, but like you, I dreamed about living in that beautiful part of the country. What a peaceful time, how young we were, how much love we had, we still do," she said kissing her husband.

Bob kissed her back. "Of course, we have problems, show me parents that have no problems raising their children, but we did the best we could and overall, I feel blessed by God to see all of them, not only our children, but nephews and nieces also, being on the right path. As long as they believe in God, they will receive His guidance and the only thing they have to do is to follow Him."

"You make me feel good Bob. Thank you for opening your heart today. It isn't easy to judge yourself, questioning your job as a mother, as a parent. But now, after listening to you, my conclusion is that I did the best I could and looking at the way our children turned out, I think we did a pretty good job. Let's talk about selling the house, our home and like you said, rent something. Until we'll know for sure what we would like to do with the rest of our lives, once we retire."

"I agree, let's sell it and we'll figure it out after wards," Bob agreed.

Their house was so nice and well maintained that it was a fast sell; they hadn't even had time to think much.

"I can't believe how fast our home sold, in the blink of an eye. So what are we going to do now?" Mary Rita asked.

"One of my friends told me about a penthouse that's available, somewhere in the suburbs. Do you want me to find out more details?" Bob asked.

"Of course, we have to empty our home fast."

Bob called his friend and arranged with an agent to go and check the apartment to see if they liked it. The area where

NUMB

the penthouse was located had a breathtaking landscape and the view from the penthouse was more than divine. No buildings, no factories, nothing, just plain forest. It wasn't hard for the couple to decide and soon, they moved in the penthouse apartment with Anne, Mary Rita's mother.

Kathleen Petrovich called her parents with good news,

"Mom, do you remember my desire to adopt children? Well, it's getting closer and I would like you to come and visit before we bring the baby home. After that, I know you'll be here all the time to be with your grandbaby."

"Of course, we'll be there soon. I cannot wait to see you and I'm so excited about the baby. He or she will be blessed to have you both as parents," Mary Rita said.

Family, friends, coworkers, everyone knew how much Kathleen and her parents loved each other. Mary Rita would do the unthinkable, the impossible to help her daughter and Kathleen was the same way. Even if she was their daughter, it looked like she was the one protecting her parents, always aware of what was going on in their lives. She did the best she could to be sure they were safe, healthy and that no one did something wrong to her parents.

At the same time, she couldn't be more grateful to God for having such a healthy, sharp minded mother. Bob, her father had some heart issues but he was doing great with doctors' care.

The thought of visiting their daughter was coming often in Mary Rita's mind and one day she said, "Bob, let's go to Pensacola to visit Kathleen, she's called many times to invite us to come and I'm ready for a trip, my mother will enjoy it, too."

A beautiful, long, but not exhausting trip with short stops, picnics, rest, a little walking made the time fly. It was like a small vacation for all of them. Anne, Mary Rita's mother really enjoyed the beautiful trip and she couldn't wait to see her granddaughter that now was a married woman. They had no idea how fast they got to Kathleen's and Mike's home, that's how much the time passed by quickly. Getting closer to Pensacola, the view was exceptional, something they saw in Mexico, and most of the places they'd traveled, but for them this area was a lot more beautiful, serene, and amazingly fascinating. Nobody spoke...they only had eyes for the landscape spreading out in front of them. Bob Wish was driving slowly; he wanted to look at the ocean and the places in front of him.

Kathleen and Mike greeted them with love and they'd already made plans for the next day. Anne was pleased to see how well Kathleen adapted to the new surroundings and how she well she was treating her guests. Mary Rita noticed the admiration her mom had for Kathleen and tried to get Bob's attention, to share with him such a good feeling, but Bob was lost in checking out the features of the house. His 'inspection' finished with a good grade, he was satisfied with the quality of the house and the way it was built.

Kathleen drove them around and showed them the beach, the churches, shopping malls and almost all the things she knew her family would be interested in. Kathleen knew her job was done when she saw that her mother, father and her grandmother were speechless.

"Kathleen, I had no idea places like this existed in America," Mary Rita said. "You know I went to Europe, Mexico, Hawaii and many other places, but I have never seen such a paradise. I'm mesmerized by the colors of the sand, the ocean ...."

NUMB

"I know, we feel the same way. I already started investing in properties, in the ones that need to be 'invigorated', fixed and put it on the market. I already did few and there is quite a profit in doing that."

"Good for you, I remember when you told me about your dream of buying, fixing and reselling. I'm glad you found something you enjoy doing. It keeps you busy and you make good money. Daughter like the mother, you're my money girl, I'm proud of you." Mary Rita beamed at her daughter.

"Believe it or not, my husband said the same thing, I hope it is a good thing," she joked.

"The first thing I would like to know is where the Catholic Church is located. You know how we are, twice a day if we can, we would like to attend the service," Mary Rita said.

"I know and I do the same thing you do. Without God, I couldn't be so happy! Does this mean you will be moving down here, soon?" Kathleen asked looking hopeful.

"You never know, we'll pray about it then stay still to hear God's words. What he wants, this is what it will be for sure."

Mary Rita, her husband and her mother went back home to Chicago dreaming of the ocean waves, the colors of the water and the sand they left behind, pleased to see their Kathleen doing so well.

The entire trip back to Chicago, Fort Walton Beach and Pensacola in particular, were part of the main conversation followed by many sighs and dreams.

Bob knew immediately that his dream of building a cabin in Wisconsin would be turned into building a Florida cottage close to Kathleen, he just had that feeling.

The time to retire was getting closer. Both Bob and Mary Rita were proud of the work they'd done and the business they had built. So many distributorships, so many strong sales persons, the company couldn't be prouder.

"Do you know what happened today?" Mary Rita asked her husband when she came home from her work.

"No, I hope nothing wrong? We're almost out of all the things that could happen I mean business wise. We've had all the possible situations to have when we worked with people," he said smiling.

"Well, the company wants me to keep working and help those that couldn't do what we did, or don't know how, or they're just lazy. Anyway, I refused the offer," she said.

"I can't believe they did that. Do you know what a huge honor it is? Do you know why it is such an honor?" Bob asked.

"Yes, I know. I'm a woman that's why it is such an event to be offered a high position, but don't forget what kind of work I did for them," Mary Rita said.

"Correct, but I'm glad you refused it. We have to live a little, I'm so proud of you, I assume it was hard for you to say no," Bob teased.

"Actually, looking back, I don't think I ever worked! No, I take that back. I did work when I was a waitress and a meat packer, I can say that *was* work. What I did for twenty six years with my Tupperware was fun and I know I had all that success because of my attitude, my energy and enthusiasm and above all, because of you. But let's go back to their offer. I know I should've asked you first but I had no time to talk to you and honestly, I didn't want to talk to you about accepting their offer. Being married for such a long time with you, my dear husband, we started thinking the same way, am I right that you don't want me to work more than I did?"

"You know me better than I know myself. Yes, I want you to retire young, so we can travel. I want to get old cars and make them look brand new, sell them and make people happy. You see, our Kathleen does the same thing with her houses that I want to do it with my cars. We can go to car

NUMB

shows, become members of some distinctive car clubs, get a boat. Mary Rita, we finally start living!"

"Perfect, now it's our time, let's enjoy it. I'm ready for some freedom." Mary Rita grinned at him.

They started thinking more and more often about retirement and all the new things waiting for them to do, to enjoy. Day by day, that dream was getting closer and thank God, both of them were still young enough to enjoy it.

Two years after visiting their older daughter, the couple bought ten acres in Florida and Bob couldn't wait to build a cottage for them. After spending twenty thousand dollars, the land was okay for construction; it needed more filling, being a wet land. The first step was done; the land was purchased. So now, it was time to build a sweet cottage, like they called it.

"Bob, you know how much I like swimming, if I can have a swimming pool here, I would be extremely happy and this won't be only for me, our grandchildren will come to visit, so they will be extremely happy to have the swimming pool right here, when they don't go to the beach."

"Do not worry, honey, you'll have it. I'm glad to have our daughters living close to us, one lives on the East and one lives on the West. Isn't this something?"

"You see, this is another gift from God, how many people can say what you just said, to have your own children living close to us, to help each other, to have fun together and help each other when necessary. Isn't this a blessing? I'm counting my blessings daily, and it's still not enough thanks," Mary Rita said.

"Same here, I never let a day pass without being sure I thanked God for everything, He is on our side all the time, guiding our steps. I couldn't be more grateful." Bob nodded.

"We hit the lottery with the price we purchased the lot for. God sent us here," Mary Rita added. "Do you remember last time when we visited Kathleen and our first question was about the Catholic Church and there is one in Fort Walton Beach, but it's way too far from here...a fifty two mile round trip. The way we go to mass daily, it will make it impossible. Maybe we should build our Catholic Church close to our home. I wanted for years to thank God by building a church. It bet we can find enough Catholic people to attend the service."

"No question about it, this place will have such a huge population soon, it is an amazing place. People like us who are retiring, want warmer weather. Not our case right now, I know as we're still young, but it will be so much better later on."

"Do you know that our Kathleen is doing really well flipping houses? She's making good money."

"Do I know about it? Of course, I do. I talked to her about doing the same thing, to work with her. I think it will be so much fun. And me, being a carpenter, it would be helpful, but I keep forgetting, we're retired people now. We need to enjoy life, not just work, work." He laughed.

"Don't worry, I'll make it fun." Mary Rita smiled."

The 'cottage' soon became their sweet home, a beautiful and welcoming home. By now, Mary Rita and Bob Wish were happy grandparents and when they started the construction of the swimming pool, they decided to make it only three feet deep, to be safe for the grandkids. Soon, their home became a wonderful place to relax, to enjoy the water view and the amazing sunsets, the home was surrounded by two acres of land and it had an amazing view of the large bay connected to the Gulf of Mexico.

NUMB

"I cannot wait to see St. Anne Church ready and to start the services, Bob. Do you think there are many Catholic people in this area? I remember our priest telling us that the Christian Orthodox believers are more than welcome to the Catholic churches, because we believe in the same Jesus Christ and we venerate our Virgin Mary. Actually, I do feel like everyone is welcomed, the only difference is the communion, but they can enjoy the liturgy and listen to the word of God. Bob, when I listen to our music in church, I get goose bumps, the Holy Spirits touches me, and when we donate money to the poor, I pray they could come and be able to hear the word of God. I want them to feel as blessed as I feel. It blesses me to see them praying, that's how much I dream of helping those people."

Bob agreed. "I know and I kind of feel the same way. I love when I see you in the morning reading your devotions, talking to God, praying with your rosaries, it makes me feel calmer, stronger and ready to start my day. You see, I have never told you this, but I think you made me a stronger believer. Growing up, I did go to church. I followed all the things church told me to do, but I never saw the other side of the world, those people that have no roof over their heads, no possibilities to get a good, solid education, to keep them away from drugs, alcohol and getting involved with gangs and really bad people. Every time I see a homeless person of course, I help. But in my mind, I wonder and I always do, what could have happened in that person's life that made him become a homeless? Why doesn't that person live in the shelters provided by the government, why?" Bob said.

"It amazes me how much we think alike! You're the man I love forever. I wish other people could see inside you, like I do. I think our daughter, Kathleen sees it too. Yes, Bob, we have plenty of money coming in our lives, so we can spread the word of God. I would like to go on a missionary trip with you and Kathleen. I know Christina loves God but I don't think she would consider spending the time, but I will ask her. There are so many people who want to help but they don't know where to start. The building of St. Anne Catholic Church is getting ready and in few more months, people will start worshiping, having daily masses and starting forming a strong community. I'm waiting for that day to come."

The Wish family was grateful to have such a church in their neighborhood, and they'd even been blessed with an excellent priest and spiritual advisor.

The priest's love for God showed in all the things he did for his church goers and he became the right person to ask for help, it didn't matter what the needs were.

Anne Carone, Mary Rita's mother, was more than grateful for what Bob and her daughter did for her. They built a nice house right next to their home so she could be taken care of. After working all her life, now she had a good life, a nice home, a good church, loving grandchildren and great grandchildren. Anne's life had many tragedies that put a sad mark in her soul but seeing her family staying together and loving each other was making her put all the tragedies behind her, so now Anne was living the time of her life, being loved by all her relatives and breathing the same air as her daughter and her family. God listened to all her prayers.

The family from Chicago was visiting more often and they had plenty of space to enjoy. Eddie Carone, Mary Rita's nephew, Beau's son was close to his aunt and he loved Bob Wish, too. He came often to visit his folks.

Mary Rita and Bob were happy to see the family love tradition going on. Eddie Carone reminded Mary Rita of her sweet brother Beau so much and it was a joy to be with him. Seeing Eddie again, her mind went back to Chicago, the city that

NUMB

brought her love, success, suffering and hopes. She would always love that city. "Eddie, if you want you can store your boat here at our property, where the boat dock is. There's plenty of room," Mary Rita told her nephew.

"Thank you, I'll do it. I love that you are so considerate. Do you know how much we talk about you and Uncle Bob back in Chicago? You see, everyone would like to move here, but it's too complicated. We are so many people; everyone has his or her own family, children, jobs, extended families... We all want to live closer to the ocean, closer to you, to have a warmer weather that's for sure. It would make us all a lot happier than we are right now. It doesn't mean we're not ok, I'm talking about almost all of us, but the cold weather, the winds, and the snow makes us grumpy! When you used to live there, you must've been the same way, or is just me?" Eddie asked.

"Bob and I were so busy building the Tupperware business that now when I look back to our lives, I realize how fortunate we had been. We had to travel for our business, so each trip was a small vacation, even if we worked. At the end of work day, we enjoyed being together, had fun and got ready for the next day. Our situation was so much different that what our family members have now. When you work in a factory, or if you have a nine to five job, things aren't as enjoyable as they were for us and we thank God every day for being that blessed. It doesn't mean that you're not blessed, but you have to be able to see your blessings. I read somewhere that when you talk to God, it is called prayer and when God talks to you, it is called intuition. We have to let Him talk to us but we have to be quiet and hear what He has to say. It's not an easy task, but if you do it every day, you'll get there," Mary Rita shared her wisdom and experience with her handsome nephew.

"Thank you for telling me all this, I'm already wiser for it." Eddie smiled and hugged his aunt.

A few days after their heart to heart conversation, Eddie brought his boat and he couldn't have been happier. He now had a safer place for his boat and would be ready to go fishing anytime, he came to visit his aunt, his uncle and his grandma...

A good neighbor of the Wish's asked Bob if he could put his boat there too. He was such a good Christian man and Bob Wish had so much respect for him. "Go ahead and bring it here, there is so much space," Bob said.

Being a really good neighbor, the man offered to pay having his boat safe and protected, but Bob would never accept his offer.

So, the boat house sheltered two boats and the couple enjoyed looking at them.

NUMB

CHAPTER SEVEN

The year of 1983 was a sad year for The Wish's, especially for Mary Rita and her side of the Irish family; her amazing, hard worker, beautiful mother passed away and went to be with her beloved husband, Ed Carone. The entire family, the Irish side and the Italian side had been united one more time. Anne Carone was the glue that held them all together, always loving and always caring for her children and grandchildren. She was the foundation they set their problems on and she always had an answer for them.

Mary Rita was utterly devastated for a time as she lost her best friend, the woman who watched each step of her life, the woman who scarified all she had for her children and for her family. Her mother was a saint. She lived her life with dignity and a love of God. Anne Carone lived for her children and she did the impossible to save her first husband, the father of her children.

For days, Mary Rita wasn't able to be in anyone's company, she just stayed in her house, looking at the water and imagining her life with her mother.

After awhile, the wounds caused by her mother's death began to heal, little by little and she became more alive.

Mary Rita rented the house out where her mother used to live, next to her home to a dedicated priest of St. Anne Church in Santa Rosa Beach, Florida. This man spent his time in prayers, searching for God's word and this made Mary Rita and Bob feel really blessed to have such a godly man living on their property. All their neighbors loved this priest and he made them feel the same way.

After twelve years, the house where Mary Rita's mother lived and where the priest resided became vacant and it became a beautiful gift for Kathleen, to have a place closer to her parents.

At the same time, their youngest daughter, Christina wanted a large home, somewhere in the country, to be able to have horses. After a year of researches, she decided what she wanted and her parents were more than glad to gift her with that property. The home had room enough for Christina's needs, the yard was large enough for her to have horses and enjoy her life style, the way she wanted.

"Bob, I think we took good care of our daughters and grandchildren. It makes me really happy to see their gratitude, to hear them saying that we didn't have to give them such monetary gifts, to hear them being so thankful. We're blessed with a large and loving family and most of all, we're blessed with good health and each other."

"I don't know about health, you know I have some heart issues, but everything else is more than true. I'm grateful too, and I see that when my time comes to leave this earth, it gives me peace of mind to see you surrounded by so many relatives. I know for sure that you'll be helped. And look at our Kathleen, not even one day passes without her calling us and asking us about our health and if there's something we need. Christina calls us too, I shouldn't complain about it."

Mary Rita agreed. "We have to go back to Baton Rouge; we have so many things to do there. Kathleen is doing really well

NUMB

with her investing properties. She's a tough cookie, going back and forth for her business. I liked it there but not like I love living here. Following Kathleen, we've gotten to know Baton Rouge though."

"Like her mama, she's got the sense of working from you, honey. I like working but I couldn't do what you did," Bob said.

Both of them smiled and got ready for a heart doctor appointment for Bob. Nothing major, but Bob needed to keep up with his doctor appointments.

The Wish's fiftieth wedding anniversary was approaching. Mary Rita invited all their relatives from Chicago as well as numerous families from church and the neighborhood.

Her brother Beau and his family, Joe's family, the brother she lost in the 1964 Chicago fire, Bob's brother's family, nephews, everyone came for the big celebration.

After ten o'clock mass at St .Anne Catholic Church, they went to a fancy resort club where they had a big lunch and a party with music.

The big fishing boat was waiting for them back home and they had so much fun fishing. They cleaned the boat and were ready to go to Sandestin, an exclusive resort style neighborhood, to the Boat Deck for a wonderful cruise. The Sandestin community was located right on the Bay, with a huge Marina full of yachts and large boats, some of them were able to cross the Gulf of Mexico or sail the ocean.

Any description of that amazing place didn't really do it any justice, that's how gorgeous it was. The Bay was large with deep water, full of playing dolphins, not scared to get closer to their boat. Coming from Chicago, people were cheering with happiness when the dolphins were jumping from the water, inviting passengers of the boat to play with them.

The air was hot and humid, typical July weather, but no one seemed to care about the heat as they were having the time of their lives.

Mary Rita and Bob Wish couldn't be happier. With tears in their eyes, they thanked everyone for coming to celebrate such a milestone in their lives, fifty years of a happy marriage.

The food, the drinks, the large boat, the cruise and above all... being together after so many years, made for a memorable celebration.

Everyone went back with lasting memories. They all hoped to see each other again in ten years, for Mary Rita and Bob's sixtieth wedding anniversary.

Bob Wish's passion for old cars made him become a member of two car clubs. Paul Stevens, a good neighbor and friend, helped him to sign up for membership as the both of them shared the same passion of buying old cars and creating real masterpieces from them. Every time Bob witnessed the amazing transformation of an old beat up car into a shiny jewel, he just kept feeling inspired.

So, one day after the church service at their new church, Bob Wish asked a lady if she knew about a thirty-six old Chevy, he wanted to buy.

The lady he asked, happened to be Mary Rita's spiritual adviser, a good friend of hers.

"I can't believe it! I just talked to my daughter that lives in Baton Rouge and she said that she has that old car in her garage."

"Do you know how old the car is?" Bob asked.

"Oh, no, I don't know anything about cars, she said it because she was complaining that someone asked her to

NUMB

keep that car in her garage and she couldn't say no. I'll ask if you want me to," the lady said.

"Please do, and if it is an old car we can go there and take a look, eventually buy it. We can take a trip anytime, it will be a nice time to be with my wife," Bob said.

"Yes, there aren't too many people who love each other like you two do. I love the way you take care of each other. The young couples should pay more attention to how you treat your wife and how she cares about you, you're inseparable," Cynthia Faulkner said.

"Ok, I'll wait for you to let me know and we'll start from there." Bob Wish couldn't wait to tell his wife about the conversation he had with her friend.

"Bob, I'm glad you talked to her, she is a wonderful Christian woman. Do you remember when she invited me and Kathleen for a short meeting with Father James, he is a SOLT priest. Do you know what SOLT is? This happened way back when we were still living in Chicago."

"I think you told me about it but I forgot, maybe if you told me the full name of it without the abbreviation, maybe I'd know."

"SOLT means, Society of Lady Trinity! The name is a lot longer: Society of Our Lady of the Most Holy Trinity and it was founded in 1958 by Father Callaghan. The Catholic Society of Apostolic Life, it is a missionary group. The Society does work in many, many countries like; Belize, Guatemala, Ghana, Italy, Mexico, and a lot more I can't remember, but I know for sure what a good job they do. What a beautiful name; I always loved the concept of the Holy Trinity, Father, Son and Holy Spirit. It is everything, at least for me. Do you know what their motto is? 'Imitate Mary, Become like Jesus, Live for the Triune God,' isn't that beautiful? I became a member of this society, remember?"

Bob wanted to please his wife because she enjoyed repeating the story, so even if he knew all the details, he said, "Go ahead and remind me, I'll be all ears."

She smiled at him, knowing what he was up to. She loved him for it too. "Well, Kathleen came to pick me up from the airport in Pensacola. She was so determined to take me to that meeting so I told her, 'Okay, Kathleen, I'll go with one condition, we have to sit in the last row so if I feel like falling in sleep, I can leave, promise?' She was so sure of my reaction that she agreed with me sitting in the last row. We went inside, sat all the way on the last seats and I was ready to fall in sleep, I was that tired. In the beginning, I tried to be polite and kept my eyes open but not too long after he started talking, I felt alive, really alive! We stayed till the end of the meeting and this is how I became a member of SOLT, so glad I did it."

Bob grinned at her.

Mary Rita stood up and kissed her husband saying, "I knew you knew it, how could you forget such a thing? I do love you so."

The more God blessed them with wealth, the more they gave to their church, the St. Anne Catholic Church, to the beautiful Arc of Covenant, or The Retreat Center they liked to call it, with a large praying room, educational area surrounded by a beautiful landscape. The campus also had two large apartment buildings with separate apartments that could offer a nice place to spend a day to rest after attending the teachings. So many Christian believers could now pray in the Retreat or the "Paradise" like the place was called.

Walton County, where the Wish family lived needed street front acreage to enlarge the highway. One of their properties was located right in the area the county wanted. This was a huge opportunity for the Wish's to get even more back from

NUMB

their investment in the property. So they could make more donations, because everything they were doing was with the idea of helping others in their minds.

"So, what do you think, should we sell the front road acres that we own?" Bob asked.

"Yes, it is needed, even if we don't need the money. We can purchase something else somewhere and still help the State," Mary Rita said.

"Okay, let's do it," Bob agreed.

So, they sold the property and the money was pouring in for the Wish family and the same way their donations for different charities became larger.

One day after the selling of the front road property, Mary Rita was relaxing watching the water from her screen porch. "You see Bob, this is my mission on this Earth, I want to help people, and I will do it."

"I know you will, but be careful," Bob warned. "This world is full of predators, charlatans, people that will strip you of the money that you worked so hard for. I know you'll say that it wasn't work, but I worked with you all the time and I saw how much you did for us, your family. Mary Rita, I always said that you were the one that made the money and you have all the right to spend it the way you want to spend it, but just open your eyes and use your judgment when choosing the people you deal with."

"You know I'll never do something stupid. I'm smart enough to read the people I want to help or work with, plus my Kathleen will always be closer to me and she is like an eagle, ready to protect me."

"I hope it will never be necessary for her to actually step in and protect you though," Bob said with sadness in his voice.Bob knew his wife, her desire to always be a winner, the desire to be in front of everything she did and this was one of the reasons she was so successful selling Tupperware, she wanted to be the best. He prayed that it would never happen to her, being taken advantage of. Or, that the cause she believed in with all her heart and all her soul, would end up not being a Godly, Christian, helpful one, a scam. He prayed about this a lot, though he never mentioned it to her.

"Hi Bob," Cynthia Faulkner said, "I talked to my daughter and I was right, she does have an old car parked in her garage and she would be very happy to not see it there any more, but it is not her car. The car belongs to my boss and my friend, Eve Garner."

"Okay, perfect. When can we go and look at?"

"Anytime you want, my daughter has a small child, my sweet grandson and she stays mostly at home. Just let me know when you both come and I'll take you there," Cynthia said.

Mary Rita packed few things and Bob happily drove them to Baton Rouge. The trip was nice and scenic; the landscape was beautiful, Bob's desire to see the old car made the trip to feel shorter. The city had a special charm, but he was interested only in the car issue.

Mary Rita though, was open to meeting more people, seeing more places.

Kathleen was now living in Baton Rouge and her house was the talk of the city. A majestic, large, old house that she'd renovated to make it impressive and beautiful.

Bob and Mary Rita enjoyed visiting Baton Rouge and staying at Kathleen's home.

They made arrangements to meet in front of Irene's house. Once they met, they entered the house together.

NUMB

"Hi, I'm Irene Floyd, Cynthia's daughter, nice to meet you."

"Hi, I'm Bob, Bob Wish and this is my wife, Mary Rita."

"I have heard so many wonderful things about you, both of you. About all the charity work and donations, you do for your area. We are blessed to have people like you. We kind of need people like you here in Baton Rouge, right Mom?" Irene turned towards her mother.

Cynthia was playing with her grandson and she didn't participate at their conversation but she understood what her daughter said. "Yes, we're in desperate need of some donations, but I don't think this is the right moment to talk about it. Irene, show Bob the car, please."

Irene took Mary Rita and Bob to the garage where an old car was waiting for Bob's renovation, Bob's love. The car looked so bad, but Bob didn't seem to care much, he knew his skills and he knew what he could do with the creepy looking car. "Okay, so whose car is this one? I would like to talk to the person in charge."

"I'll let her know you're here. She will be here in few minutes," Irene said.

A dark haired woman showed up a few minutes later with eyes looking like she had them closed. She introduced herself, "Hi, I'm Eve Garner, nice to meet you."

"Hi, Bob Wish and this is Mary Rita, my wife and Kathleen, our daughter."

"Cynthia told us so much about you and your charity work over there in Santa Rosa Beach, Florida. It is such a noble job, to serve God, by helping the needy," she said.

Bob looked at the car and he took it out for a test after he asked Eve's permission.

The moment Bob left the garage, Mary Rita felt sorry that she didn't join her husband for the test drive. As soon as Bob was gone, Kathleen and she became the target of Eve's speech.

She talked about the charity organization she founded in order to help people and she offered to take them to the church that was the main focus of her work.

Bob loved the car and he was ready to buy it, when he heard his wife saying,

"I would like to go and visit St. Bernadette, is not too far from here."

"Okay, we'll go, but first let me tell Eve that I'll buy her car," Bob said and he paid the full amount Eve asked for the car.

They formed a small group and walked to visit the church. The main image of the church, when entering it, it was the Divine Mercy, a large image of St. Faustina, the Apostle of the Divine Mercy, Jesus Christ. Eve Garner suddenly became an authority explaining how St. Faustina had daily conversations with Jesus Christ and all the orders she received from Him. She was saying about the dairy St. Faustina kept when she was a nun, in Poland and how many amazing things she did during her short life; St. Faustina died at the age of thirty three, the same age as Jesus died.

There were people listening to her, some even came closer to be sure they could hear what she was saying. She did have a way of talking about her beliefs that grabbed the attention of her audience. It was something no one could seem to put a finger on, a sensation that couldn't be explained...she made you feel like you couldn't leave the Church without pulling your checkbook!

At the end of the visit, Mary Rita and Bob left promising to return and spend more time in Baton Rouge. Kathleen promised to visit more often.

NUMB

"Kathleen, we're going to invest in few properties here, in Baton Rouge," Mary Rita said. "So you better start looking around. I love your style. You did a fantastic job with your house."

"Thank you Mom, I do enjoy what I'm doing. The houses that I buy look so bad but once I renovate them, it is so easy to sell them. I think I told you about this few times already, but I'm more than happy to work with you."

"I would like to talk to you about that lady that took us to St. Bernadette Church in Baton Rouge; I understood she is a poor lady or I should say 'not wealthy' and gives almost everything she has to the poor. I'm very impressed to meet someone that has such a Godly heart. I didn't like her in the beginning, but when she started talking, something transformed her, illuminating her face. She really believes in God and in her mission, I think I would like to listen to her few more times before donating for her charity."

"Mom, I believe in what she says. Some of her prophecies did happen, but people are divided; few people listen to her and follow her, others want her isolated from Church. She was even the subject of few meetings among high rank priests. There are priests that accept her, but most of the others stay away from her. The reason I'm telling you all this, is so you know what I think and to be aware of that woman's spiritual power. I cannot say this for sure, but few things she said shook me. Even though I try to keep my faith in God unaltered."

"I had no idea she talked about prophecies, do you think she really is a mystic, like she proclaimed herself?" Mary Rita asked.

"Who am I to know the answer? High priests were not able to say black or white. But some things she 'saw' before they happened, they really happened. She has some followers that will testify that everything she said was said before it happened. I will tell you everything I find out about her, so you can decide what to do, if you want to donate something."

NUMB

CHAPTER EIGHT

Mary Rita and Bob went back to their home in Florida where their paradise waited for them.

Mary Rita's friend Cynthia, who lived in Ponce de Leon, Florida and split her time between Baton Rouge and her small town, was coming frequently to St. Anne Catholic Church and that's how they became friends. She seemed to have a mission to accomplish. Every day she was telling Mary Rita new things about her friend from Baton Rouge, Eve Garner. How much she helped some women that showed up to their church, how much she dreamed about starting a missionary trip to Poland where her favorite Saint was born.

Mary Rita had her own charities in mind that she wanted to help, and the list was getting longer and longer, but she listened to her friend, trying to be polite. But the more she heard about Eve Garner, the more she wanted to get to know her. They'd met once when Bob purchased that car from her, parked in Cynthia's daughter garage. The moment she met Eve, Mary Rita wasn't really impressed by her, not at all, but at the same time, she knew to not judge the book by the cover, so she really paid attention to what her friend said about the woman.

"How could be possible that your friend Eve Garner had such a car? I'm talking about the car that my Bob bought."

"Well, there are members of the mission that donate cars, homes to her, so she sells them and makes contributions to the charity. But she doesn't keep anything for herself; isn't this a Christian thing? She is a Saint. Indeed, I don't remember knowing about people doing this. Even for me, it would be difficult, and you know how much I want to help the charities in our local area. You and Bob already donated more than a million dollars to our places that needed help and this means lots of money for our times. They need someone like you there in Baton Rouge. My mother believed in Eve for more than twenty years and when she passed away, she donated a large and I do mean a very *large* sum of money to St. John but Eve has lots of expenses in order to fulfill her promises to follow God's orders. The organization that her husband and she formed is a non-profit one and I know for sure, she reports everything to the government."

"Cynthia, you must believe in her mission. The way you talk, I have never heard you talking like this in our church, but you know more about her than I do. I know your daughter lives there and she needs you now to help with babysitting the baby. Are you going to move there permanently?"

"I'm not sure, because I have properties here to take care of and my husband's health is not the greatest," Cynthia answered. "I have been traveling back and forth to Louisiana and it has been tiring."

"I know. My Bob's health is okay, but not great. I'm so grateful we can go places together and have all the wonderful trips with our daughter, Kathleen. She likes taking us everywhere, cruises, trips and she loves going to Europe. I never thought I'd have so much fun after retiring."

"Mary Rita, we've been friends for more than twenty years, both of us have older husbands, we should make a pact, a promise to each other, that if something goes wrong with either of them, we'll be there for the each other, to help."

NUMB

"We don't have to have a pact! Once you're my friend, you will be my friend for the rest of my life, and I know you'll do the same for me." Mary Rita hugged her.

"Would you like to go with me next time when I go to stay with my daughter? You can stay with Kathleen?"

"Good idea, I'll see what Bob says."

"You know exactly what Bob will say, even before you'll ask him!" Cynthia laughed.

"You're right, but he is the head of the house," Mary Rita replied with a huge smile.

"Kathleen, I'm coming to Baton Rouge to stay with you. Are you happy to hear this?"

"Of course, I was going to call you. There are few houses I think that would appeal to you, Mom. It's about time to start working," she answered feeling happy to see her mother and spend some time with her, while 'working.' "

Mary Rita started helping St. John Charity, being convinced that everything she donated went to the right purpose, for the mission of helping the poor.

Kathleen became a good helper too, getting closer to the members of the charity group. One day, she remembered, back in Florida, Eve Garner was visiting her best friend and secretary, Cynthia Faulkner in Florida, where Cynthia had a house and where her husband lived. Cynthia's husband's health wasn't the best but still allowed her to go back to Baton Rouge and help her charity group. She was a long time friend of her mother, Mary Rita Wish.

That day, Eve suggested to Kathleen to go out with Arthur Walker, the spokesman for Eve's charity group.

Arthur was a real estate agent dealing with insurance issues, too. Kathleen thought it would be helpful to get to know Arthur considering her type of business, buying, fixing and selling houses, it was something they had in common.

At that moment in their lives, both of them had been divorced. Kathleen's children that she had adopted were older now and ready to start their own lives, so Kathleen had an open eye for her own future. She liked hard working people and she thought it wouldn't hurt to go out with Arthur.

He was a tall man, presentable and he divorced his wife after more than twenty years, to follow Eve. It was a type of adoration, a blind relationship; whatever she said, he did.

He was the man that was always there to testify for Eve's actions, ready to jump in fire for his boss, Eve Garner.

Paul Garner, Eve's husband knew he had no reason to be jealous, physically the man was inoffensive, he wasn't like other men, so he trusted him also with whatever his wife was telling Arthur to do.

Kathleen went out with Arthur as Eve suggested, but she didn't feel attracted to him, so they kept a nice, friendly relationship.

Kathleen wasn't sure about this whole mission thing with Eve though, and it bothered her that her mother seemed interested in joining Eve's group now.

Mary Rita became more and more involved in the charity trying to see the mission started. Eve advised Mary Rita to change her accountant and went with a large accounting firm in Florida to protect her money. She followed her advice and not too long after, that CPA she'd had before was indicted

NUMB

under federal charges and much of his client's money was tied up in court. She had her own doubts about how Eve was able to know this in advance but like any other thing she'd predicted, it had been claimed as coming from God.

Even if she knew all the logical factors, she felt obligated to do mostly everything Eve ordered, like when Eve Garner needed funds for few nuns from Poland to come and visit, or she needed funds for their group to go to Poland and many other projects.

Few days after Mary Rita had those inner debates, when she was back and forth from Santa Rosa Beach, Florida and Baton Rouge, Louisiana, Eve approached the group saying, "We need to have a room for worship, inside the church and we need money for it. That room has to be on the left side of the altar, this is what God told me to do."

"It will be done," the group had answered. While hypnotic waves seemed to be controlling everyone's mind and body. No questioning, no arguments, no one said anything in refusal...they would give the money to the cause.

Mary Rita was more than excited to be part of such work in the name of God. The more time she spent with the group, the more she believed in their mission. Those moments when she mentally asked questions about the group being legit, about where the money went, became less and less frequent.

One day, she called her daughter. "Kathleen, I want you to check on this property, please? Then tell me if the price is right and call me back. I don't have too much time; they want me to buy it right away."

"Who are they?' Kathleen asked.

"You know who! Eve wants us to buy a nice home and renovate it so we can have a nice shop where the pilgrims can come, shop and relax. And I like the idea. It will be a beautiful place for everyone, an antique store, and a coffee shop."

"I agree, but don't you think that you and dad already spent more than you should? Let other people do their part, too," Kathleen urged.

"Oh, I'm not sure your dad wants to know about all my investments, it drives him insane! He said the same thing you said, enough is enough, and that we should do other things other than helping this charity, but I see all the good things they do for people."

"Do you really see those good things? Mom, I did some research and I already requested my five thousand dollars back, you know the membership money?"

Mary Rita gasped. "You did what? How could you do that? The group needs all the money we have. They want all the properties we purchased to be left by legal wills to St. John Charity!"

Sounding disappointed, Kathleen finally told her mother the address of the property. "I had already donated 35,000 to this house, Mom. You do what you want to do, like Dad always says, 'she made the money, she can do whatever she wants with it.' And it is true, you made all this money, but you have to open your eyes, like I opened mine and see the reality. I'll go and check the property one more time, because I did it before when I donated the money, but remember, nobody in this world loves you more than I do, of course Dad loves you a lot, but it's so much different than the love I have for you. Do you remember all the trips we took together, the fun we had when we took classes together, the time we spent together? Mom, we are not only mother and daughter, we have a special bond. I respect you but you have to promise me that you will be more cautious and pay more attention at what is going on around you. One more thing, I don't like the

NUMB

fact that some of the things you do here in Baton Rouge, you consider it to be not important enough for Dad to know about it. You always did everything together, why not now?"

Mary Rita sighed into the phone. "I will think about all that you have said. I love you." She hung up the phone and suddenly started thinking if she should hide most of her donations, most of her actions from her own daughter!

Oh no, I would never do this to her; she loves me more than anyone else, how can I even think this way?

Eve Garner was busy in her office thinking about her missions, trying to choose carefully the persons to go to Europe and to be her tools. But for sure, Arthur Walker, Cynthia Faulkner, Irene Floyd, Deanne Jones, Cynthia's daughters, and Mary Rita Wish would be part of those trips. Something made Eve think that it would be necessary first for one team to go to Rome, Italy and accomplish the unthinkable. To put some documents in Pope's hands through his Swiss Guards and after that, another team could to go to Poland, to the monastery where St. Faustina lived and where her relics were. She already had everything lined up but she wanted to be sure no details were missed. She knew she had to work on people's minds, to make them want to spend their time and money for her 'visions' to become true.

Feeling a lot lighter and content with her thinking, she left the office and when she saw her husband, she said, "Well, these missions will require all my mental focus. It will be a hard work to arrange all the details, to make them a success. But that's what I'm here for. You have a smart wife, Sir, be grateful. I make your life so easy, right?"

"Not only are you right, but I'd feel lost without you," Paul Garner said, kissing his wife who always mesmerized him. He continued to feel very much attracted to her and he knew that her 'beauty' wasn't the top of the reasons. He was never able to explain why he divorced his wife after a long, loving marriage. Why he'd followed Eve everywhere she wanted, why he was physically attracted to her. Paul knew it was more than physical attraction, he knew it was part of her plans, she needed him to be around her, she had to look like a normal, devoted woman, having a family, going to church and helping the needy.

Kathleen Petrovich knew that these people would not stop draining her mother's assets, she knew this, but she'd already moved to another state where she'd opened a fabulous business and she worked long, tiring hours, but with great success. Whatever she was doing, whatever she touched, turned to gold just like it had for her mother, that's how smart and inventive she was.

People who worked with her felt blessed, their boss treated them with respect and consideration.

This business required a lot of Kathleen's time, so it was hard for her to get in touch with people she knew, to ask them to check on her parents. But she trusted a lady at St. Bernadette Church who told her what was going on with her mother; her name was Tracy and she was a real friend. Kathleen felt really grateful to have someone she trusted. To be able to know step by step what her mother's actions had been. She never thought she would get to this point, to need to check on things about her own mother, the woman she adored, the one she had the most fun with her entire life. Kathleen hurt in her heart every time she had to ask her

NUMB

friend about Mary Rita, it made her feel like she didn't trust her mother. She knew if Mary Rita found out what her daughter was doing, she would feel insulted and would be very upset, but Tracy could be trusted not to say anything

Kathleen felt sure that to some extent, her father had to agree to sign documents for Mary Rita and him to purchase the properties they talked about. She was able to look in the public records and see that the majority of the properties the Wish family purchased and they had been purchased at an inflated price, tens of thousands over the appraised value. A lot more than the other houses in the vicinity had been sold for and she didn't want this practice to continue.

She began to panic and inquired what she could do to protect her parents from becoming poor, after a long life of hard work and earning money honestly.

Time was short now and Kathleen already knew that the St. John Charity wanted more and more money to create funds for different, sometimes, imaginary needs.

CHAPTER NINE

One day, Father Timothy visited Bob Wish and both of them were relaxing looking at the water. For some reason, the water front property Mary Rita and Bob owned in Florida was never a subject of any discussion connected to the charity group. Father Timothy had only negative thoughts about that group. "Bob, I think Mary Rita is a saint. Look how much she does for that group in Baton Rouge. I know both of you donated a fortune here too and I would like you do other things, take care of your health, have fun and at the same time, serve God too. I would like to talk to her when she comes back."

Bob nodded. "I think the same way. She even made me purchase a building that I didn't want to, but she insisted, so we bought it. Our daughter, Kathleen knows the real estate business really well and she was completely against us buying it and she was right. Now is too late, let's hope that it will be put to work for a good cause."

The priest was deeply troubled over this subject. "With the donations they received from only what I know, this St. John Charity group should be well known by now, but nobody talks about it when we have our meetings with our bishops. Bob, I feel that something isn't right. There are people looking for the most devoted Catholic believers, I'm talking about us, but it can be in any other churches, the procedure is always the same. They look for the women mostly, because men are by nature more logical than women. The women are

NUMB

the most spiritual as well, they go to Mass everyday, say the Rosary everyday, sometimes few times a day, and they are always seeking new and better ways to serve and worship God, and this is your loving wife. All the things she does for the charity group that she's a member of, is coming from her pure heart. She never thinks twice if she needs to help. Mary Rita is one of the best and godliest women that I have ever preached to. She is God's instrument and this is exactly what she does, helping others with everything she has. My only concern is Satan. You see Bob, when so much money is pouring in and nothing shows, it is Satan that is working in full force to destroy what you, your wife, your daughter and many more other believers have built. They tried to have a solid, strong financial organization and Satan is doing his demonic work. Demonic means 'to divide' and it is working. I heard that Cynthia ran away and nobody knows where she went, not even her daughters."

Bob sat forward, looking upset as he listened.

"I'm not sure if you remember that Cynthia was coming to our church like you and Mary Rita did all the time. I was her spiritual Father, she would ask me anything but she did not tell me where she was going and this is strange, very strange. I pray for her safe return. Kathleen could feel Satan at work and slowly, she detached from the group and now, she told me she feels free, like almost feeling liberated from a prison. Her main purpose now is to see her mom, your wife free as well. I remembered one time Mary Rita telling me that every time she was looking in that woman's eyes, she was getting dizzy, she felt almost hypnotized, numb... It is very possible too, because those 'Leaders' have a strong will and their desire for power and money has no limits. One of the things those people say every single day, to every single person of their group is, 'Wait, God will do it. You only have to wait and pray.' Those leaders have a desire of being someone special, and you can be a real special mystic if your followers believed that you communicate with God. Bob, I wish I could open her mind and pour in the truth. But for her, everything she does is in the name of God, helping the needy."

Bob looked out over the water and sighed. "Thank you Father for visiting me, it means a lot to me. It has made me feel better and I will drive tomorrow to Baton Rouge to see my lady, I miss her."

As soon as Father Timothy left, Bob's eyes remained glued to the bay water. Dolphins were swimming slowly, bringing joy and peace to him. He started talking to the One that helped him and his family with each endeavor they went through. *God, help my wife to see her actions clearly, to open her eyes she can see the real face of that woman. I won't even want to say her name. Mary Rita believes with all her heart that all the money and all the properties she donated really helped the poor. She really believes that the word of God will be spread by that charity! God, make her see what I see, what Kathleen saw and so many other people from Church can see.*

Bob left the bench he was sitting on. With a heavy heart; he went back inside his beautiful home, where he could see the water from every corner, every place.

Not too long after Bob went inside, the phone rang.

"Dad, how are you? I miss you. Where's mom?" Kathleen asked.

"You know where she is. She went back to Baton Rouge and I'll leave tomorrow to see her over there. I miss her; it's hard to be alone."

"I don't like what she's doing Dad, and I don't like that she goes there alone. That woman with her charity is taking all your money that you worked your entire lives for. We have to do something to get her out of there, to protect her from those sharks. My God, do they have sharp teeth or what?"

NUMB

"You're right! What can we do to see her out? Eve Garner and her missions; it's all what your mother talks about. Kathleen, I don't see an exit for us. Mary Rita's mind is only on the charity."

"You just said the right word... mind, her mind! This is what you and I have to do. We need to find a way to show her the mental abuse she is under. Dad, I really believe what I just said; she is under a severe mental abuse, isn't she? Do you think she would ever agree to have a doctor exam? I do think that woman does something strange to my mother; besides hypnotizing her. And not only to her. I believe she does this, whatever it is, to all of her followers. I know that woman had some other issues of her own. Let me tell you what that woman did, you will not believe it. One day, she talked to her 'Group' and explained that their St. John Charity had to have a lawyer, but not any kind of lawyer, she told them that it had to be the best lawyer because some people were aiming get them in trouble, like suing or who knows what. She let them scratched their minds to come up with the best lawyer names and a few minutes after everyone suggested different lawyer names, she said that she already knew who the best lawyer was, and she told everyone the lawyer's name. She was prepared with the name because she knew why that lawyer had to be the only one. My mother pulled her checkbook out and without any hesitation, she wrote a check for ten thousand dollars in the name of the St. John Charity, but she made it payable to Eve Garner! You see dad, I knew where this money went, but my mother didn't know it. If I try to show her that I was right, she will get really mad at me. That's how much she believes in Eve Garner and her work of charity. Dad, we need legal help to protect her."

"No, Kathleen, I'm not sure if she will get angry but for sure, we do need legal help."

"Dad, that woman was caught with drugs and she had been arrested. Nobody knew, because she pretended to be just absent because she 'needed her time alone with God' and there was not even one single person that really knew the truth! That fat check went for her lawyer fees, not for the poor. When she couldn't be present and run her group, but the truth was that she had to spend time in jail, a short time, but still time. The lawyer she paid with my mother's money made all the arrangements for Eve, so she was out of jail pretty soon."

"What? That's impossible; she cannot be that evil."

"It's true, Dad. One day, Irene, Cynthia's daughter was home taking care of her new baby. Well, someone rang the bell and dropped a package at her door. By the time she opened the door, the person who delivered the package was gone. It wasn't delivered by the mailman, had no stamps, nothing, when she looked inside, a suspicious powder covered the cardboard. It wasn't even properly packed. Irene was so scared and she waited for her husband to get home then she showed him the package, the powder. Their first impulse was to go to the police station but then both of them realized how much trouble this would cause Cynthia, Irene's mother, because she's the secretary of the St. John Charity."

"Why? What had Cynthia or St. John Charity to do with the package?" her father asked.

"You see, many times people were dropping donations for the charity group right at Irene's door, knowing her mother worked there and knowing how involved Irene was with the group, that's why the first thought was about the implications caused by the package. They were afraid of interrogations, the police questioning them, lawsuit, houses being searched and who knows what else, so both of them decided to talk directly to Eve Garner.... *'Do you have*

NUMB

something to say about this package and why it was delivered to my door?' Eve told them, 'I have no idea what you're talking about.' And she tried to grab the package. 'But if you are thinking about going to the police, your child will die in few days and only because I say so. You should know by now how powerful my prayers are. I can predict everything and you should remember how many things I predicted that came true. You better give me the package and I promise nothing will happen to your living child. It is not the child's fault that his parents are so stupid.' Suddenly, the woman they wanted to expose and be incarcerated by the police was the one holding the victory in her hands. Fear paralyzed the couple even if their rationality was telling them the logical answer. When your child becomes part of such a horrible blackmail, there is no rationality that can face the cost of being brave."

"That is horrible. I never knew all this was happening. I will tell you something though. Your mother doesn't think I know all that she invests and do you know why? She wants to protect me. I'm concerned about our wealth but not because of me, no, but because of our children, grandchildren and great children. Charities always have been part of our donations but not to strip you and your family to the bone!"

"I don't think God wants this from anyone," Kathleen agreed. "Let me know if you come up with any idea how to help Mom."

"I will. Love you so much. Call me soon because I'll think more about our conversation, but remember, my love for your mother is bigger than all my worries about the money. I love her... period."

"I know Dad."

They hung up; each one worried and tried to think of a way to get Mary Rita away from Eve's clutches. Both of them declared war on 'Satan', praying hard to bring Mary Rita back to reality, to be able to see the truth. They knew how hard it would be to get through Mary Rita's Faith screen, the one she'd worn... for all of her life.

NUMB

CHAPTER TEN

Somewhere in Baton Rouge, a small group of people were making arrangements for some important trips across the Atlantic Ocean to Europe for a few missions that had to be accomplished according to their group leader's orders.

The group had been aware of some changes in their boss' thinking' and her revelations, now her story had changed... she had to get some important document, according to her beliefs, she had to convince at least two women to spend the money and the time to make that trip. The mission and for the leader of the charity group as the 'scroll' as she named it, had to get into the Pope's hands.

"Do you understand me?" Eve said. "I mean John Paul the Second, no one else, the Pope. Those documents have to get there, our mission, our charity depends of the success of this trip."

Cynthia was working fast to see if she could convince one of her daughters to go with her, spend the money and she wasn't sure if her daughter would have the necessary time to spend abroad. She would have to make many arrangements so her family would have what they needed till she came be back. Cynthia knew she was asking for a lot but at the same time, her daughter would do anything in the name of God.

"Deanne, do you have few minutes to talk?" Cynthia asked one of her daughters.

"Hi mom, how are you? Of course I have, what is going on?"

"Well, it seems like you and I have to go to Rome!"

"Are you inviting me to go with you to Europe for fun? Let's go. Actually, Chris came home from work, few days ago and suggested we should go to Rome. What is going on here? Is this a secret plan?" Deanne giggled.

"Oh, I'm so happy to hear he had the same idea. It will be fun and also, we will have the rare occasion to meet the Pope!" Cynthia couldn't believe that her son in law had such an idea.

"You mean *our* Pope, John Paul? No, it's impossible. Do you know how hard is to have a chance to meet him in person? People have to get tickets months in advance to be able to have even a short audience with him. He's the leader of the Catholic Religious world! It can't be that simple, he is such a powerful figure."

"Eve had no idea about you and Chris going to Rome, and I just found out about your trip. We have to try, it could be one chance in a lifetime," Cynthia insisted.

"Okay mom, this isn't something to decide in a moment and over the phone. I will fly down there to spend some time with you and Mary Rita and of course Eve. How's Mary Rita doing by the way?"

"She is the most efficient members we have. We just ask for things we need for our charity and she is ready to help, all the time. She never asked questions because she believes in what Eve says, 'God knows you have it, you have to give it' and she does. I have never met anyone so dedicated to our mission like she is, maybe my mother, your grandmother was like her. And me too, you see, this trip will cost me a huge amount of money but my heart will be fulfilled. I have to see the Pope!"

NUMB

"Mom, let me talk to my husband about coming to visit you in Baton Rouge, and it depends on his schedule. Maybe we can have a short, nice vacation in Baton Rouge. I'll let you know as soon as I can, love you mom," Deanne Jones said.

Few days after mother-daughter conversation, Cynthia's daughter, Deanne and her husband, Chris Jones, came down to spend some time visiting Cynthia and her charity group friends.

While spending time with everyone there in Baton Rouge, they put together a plan in order to accomplish their mission that Eve had charged them with.

The trip was well planned. They got ready with all the thongs necessary to accomplish their 'mission.' They prepared the documents to be sure there will be no problems at the airport. The day they flew and crossed the Atlantic Ocean, was a day full of clear skies as the weather was soft and pleasant. Everyone hoped to have a little bit of vacation, being sure their mission wasn't so hard. Once Cynthia, Deanne and Chris Jones arrived in Rome, they started their mission to deliver the scroll, identical to the one they held high when the Pope's car drove by them and he looked right at the sign they held.

This time, the scroll had to be placed in the Pope's hands or someone from his guard.

After following Pope's schedule, going from one place to another, they arrived at St. Peter's Basilica. It was late being really dark inside and around the church. It felt like a divine experience even while feeling watched by the Pope's guard, the Swiss Guards.

Cynthia talked to the officer in charge and after answering the entire questionnaire, he asked of her, he agreed to take the scroll from Deanne's hands. After checking the outside of the scroll, the officer said he would deliver the document to the ones close to the Pope.

The two women couldn't have been more grateful and relieved.

The flight back home from the Vatican was smooth and once they touched dry land, everyone went to their homes. They had been received with very nice greetings and appreciation for what they were able to achieve.

Back in Baton Rouge, more and more people were associating Eve with Sister Faustina and she was glad to 'feed' the image, as it was serving her goals really well. Most of the people who knew her almost forgot about her Japanese origin, about her adoption. Now her claims moved to another part of the world from Japan, the place she initially pretended she had been adopted, to Poland, the place where St. Faustina lived. Going to Poland, could be quite a trip, a trip that her imagination had to work hard while figuring out all the details, to be sure everything would go according to her plans.

Eve called her friend-secretary and invited her to sit down.

The moment Cynthia heard the invitation she knew something important was coming up, she knew she was going to be asked to do something major.

"Cynthia, you have to help me. I need you to go to Poland. I need you to take a scroll and a document from me and give it to the Superior Nun, the only living nun who knew Sister Faustina in person. She is the one who knows what my 'documents' talk about."

"Do you mean Poland, Europe? Don't you think I'm a little old for that kind of trip? What about younger people?"

NUMB

"No, you, Mary Rita and your Deanne are the only ones to make this trip a success. You all are smart and I believe in you all. I'm going to join you this time, if the things go well here with the St. John Charity, I don't want people to miss me."

"Okay, tell me what it's about," Cynthia said.

When Eve started explaining to her secretary about the trip in Poland, she suddenly remembered what Cynthia's daughter had in her house and how was she able to obtain something that could be part of her future dream. Deanne was in possession of a few of the St. Faustina's relics and suddenly... the entire story came clear in her mind. Eve Garner had another plan now, a very important plan to accomplish.

Deanne lived in Atlantic City, New Jersey and she asked her pastor to write a letter to the priest of the monastery where the saint's relics were, asking for some of those relics to bring them to their church for veneration.

The pastor wrote the letter and when Deanne and her husband visited the monastery in Poland, she was thrilled to be approved to take home with her some of the relics of St. Faustina, and to offer them to her church.

The relics had been carefully packed and sealed with the monastery seal and they had been placed in a special box, so the American custom officers would know what was inside and let them go through their scrutinizing rules.

The next Sunday when she went to her church, after the Service, she talked to her pastor and handed him the precious box, being excited that she could offer such a fantastic gift to her church and to see those relics there, where people would worship and pray at.

The priest thanked her and he really appreciated what Deanne and her husband did for their church but he'd asked

Deanne to keep the relics in a safe place until he was cleared by the dioceses to receive them and put them in the right place close to the altar.

But it wasn't as simple as Deanne thought it would be.

Years went by and she was never asked to bring the relics to her church because the new priest, who replaced the one she talked to, wasn't ready either, saying that the church needed to have a really big ceremony to receive the relics. It didn't make sense to Deanne, but she kept saving the box in her house.

Eve Gardner knew she now had a plan for those relics. They were an important part of her 'visions' and her mind was working already, way in advance, to see it happen.

One day, she asked Cynthia to talk to her daughter, Deanne Jones about it, "Cynthia, don't you think it would be a lot better to have those relics that Deanne keeps in her house, to have them here. So everyone can worship and venerate them, instead of staying in a box?"

Obediently, Cynthia asked her daughter about the relics.

"Actually, I completely forgot about the relics, it was so long ago. My priest said that he wasn't ready to receive them. I suppose it would be alright to have them at your St. Bernadette's"

Eve was so happy that she really helped few poor women that day, giving them a twenty dollars bill for each.

The summer was getting closer and so was the vacation time. Deanne and her husband went to Baton Rouge at the end of their long and beautiful vacation and everyone was happy to see them, but the most excited one was Eve Garner. After Deanne and her husband left, she was holding the relics in her arms and soon all worshipers knew about the St. Faustina's relics.

NUMB

The woman who ordered the trips, using other people's money, their time and their funds, was now holding the missing piece of the puzzle, the relics.

Cynthia expected to get a 'thank you' at least, besides the greeting they all got when coming back from Europe. Thanks for doing such a good job and all the things the group achieved for their team's expenses. Or for even how she was able to make her daughter donate the relics to St. Bernadette Church but then she realized who the person she worked for was and she gave up the hope of being appreciated.

Next day, the relics of St. Faustina had been placed on the left side of the altar of St. Bernadette Church where the worship room was, so people would come, pray and venerate the relics and the Divine Mercy, the large painting representing Jesus Christ with two veils springing from His heart. One veil was red and one was pale. The Divine Mercy painting was getting ready to bless the church and those entering and praying to God. But at the same time, being convinced that Eve Garner and her mystical powers made all this possible, the worshipers had no idea who her real Master was and how much they were under her Master's influence, Satan.

Then as usual, she wanted more. There was always something needing to be done in order to proclaim her prophetic power. She could see herself in a near future traveling and teaching people about Sister Faustina and her teachings, her prophecies, her visions. She prepared the road of lies with people's fear of the unknown.

Traveling around the world to spread the word of God and her plans required some funds, financial funds, and her mind was set on this. Eve envisioned her future, surrounded by a small group of people formed by her husband Paul Garner, her spokesman Arthur Walker, her secretary and best friend and follower for more than twenty years, Cynthia Faulkner and of course, Mary Rita Wish, the follower whose presence was making Eve's 'vision' possible! Eve knew how much she needed Mary Rita's deep faith in doing what God tells you to do, to follow His commands and she was sure to make those commands coming through her, through her voice. Everyone believed it, not only Mary Rita Wish.

Looking closer at this group, everyone had a well determined role, and Eve knew how to use this to the maximum of their potentials.

No detail was left unthought-of. Everything was planned step by step by her brilliant mind, a mind used to serve the 'one' that her mission was supposed to be against, Satan.

No one could see who the real Master was that she was worshipping, the real Master behind her predictions, her visions and all her actions, while going to church and praying for the poor, making her appear to be a devoted Christian woman.

Eve was gaining more and more popularity and Mary Rita Wish was giving away more of her money, helping the world wide mission to grow.

NUMB

CHAPTER ELEVEN

"Mary Rita," Bob said when he finally saw his wife. "How's everything going with you? I didn't get a chance to see you for two weeks. I missed you a lot. We need to start a new construction project together, let's renovate few more buildings."

"And I missed you too, my husband," Mary Rita replied getting closer so she could give him a big hug. "There is a house close to St. Bernadette Church and it could become a commercial or residential rental. My problem is that our daughter doesn't want us to buy it. Something about this building that she doesn't agree with. Maybe she's right. Let's wait a little longer and pray for it. If it has to be ours, it will be. If not, we have to look at other properties. How are you feeling? You're right, I should spend more time home, and I'm on the road all the time. We have to go to Indiana to see our daughter's gorgeous home and we should spend few days there, what do you think?"

"Anytime, I would love to go with you, we have to let her know about us coming." Bob nodded.

"Well, when we come back from Kathleen's house, I have to get ready to help Eve Garner to put together future plans for St. John Charity; she has important plans for almost everybody in our group."

"Mary Rita, you look so radiant when you talk about the missionary trips or jobs you have for the group."

"I do love you so much Bob. I'm almost seventy five years old and when I look at you, I feel like a young woman. I know sometimes you don't agree with what I do or how I do the work around here in Baton Rouge, but I believe in everything I do with all my heart."

"You don't have to tell me, it shows your dedication, but I have moments when my heart bothers me and I need you more and more."

"What's wrong with you? Are you sick?" Mary Rita asked.

"Like I said, I get tired easily, as soon as I do something that requires more effort."

"Did you see the heart doctor?"

"No, but I will," Bob promised with a sad voice.

Mary Rita knew something wasn't right with her husband of fifty seven years and she realized she needed be with him more often.

No one could see that Bob was getting tired doing things, physically tired.

His love for old cars was keeping him active and his good friends and neighbors were spending a good amount of time with him, but he still wanted his wife home.

Mary Rita started the preparations for her first missionary trip and lots of money went into those preparations; air tickets, hotel rooms, meals, and she generously contributed financially for the cost of the trip, financing the mission.

The mission that Eve kept talking about for years would finally start and Mary Rita felt honored to be part of it. The other side of the story, the money spent, it was just additional, not as important, and so, she never asked why the total cost of the trip had to be covered mostly by her.

The arrival in Poland was perfect timing; everything fell in the right place, the driver/interpreter was already known to

NUMB

Cynthia and Deanne. Mary Rita was impressed by how well he spoke English. An important part of their mission was to be able to have someone that spoke Polish to communicate the purpose of their mission to the right person. This person was the Superior Nun of the monastery where sister Faustina was born.

Mary Rita was so touched by the Holy Spirit that she had tears in her eyes all the time she spent in the presence of the nun. The Superior Nun was the only living person in that monastery in Krakow, Poland who knew Sister Faustina when she was alive; the only resident of the monastery who knew the real story of Saint Faustina, whose relics were kept at the Shrine of Divine Mercy in Lagiewniki, a suburb of Krakow.

After a long ordeal, 'the representatives' of St. John Charity as both women, Cynthia and Mary Rita had been instructed by Eve Garner to call themselves; they met the Superior Nun and knelt before her.

The Superior Nun made them get right up; she didn't want them kneel before her.

The Chapel where the meeting took place had few nuns that spoke English.

One of them came and helped them to understand each other. At the end of the meeting, Cynthia and Mary Rita had been told by the interpreter nun that the document they had presented to the Superior Nun was from evil and that it was evil!

The Superior Nun kept her head down as the interpreter spoke; as though she didn't want to look at the women in front of her. She almost threw the documents on the floor, that's how disgusted she seemed to be.

Mary Rita and Cynthia had no idea about what the document said.

The interpreter nun said that Cynthia and Mary Rita should leave and to not come back and to *not* leave the document there.

Eve Garner's 'representatives' were shocked.

The deep faith of those nuns made it possible to see the evil work in that document.

Cynthia and Mary Rita informed their leader right away about the ordeal they had to go through when giving the scroll and the document to the Superior Nun in charge with scrutinizing all the documents.

When Eve heard what happened with the document she wanted both the scroll and the document to be at that monastery, so she told Cynthia to go back, give it to the Mother Superior and be sure she got them.

It was easier to say than to do, but next day, Mary Rita, Cynthia, and Deanne were heading again to the chapel, to try to leave the document and the scroll in the hands of Mother Superior.

It was a day full of success for the 'representatives' of St. John Charity, or better said, for Eve Garner's goal. The two women were able to hand the document and the scroll to the Mother Superior's assistant and they left the chapel feeling joyous.

Their mission had been accomplished. Now Eve could claim what she kept claiming all those years.... *"I'm who Sister Faustina talks about and who John Paul II knows about. That it was all true, because both missions had been accomplished."*

Yes, by using people faithful to God, who'd, spent a fortune to make her plan feasible. It was a big celebration for St. John Charity. Eve Garner, the woman who kept everyone on her leash, would now be able to make affirmations that for the first time in her 'career'... were true. Her devoted followers made so many sacrifices for her, in the name of God,

NUMB

hoping this event would bring more people to believe in their leader, Eve Garner.

All those women worked hard and spent money for Eve's glory. Eve couldn't have been happier.

It was time for Mary Rita to go back to Florida and be with her husband, Bob, but before this, she had a talk with her friend, Eve because she wanted to tell her something.

"Mary Rita, you should start talking with Cynthia and have an agreement between you two that if something happens, you know what I'm talking about, as you both have sick husbands, older than you are, so you should look out for each other. It is hard to be alone. Your daughter is not happy with your actions here, helping St. John Charity and helping the poor, everybody can see it. We already had been informed that she is trying to get you in a nursing home to protect your assets."

"What? My Kathleen would never do such a thing! We are best friends and she calls me all the time to be sure that I'm doing well. You know better than anyone how much she loves her father and me, how could you say this?"

"Well, ask your friend Cynthia about what had happened when *your* Kathleen talked to your priest in Santa Rosa Beach, Father Timothy. Just talk to her before you leave. I want the best for you and I'm so grateful for all the donations you gave to our charity, but I also consider myself your friend."

"I know and I appreciate your friendship, but no one can convince me that my own daughter that I adore would put me in a nursing home. Why? She knows how sharp my mind is, how bright my memory is, no doctor would ever diagnose me as incompetent."

"You should get a document stating what you just said; we all know how smart you are and we all can testify, but we are not psychiatrists, or doctors. I can have an appointment set up for you and this way you'll be ok."

"Okay, I'll go and have a doctor examine me, if this will protect me from going in a nursing home, I'll do it. I'm not scared about being in a nursing home, people get help there, but I'm too sharp and physically able to do everything that I can't see myself living there, not yet....."

"Better have documents from at least two doctors, to be sure you'll be covered."

Mary Rita nodded. "I know lots of doctors in Florida even if I've never been sick!"

"Do not worry, I know plenty.

"How soon can you get those appointments for me?"

"Why? Are you in a hurry?" Eve asked.

"Kind of, I have to go back to my husband. I miss him."

"Is he okay? Do you want me to go with you? I can take few days off and we can drive together?"

"Thank you, Bob is doing well, but he's missing me a lot, and he is at an apartment we have here." Mary Rita tried to avoid the real reason she needed to go back home.

"Alright, I'll let you know about the doctor appointments as soon as I get them set up, see you at six," Eve said.

As soon as Eve left, Mary Rita put her head on the table and could not stop her tears coming down her face. Her heart was heavy, and her sharp mind kept analyzing everything that had happened, knowing something had changed. Somehow, deep in her conscious she knew that God would never require the kind of spending that would leave her family heirs depleted of their inheritance. That was the

NUMB

real subject she'd intended to bring up to Eve, then Eve brought up that horrible bit about Kathleen.

"God, they keep telling me that I can do whatever I want to do with the money I made, but I have two children, grandchildren and a large family that loves me. I could give them a huge chunk of what I have spent in donations and still have plenty left for church and for me. Why is everything going to this woman? I'll tell you why... I'm scared that something really bad could happen. It's the fear that makes me keep giving and giving. I do you remember when she told my Kathleen that if she donated a large amount of money, I don't remember right now exactly, but it was about few thousand dollars that her father would live an extra period of time! Eve knew my Bob has heart problems, she knew he would have to have a special type of intervention. When I'd just found out about my husband's heart condition 2 years ago, Eve knew way before me, from her spies. My Kathleen believed in her so much that she gave her the money. She wanted her father to live a longer, healthy life and she is trying to convince me that such a loving daughter was looking to put me in an institution? No, this has to be her working on a way to separate my Kathleen from me and her dad. "Well, this would ever happen," she firmly stated.

The psychiatrist appointment was arranged and Mary Rita went to her appointment, being confident in her mental sanity, her mental health.

It was a long visit, to fill all the blank lines with her answers. The doctor asked her a myriad of questions and in the end, the doctor said, "Ma'am, I don't know who sent you here and why. I have wasted my time but I enjoyed meeting you. It was my pleasure to talk to you. You are mentally healthier and fit, than all of us put together."

Mary Rita knew she would be diagnosed as normal but she was afraid that if it were true that Kathleen wanted to put her in a nursing home, this wouldn't be enough. She knew she had to go to a doctor that didn't know Eve or Kathleen, someone neutral.

Eve already knew the results as she had her antennas all over the city.

Mary Rita called her, told her how the doctor visit went and what she thought about going to a completely neutral doctor.

Eve was surprised by Mary Rita's thinking but she agreed with the idea. The second psychiatrist signed the same diagnosis, that Mary Rita Wish was competent, alert, and healthy in all her faculties.

Eve knew she had to work harder than she did with the other followers, because being that smart, Mary Rita would need more convincing arguments to make her donate even more than she already had. It seemed like Mary Rita became Eve's main goal, to plant more powerful 'seeds' into her mind, to make her even more sensitive to people's sufferings. She had her own Master to pray for more strength, for more convincing influences. The more she was getting for her cause the more she wanted.

Kathleen Petrovich's idea to put her mother in a safe place where no one could access her funds had failed. Now she had to find another way to protect her mother from being ripped off by that group, the way she called it, in a nice way, but everyone was aware of what that 'group' was all about.

Kathleen had to talk again with the attorney that advised her to take action to protect her mother and her assets. She

NUMB

would never have such thoughts about her loving mother, but if this 'method' represented her last resort, she would have no other choice but to do it. Her sister, Christina offered her all the help she could get but Kathleen was too far away to be able to 'work' together with her sister, but she was grateful Christina offered to help.

She gathered all the letters from their family members and all the bank statements while trying to put together a solid plan, a perfect argument in front of authorities, so she could save her mother from Satan's clutches.

She knew what this group would do to her mother, the woman that Kathleen considered a saint. Looking back at all the things she did for her community, for her church and the people that needed help, she was a saint for them. Kathleen believed in her mother and she prayed to God to get her out of that group.

Kathleen knew the forces she was fighting against. The powerful bondage evil created around you, hugging your mind and body like an octopus, contaminating your brain and soul. There were no medications against this, only prayers and patience. Her own life was now becoming centered only on her mother's salvation, neglecting her family and her business. She had to work longer hours to be able to have the extra time she needed for her 'legal' appointments and to spend money on things that she never though she would have to.

Kathleen kept asking her inner self, " *How is possible that such a strong, smart, a self made millionaire, whose mind is so disciplined and organized not see what everyone else sees? She worked everyday to help others to help themselves, training them to fight for a better life and now, I am the one fighting for her life!?*"

She knew she would not give up. Her fight would go on till her mother would again be the woman she used to be. It wasn't her own doing that she was giving all her money and life away to some cult. Mary Rita was simply a woman who was convinced her actions were the right ones and everything she was giving away was in the name of God, for His purposes.

Kathleen's mission was harder than she thought it would be for the same reason Eve Garner knew why she had to work harder on Mary Rita's brain and soul, using her passion for what she was doing as a weapon.

"God, I put all my hopes and my mother's situation in your hands. I can see in my mind the diabolic plan Eve has for my mother, actually for her money because she doesn't care about her as a human being. I see how she already has a plan for my mother when my father is gone, that woman guides everyone's steps to the road she wants them to walk. God, I walked that road. I was a believer and she kept me under her influence through fear that my dad would die if I didn't do what she ordered me to do. She even said I'd be raped if I didn't move from my house that my parents gave to me and that I had to sell my house in Florida and move to Baton Rouge. God, I see now what I couldn't see back then. I see why she had to have all the properties in Baton Rouge, so she could control any transactions and it was a lot easier for her to be present in people's lives, making them to donate their homes, legally, to St. John Charity, to the mission that never started. Help my mother to see what I see now, once I got out of her evil circle. God, I'm fighting a strong enemy but you're the one that will show me the way, you're the only one I put my hopes in, help me God."

Kathleen started crying and her heavy heart was feeling lighter and full of hope for the future. If someone would have

NUMB

seen her crying, that person would think Kathleen was on her mother's death bed—that's how deeply worried and trouble she was over this cult entrapping her sweet mother.

CHAPTER TWELVE

Mary Rita went home to Santa Rosa Beach, Florida and spent a good amount of time being with her hubby and both of them had the time of their lives.

One day, driving around their beautiful town, looking at the emerald water of the Gulf of Mexico and the sugar white sand, Mary Rita became nostalgic and this was something that didn't happen too often to her. Being a practical working woman, that didn't know what slowing down was, to relax was a foreign concept to her.

But this time, the beauty of the surroundings calmed her and brought long time memories back into her mind and smiling she asked, "Bob, do you remember the Tupperware award we received in 1974, when we were still living in Chicago? For some reason that huge event just came to my mind. Back then, it was a special award, not like now. It was given only once a year to the person or couple that had many years of achievement. It was something like a well rounded award? I never understood exactly what it meant."

Bob smiled. "A well rounded person is someone who is skilled, capable in a lot of different things, someone that is an achiever. A person that helps people work and become successful."

She smiled back. "It reminds me about our life there in Chicago, with so many family members around us. We've had so much fun in that city, so many memories. We built

NUMB

our fortune there and this was the place we started our family, our daughters were born there, so many things to remember..."

"I still remember that evening when I drove you home and we had an accident, the car that hit us, when I broke my front tooth," Bob added with a smile.

"I knew that moment would mark us, I knew you'd remember me forever," she said and she couldn't stop smiling.

"It did and I've been the happiest man since then Mary Rita. We had a really good life because we did the right things. We never got involved in bad things. We helped people around us and took care of our family."

"Bob, I miss my relatives, but thank God, they come down to our home pretty often and visit us, they love our 'paradise' as much as we do."

"It was a good idea to move to Florida, it is really a heaven on earth," Bob agreed.

"So that day when Mary Rita and Bob Wish were the talk of the ceremony representing the success of the Tupperware Company, showing everyone that working hard the American dream could happen, became one of moments of my life that I'm the most proud of! I've been awarded many times, but that special award was the one that impressed me the most. I remember we were talking and laughing, having a good time. I didn't pay attention to what the speaker was saying, but when I heard the words, *this couple started the Tupperware business when they were still living in an attic apartment*, then I realized he was talking about us, you and I!"

Bob laughed. "I was shocked too!"

"We were so surprised and it was overwhelming. I had tears in my eyes. Bob, I'll never forget that moment and the fact that I didn't know about it, it made it even more impressive, at least for me," she said full of nostalgia. "We

~ 296 ~

have the most blessed marriage a couple can ask for." She put her arms around her husband and tears were streaming down her face.

They were tears of gratitude and love, something that had never changed in her heart, even if there was an invisible force pulling her away from the ones she loved the most.

The couple had a really soul nourishing time together and they were back at their home, the beautiful waterfront home in Santa Rosa Beach, enjoying each other's presence. Mary Rita didn't want to tell her husband about Kathleen, about her trying to have her declared incompetent.

First of all, she still didn't believe this was possible. Secondly, she wanted to protect Bob from having to go through such a conversation, but after awhile Mary Rita thought that it was important for both of them for her to share her thoughts about Kathleen even if she had doubts about it. So she tried to present the situation like she wasn't affected by it. Mary Rita postponed the conversation a few times now, but after taking few deep breaths, she asked with a soft voice, "Bob, explain to me how it's possible to be awarded with the highest award of our company and being recognized as a top achiever. Then at the same time, to be tested for 'mental capacity' for competence, for being able to make decisions on my own, to keep our financial documents in order and all the stuff that comes with being tested by psychiatrists?" Mary Rita asked her husband.

For few moments Bob was quiet and didn't know how to react to his wife's question, he had no idea if Kathleen did something to have her mother liberated from the influence of that group and she didn't mention anything like this. Mary Rita had no idea that he already knew everything from

NUMB

Kathleen, all her plans to save her mother, but he hadn't said one word, he'd decided to leave it to God.

Bob knew his daughter very well and he knew she would never do such a drastic thing without telling him first. He knew about Kathleen's plans, they both agreed that something had to be done, but he knew for sure Kathleen did not yet start the process of having her mother examined by doctors for incompetence.

He knew it for sure so he took a deep breath and asked, "What psychiatrist are you talking about and why? I'm confused."

"Oh, don't worry, I was just saying—"

"Mary Rita, did you go to the doctor? You're strong and healthy, why did you go?"

"Bob, forget about it, let's have dinner and spend some time together. I loved the time we spend together. I know I said it again, but we have so many memories, so much love that kept us together for so many years. I pray to God to be healthy and strong, like you said, for many more years to come, you and me to be here on earth for a long, long time."

"I pray everyday for the same thing and hopefully my heart condition will hold off. I'm not ready to go yet. Mary Rita, we never talked about what I would like you to do after I'm gone but we have to be realistic. I'm older than you are, five years older and my health is not so great so let me tell you what my heart is telling me. You cannot be alone, or better said, you shouldn't be alone after I am gone. You could be alone, but I don't want you to be. You're a joy to be around, your positive attitude, the energy you have is contagious and any man, any unmarried man," he corrected himself with a smile. "Any man would be glad to have you as a companion, even as a wife, even if I would be jealous in my grave."

The time came and he said something that was in the back of his mind, something that he was waiting for the right moment to get it out, "Just do not marry Arthur Walker, anybody but him, please, that man shouldn't be around you ever. I remembered when he tried to be with our Kathleen. Do you know what I told her?"

"No, this is the first time I've heard you talking about that man. What did you tell her? How come his name came into your mind?" Mary Rita asked feeling really curious.

"Well, I never thought such words would come out of my mouth, but they did. I said to her that even if Jesus in person told her to marry that man, to not do it! I know you're going to condemn me for saying such things as this, to have such a strong opinion about a person when one of the Ten Commandments is to love each other and to love your neighbor like you love yourself. I know you'll condemn me for what I said, but Jesus knows what was in my heart. He knew why I said what I said. He will forgive me because He knows I was right. Kathleen said she never intended to marry that creepy man but she hoped that none of the women in that group would fall into his trap. I have never told you what I really think about the mission you serve, financially and spiritually, because I love you. But I don't want you to be hurt by these people. Mary Rita, it is a trap... and I hope you'll never fall into it, but lately your actions lead you closer to that trap. I see it day by day. It seems like my monologue today represents my confession, my will. The only thing is that it isn't in writing. I love you, I have never loved anyone more than I've loved you. The love I have for our children is different, but if someone would ask me to give up my life for you, I would do it in a heartbeat. My entire life was laid down for you. Our family and Jesus were watching each step I took. This is the reason I know He will forgive me. I have to rest for a little while. I've never talked so much."

NUMB

As soon as he stopped talking, he tried to figure out how his wife had found out about Kathleen's plans, who knew about it? Bob was almost positive that only someone from St. Anne Church made the connection when she or he saw her going into Father's Timothy's office crying. Kathleen told Bob everything... how she came out of the priest's office with a smile on her face and peace in her mind.

Someone, but whom, what person could put those things together? He remembered that Cynthia was in Ponce de Leon, not too far from Santa Rosa Beach, staying at her home for a few weeks only, because the mission was calling her to go back to Baton Rouge and she saw Kathleen going to the priest office. Now everything was clear in Bob's mind, now he knew who told his wife about Kathleen's plans. He wasn't sure how she found out about the 'Nursing home salvation plans' but somebody must have heard something.... *Oh, Lord, even in your church there is room for gossiping!*

Since that visit and afterward, he noticed how properties were given to the cause of the mission, Bob hadn't had good feelings about the mission and the leader of the group.

He knew his wife had dedicated her entire life to that mission, but at the same time he knew that it was an ingenious, elaborate trap that wasn't created for regular people, it was made to attract the most religious and devoted believers. A trap made of years of diabolic lies and statements, visions, and prophecies that put mental chains on people's minds. Controlling them with a fear that something bad, really bad would happen if they didn't give everything they had, money, investments, and properties to St. John Charity.

After few days, Cynthia called Mary Rita and said that Eve, her husband and Arthur, were coming down to Florida for few days to relax and enjoy the Ocean.

Bob tried not to be negative about this event but he wasn't happy either.

Eve and her entourage were coming to Florida and Mary Rita liked to be a good host and spoil everyone.

Eve was like a spider waiting in her corner for her victim, she had to watch everyone's moves and plan the next action, like a chess player. She mastered the game and all the 'chess' figures were moved or interacted with the others, according to her brilliant thinking and she did have a superb mind, an evil one, but brilliant. "Mary Rita, we are staying at the hotel, would you like to have diner with us? We would like to go to a not so fancy restaurant and spend some time together?"

"Let me talk to Bob and I'll call you back."

Bob already heard the conversation and he was waving his hands in the air while mouthing, *no*.

Mary Rita knew he never enjoyed being with these people, as he'd never liked them.

His logical feelings, if you could call them that, were telling him to stay away from them, even if he realized it wasn't always possible. Sometimes he'd had to pretend he enjoyed being with these people, but he made those efforts for his wife only.

Mary Rita noticed that Bob wasn't even mentioned in the invitation and she was afraid Bob heard it too and that it hurt his feelings. But Bob's answer would be the same, invited or not, so she called back and asked, "What time do you want me to be there and where are we going, so I know how to be dressed?"

"Can we pick you up by six pm? And do not worry about your wardrobe, casual is fine," Eve said.

NUMB

Mary Rita didn't like to go to dinner that late and driving in the dark after dinner, so she felt grateful that Eve and Paul Garner were coming to pick her up and that she didn't have to drive. They were visiting her town and she wanted to be a polite host.

The hotel were they were staying was right on the beach.

"Why aren't we going directly to the restaurant?" Mary Rita asked once she was in the car.

"You'll see why," Eve replied.

The apartment where they were staying was nice and the view was spectacular, the ocean waves were bringing peace to people's souls and the sunset was almost ready to show its amazing dark and orange colors.

When they arrived at the apartment, Arthur Walker was the one opening the door for them to enter. Of course, he had to be there, he was Eve's spokesman. "Hi, nice to see you, I'm glad you came. Let me take few chairs and join them on the balcony."

Eve and Paul went directly on the balcony to relax, waiting for one of the famous Emerald Coast sunsets to happen.

"Mary Rita, have a seat and watch the sunset with us," Eve greeted her.

Mary Rita wanted to say that she could see the sunsets every day from her waterfront home, next to her loving husband, but she was polite and sat down to watch the sunset.

When the sun disappeared, Eve said, "We're going on the beach for a walk, you two get to know each other better, and we'll be back soon."

Mary Rita wanted to say something but she kept it to herself.

This Arthur...What can I do to not see him? Even if Bob would've never told me what he thought about this man, I had the same feeling in my heart. It's something about him that gives me negative vibrations, bad feelings. Why I do feel like suddenly the apartment is hell on earth, and a horrible breeze covers my body? I never liked this man, not even to talk to him.

"Did they really go on the beach? They invited me for dinner. I cannot stay that long." But she realized she had to take things the way they were. Eve could make something bad happen to Bob or her at anytime! That fear, the eternal fear lived like a flame of fire inside her. Logically, she knew nothing wrong could happen but she still obeyed the master.

Arthur was a tall man and his body looked impressive in appearance. Mary Rita felt like a granule of sand next to him. She felt grateful she didn't have to be next to him for long, as the apartment was big enough to be far away from him.

"Tomorrow, I have to be in Panama City. Eve always sends me there with a package every time I come to Florida," he said.

"Oh, maybe she has relatives there? It is an easy drive, straight there and if you take the beach road, you'll be amazed by the new sky rises. Sometimes when I go there, I cannot believe how fast they go up. In few months they are finished, more residents, more visitors," she said, trying to have a conversation and to make the time go faster.

Arthur nodded. "I see and I noticed this too, it is a huge change every time I visit. It truly is a different landscape, it seems like there's lots of money here, on the coast."

"It's not just the money. I think it's the beauty of this part of the world. You see, when we visited for the first time Florida, years ago, Kathleen, our daughter was living here with her husband. We fell in love with the area and decided to move here when retiring. And that's exactly what we did,

NUMB

the rest you know. Cynthia told me about Eve and her charity and since then I don't feel retired anymore," she said and started laughing.

That moment Eve and Paul entered the room, Eve looked pleasantly surprised to see Mary Rita and Arthur having a good time. Eve's mood was happier than ever, her plans were getting accomplished day by day, everyone following her orders. "Okay, let's go for diner. Hopefully, we can still find some restaurants open."

Most of the restaurants were closed by then, so they had to go to an obscure restaurant that was still serving food.

As soon as they sat down, Mary Rita's phone rang, she tried to answer it, but Eve pushed it away. "You are tested by God and HE doesn't want you to answer!"

"It's Bob and he worries about me being out in the dark and being so late. I have to answer him."

"No, you're not obeying God. He's testing you."

The phone rang few more times and each time, Eve didn't want Mary Rita to answer the phone, knowing how bad this would make Bob feel.

Mary Rita was almost crying, how could she do this to her husband and to not answer his call? She wanted to leave the place and run to Bob, but she held her emotions and politely, sat down till dinner was finally ready.

Late at night, Eve and her two men took Mary Rita home. As soon as they pulled the car in her driveway, they saw a police car; they opened the door for Mary Rita to get out of the car and turned around in a hurry. They didn't even wonder or ask about the police.

"Ma'am, are those your friends?" one of the two police officers asked.

"Yes, sir, they are, why?"

"It's strange that they didn't stop to talk to your husband or to ask what happened. Not even wondering why were we here, in your driveway. Strange, very strange, but they are your friends not mine," he said, and she could see his disagreement on his face.

The officers left.

Bob and Mary Rita went inside the home.

"Why didn't you answer the phone all evening? I've called a dozen times. How could you do this to me? I now know why I don't like those people!"

"Bob, I'm sorry, I don't always have the phone near me."

"Mary Rita, this is absurd and no one should take your phone from you. You should come up with a much better explanation. One day, when I'm gone, these people will take over everything," he said even though he did not want to continue the conversation knowing he would make his wife lie and that would hurt him more than the truth.

Mary Rita felt surprised to witness her husband's reaction. He was a man that had never shown his temper over the lifetime she'd know him. He had good cause though, this she had to face. And she felt sorry for causing him so much aggravation. She knew he was right and she couldn't believe she even did what she did.

NUMB

CHAPTER THIRTEEN

Back in Baton Rouge, Eve was waiting for Mary Rita to make more 'arrangements' in the name of the St. John Charity.

"Mary Rita, Irene Floyd and her family need a place to rent for a year or so. What about removing the tenants that you have now and rent to Irene instead?" Eve asked.

"How could I do such a thing? They pay seven hundred dollars a month and take care of the home, I couldn't do that."

"Irene is Cynthia's daughter and she did so much for us, especially for our charity, I'll solve the problem. They are going to pay you five hundred dollars a month and do some repairs around the house, okay? You are going to ask me why I am helping Irene, when she is not a member of our group anymore. Well, I do it for her mother, Cynthia."

Mary Rita wanted to say that it was her own house and why would she get rid of her good tenants that were paying seven hundred for someone that would pay only five hundred dollars! It just didn't make any sense to do it.

Soon, Irene and her family moved in and in less than a year they said, "Mary Rita, we don't need to rent from you anymore. We have our own house now and this is the bill." Irene looked upset though even as she handed her a piece of paper.

"What is this? A bill for what?" Mary Rita asked.

"This represents all the repairs we did inside and outside the house, in detail." Irene shook badly as she wouldn't look Mary Rita.

Mary Rita almost fainted. It wasn't about the money; it was the situation. This was Eve's doing. She knew it as Irene didn't look happy either. *So, I gave up my loyal tenants for these people because the Master ordered, promising that if they paid less rent, they would fix things around the house and now, I have to pay for it. Well... I'd better pray for me to stay calm.*

Being calm wasn't an easy thing for Mary Rita to do, she had to do something all the time. The house across the street from St. Bernadette was Eve's favorite place, where her office was and where people were coming to get books and sometimes twenty dollars bills, but only when other people were around, so everyone would notice her generosity.

"Mary Rita, did you make the agreement between Cynthia and you about your husbands legal on paper?"

"How can something like that be on paper, if one of us doesn't want to help, it's nothing illegal, am I right?"

"Yes, but people feel differently when they know they have signed a document."

"Maybe this is true in a totally different world. But Cynthia and I are Catholics and we believe in God. Everything we do, both of us do it to glorify His name. I will help her if she needs me and she will do the same thing for me."

"Okay, don't say I didn't tell you," Eve said.

Once the conversation ended, Mary Rita tried to figure out why this subject was so important to Eve, what would be her gain, but she had so many things waiting for her to be done that she forgot about Eve's advice.

NUMB

"Dad, I'll be coming down there soon. I have to see you and mom, if she's home. I'll be staying at Grandma Anne's cottage." Kathleen still called it this even though Anne had passed away years ago.

"Oh, I cannot wait to see you, come as soon as you can," her father said.

"Well, you know my business, the hotel needs me here all the time, but if I don't make myself invisible, people will always ask something from me. Dad, you should come and spend a few days here. I can take you back with me and I can bring you back home. You and mom should take a short vacation here, but till then, I'm coming to see you, hopefully both of you," she said.

"Your mother is in Baton Rouge but if I tell her that you're coming, she'll come," Bob assured her.

"Dad, I don't think she'll want to see me. That woman put strange thoughts in my mom's mind. Now she's afraid of me, she thinks I'll hurt her. Dad, I don't know what to do anymore, she is the love of my life, you too, but you know what I mean, woman to woman, I love her. We always had fun together, I told you this millions of times."

"I know," her father said.

Not too long after their conversation, Kathleen stopped her car in her parent's driveway that was connected to her driveway, so she was home.

Bob Wish was really happy to see his loving daughter. Both of them went to the screen porch where they sat down and relaxed. It was a blessing to just be next to the other. They didn't need words, everything was said on the phone and both of them wanted to enjoy each other's presence.

Bob could see how Kathleen's shoulders relaxed as she closed her eyes.

Not even the view of the water could make her forget that she had her heart broken though. She lost track of the time she spent going from lawyer to lawyer, spending a fortune and no one could help her. "Dad, sometimes, I want to give up, because like I told you before, everything in my life went down from the moment I started looking for ways to save her. That woman's evil tools are reaching me everywhere I go. I talked to my priest in Indiana, he came and blessed my house, my business, and everything and I had a chance to talk to him. He listened to me. I could see his expression becoming sad and he looked at me with compassion. He'd said 'Kathleen, if you were a believer whose faith is lukewarm, this wouldn't have happened to you but because the both of you, your mother and you are such strong Christians, because you follow God's teachings, the evil that has that woman's face and body, is fighting hard to get you both on his side. You have to wear God's armor every single second of your days and nights.' Dad, I'm still touched by his words. I feel blessed and somehow, even if I know how hard it will be, I do feel my mother will be out of that evil influence. I don't know how long it will take, but she will be my mother again, the one that I miss so much, the one that I love so much."

"Don't give up; you're all that she has even if she doesn't realize it, Kathleen. I'm not blaming her because in her mind she is convinced she has a mission to accomplish. This is not about being mentally incompetent, this is something between her and her God, the one she loves so much. Your mother is perfectly capable of taking care of herself and her mind is sane and healthy. Do not waste your money anymore, only God will get her out of the mess she is in. Unfortunately, she doesn't *see* the mess, she sees only the poor, the needy. I

NUMB

have wished and prayed for her to open her eyes and shake her to reality myself but she must see it for herself."

"What can we do? It is so hard to follow my priest's advice, but at least I'm trying."

"Kathleen, once I'm gone, those people will devastate our family. Do what the priest told you, I love how he explained it all to you. It's so true. Wearing God's armor everyday will protect you with his shied, and Satan cannot get through, he is so right. This all what we can do, my sweet daughter," Bob said, wrapping his arms around her, "Thank God, we love each other."

"Dad, it seems like we are having a time of confessions, the time of remembering things that we went through. This one you have to remember because it was something that it shook our obedience, back then. You have never trusted that woman but because of mom and me, you decided to listen to what Eve had to say. I hate saying her name and I prefer to call her *that woman* and even that I don't like saying. Do you remember when she said the Pope would move to Baton Rouge? And millions of people would come to Baton Rouge because of this and the property value would reach exorbitant prices? Well, the Pope never moved from the Vatican to Baton Rouge and now, looking back, only a weak mind would believe such idiocy, but back then, they all believed in her prophecies so much that they did everything she wanted them to do. The house that I hated, you and mom hated, well that house, according to her *vision* was going to become the Pope's favorite place to relax and have friends visiting! You and mom never took an initiative in real estate, so you both had always asked me for my professional advice and I had already told you to not invest in that property. For few good months, you agreed with my opinion and stayed away from purchasing that mansion but it was a short joy for me that woman wanted the building so bad that she used all the forces she had to make mom buy it. And mom did it, and thousands of dollars have been wasted in renovations, additions, you name it. Just the front gates cost my mother and you over thirty thousand dollars!" Kathleen stopped when she realized her father didn't really know all the details of her mother's missionary donations, activities and purchases, so she tried to change the subject of the conversation. Kathleen knew her mom had a heart of gold, but her 'gold' was getting into other people's pockets.

She prayed to God to keep them healthy and active. Kathleen knew how grateful she should consider herself for having such good genes. "Dad, I forgot to ask you how your heart is doing lately. And I'm not asking about the one with the love feelings!" she joked.

"Well, both are doing just fine," Bob answered. "But the 'pumping' one needs some fixings."

"What do you mean? What's wrong?" Kathleen asked.

"I'll have to have an intervention soon but I don't want to worry your mother and you, everything will be ok. The doctors said I'll do well once the procedure is done. It will help me breathe better. I have never smoked in my life, but my body sends signals of slowing down, it's getting harder to walk longer distances like before and I get shortness of breath. My concern is Mary Rita. I want to have peace of mind when my time comes, to see her here without being persuaded by you know better who, I'm trying to avoid saying her name, for your sake," he said.

"Dad, you see? The small things like you just said make you unique, a special dad with a huge heart. I have to know when you plan to have the procedure done so I can be with you all the time. Now I have good employees and I can take

NUMB

time off from the hotel I own. Do you promise me that you are going to tell me when?"

"I promise, you'll find out when it will be." Bob nodded.

What a beautiful love, father and daughter holding each other's hands, without knowing that it could be the last time....

CHAPTER FOURTEEN

Mary Rita was so active and busy with her projects in Baton Rouge, the antique and coffee shop with church activities, the mansion where' the Pope' would visit and bring his friends, she already could see herself lifted spiritually in the Pope's eyes.

Meanwhile, the leader of the group told everyone that between two and four pm, was the time when God spoke to her, so nobody could call or talk to her, the time when she would get her visions.

Kathleen was still spending some time in Baton Rouge mostly to keep an eye on what her mom was doing.

On one of those days, Eve approached her. "I don't see you as often as before, are you okay?"

"Yes, I'm perfectly fine but I'm not happy what my folks did."

"What do you mean?" Eve asked.

"You see, they purchased that stupid building hoping that it would be worth millions when the Pope would come here and we all know, that will never happen. Then they purchased a home from Irene, Cynthia's daughter for a much higher price than the property was appraised for. It seems like my parents just buy homes so other people will benefit from it." Kathleen wanted to say that she knew how much profit Eve made from that sale. Thirty five thousand dollars, just because she suggested the transaction...

NUMB

Kathleen made a quick calculation figuring out how much money Eve made by 'suggesting' homes to be bought by her members and she pretended to be a poor woman...

Eve knew she had lost a valuable member of her group, someone financially reliable. "I wanted to talk to you because Irene's husband has a small camp on the river and if we would have a pontoon or a boat, we could entertain people that will come to see the Pope and pray here, the pilgrims. Maybe your father will buy your mom a boat, a pontoon boat," Eve suggested.

Kathleen felt furious. This woman just ignored all that she'd just said. Eve knew exactly that the Pope would never come to Baton Rouge, not even for vacation. Then the way she was controlling everyone's life and emptying their pockets. Now she wanted a boat for her charity, a boat for the pilgrims, and a boat for entertainment.

Kathleen was speechless, then her dad bought a twenty thousand dollar pontoon boat for his wife's birthday, Kathleen's mother.

One more donation for the group to relax from their hectic lives!

Kathleen Petrovich couldn't take it anymore. She left the city, determined to visit the Bishop, and to let him know what was going on in Baton Rouge at St. John Charity.

At the end of her visit, she was given a letter saying to stay away from the group and that nothing Eve Garner said was from God.

On the way back home, Kathleen remembered how on several occasions Eve gave Cynthia's daughters good sums of money, and this was one of her methods to have them all agreeing with what Eve said God told her would happen did happen, indeed.

One day, when Kathleen had threatened Eve that she was going to tell her dad about what was going on inside the group, to call it in a nice way, the *cult* would be the right name for the group, so she told Eve what she intended to do. Eve and her husband, Paul came to her house and Eve had her hands bandaged and she said that she 'had the wounds of Christ' and she was bleeding and if she told her dad anything about her, her dad would have a heart attack and die!

Kathleen shook her head.

How can someone say things like this? Why, even though I'm not her follower anymore, am I still afraid that this could really happen? Why I'm scared to death that if I opened my mouth, my dad will die? How can I be so numb with fear? All these thoughts went through her mind on the way to meet her mother.

Mary Rita agreed to meet Kathleen and spend few hours together, and this was the moment when Kathleen pulled the Bishop's letter out and gave it to her mother to read.

When Mary Rita finished reading, Kathleen could see the change in her mother's face, and she could see the end of their relationship.

It was the fear of losing her dear friends, the members of the group, the fear that now her loving daughter would really start the process of putting her into a nursing home.

It was a fear that wasn't translated into words, but rather an ice shield that Mary Rita covered herself with, instantly, to not let her daughter to see inside her.

Her own mother suddenly became distant and cold. All their love, a lifetime love, a lifetime of having amazing fun together, all the time spent learning together, working together on projects—everything disappeared in a blink of an eye.

NUMB

Love, friendship, memories, their lives together, mother and daughter, was gone forever.

Kathleen didn't need to hear the words, her mother's face said it all.

Kathleen went back to Indiana with a very heavy heart, knowing that nothing could be done to get her mother out of there. She hoped that once her mom recovered the clarity of her actions, their relationship would become stronger than ever.

So, she put her God's armor on and patiently waited for something good to come out of that ordeal.

Year after year, Mary Rita was one of the best tools for Eve's ambitious; the smartest woman of their group became the most humble and dedicating herself totally to the poor and needy, even if she didn't witness much charity done by the organization.

The list of her donations was full of tens of thousand of dollars spent for people to go on missionary trips, a donation of ten thousand dollars for six people to go to Mexico to visit the shrine of Mary at Guadalupe. And the list went on: the twenty thousand dollar boat, the attorney's fees for the charity group that was in fact, used to pay Eve's drug trial's attorney and houses, many houses; tens of thousands of dollars for renovations, buying a house on a golf course, money for other people's hospital bills. The list of Mary Rita's donations was longer than a book, and all in the name of God.

Mary Rita believed that God wanted her to be there and help people the way she did and no one could convince her otherwise. Not even Kathleen's love could do it yet, but God was working, one day at a time, on his time.

October 2011, Kathleen wanted to spend the best month of the Emerald Coast at her Florida home ay her Grandmother's cottage. The weather was exceptionally dry and pleasant. All the locals knew this was the best time for them to enjoy their area; the tourists were gone, the humid days left room for drier air. Neighbors that almost didn't see each other the entire summer were doing yard work and enjoying being outside.

Bob Wish started having breathing problems, so Kathleen and Mary Rita went to the heart doctor and he recommended for Bob to see a specialist in Georgia. The doctor suggested that Bob get a special valve, a brand new technology that would make a world of difference in his heart condition.

While in Georgia, Deanne Jones, Cynthia's daughter came to visit Bob in the hospital.

Bob was really upset to see her there. After few days, they went back home and as soon as they got home, Cynthia came to visit him. Bob couldn't be more upset than he was, he just didn't like seeing these people from that group, none of them. Bob behaved like a real gentleman that he was, even if these people upset him inside, he was pleasant for his wife's sake.

When Kathleen went back to her home in Indiana, not even two weeks after she came back home, Mary Rita called. "Kathleen, your dad died. He had a massive heart attack," she said and her voice was choking. "I was with him. I'm devastated I don't know what to do."

"Mom, I was just there, he was feeling so well when I left Florida, two weeks ago, how did it happen and when?" Kathleen was crying at the other end of the phone.

"He was getting in the bed and suddenly, he could not get both legs in bed and he asked me to help him. He said he was kind of stuck. I tried to bring his legs on the bed but he couldn't move them. He suggested starting all over again,

NUMB

hoping he would be able to do it, but he couldn't. When he got off the bed, he wanted to rest a little, to gain some strength. I helped him to put his head on my lap and I sat with him on the floor. I told him that I was going to call 911. He didn't want me to call the ambulance but I did anyway. They came and worked on him thirty minutes or more, they took him to the hospital and he died about two hours later," Mary Rita said while weeping.

Both, mother and daughter were silent, but they could feel each other's pain. The man they loved the most, the best father, the best husband, the best human being to be around was gone. Their pillar, the man whose faith was stronger than evil's force, the man that Eve and her group were never able to convert to their 'faith', was gone. Bob Wish was one of the few people able to resist Eve's evil's temptations, he stood firm in his faith but he helped his loving wife to do the work of philanthropy, the work of giving to the poor, and he knew Mary Rita believed in this with all hear heart, so he did it. For sixty seven years, he was his wife's protector like he said in church when he married her, a real gentleman, and a man of his word. That wonderful human being left to be with his Father that he loved so much.

For a second, the words poured into Mary Rita's ears by Eve and the entire group became alive, and she could picture herself in a nursing home. They'd told her that her own daughter would put her there.

Words spoken over and over, everyday, for many years by these people, now it would become reality.

She will put me in a nursing home, I know it. Eve and Cynthia knew this would happen when my Bob was gone. They told me every day that this would be the end of my freedom. I won't be able to continue my mission. I cannot believe the pain I have in my heart by losing my dear husband of sixty seven years of marriage is shadowed by the huge fear I have of my daughter, my own daughter, my loving Kathleen. God, this is not possible, don't let it happen. I served you my entire life and I will keep doing my mission, if you protect me from her, I'm afraid of her, really afraid.

She looked around her empty home and cried until she had no tears left.

"God, what I feel now is what I believe people feel in your presence. I feel numb! Father, being separated from my loving husband has made me felt numb. If I hurt him in any way, by word or actions, forgive me. I didn't intend to hurt the man that I loved since I was a teenager. I loved Bob with all my soul and body. I have a huge emptiness inside me."

She made efforts to call her relatives in Chicago, her daughter Christina, her nephews, all their family members, to let them know that their loving Bob, father, uncle, brother in law, and their grandfather went to Heaven. The family knew Bob was getting older but he was healthy most of his life and he never suffered or he didn't stay in the hospitals, so it took them by surprise, even considering his age.

Cynthia Faulkner, the woman that followed the group, the mission for years and whose mother was an avid follower of Eve for more than thirty years, was there, before any relative could come to Mary Rita and Bob Wish's home. She had a house in Ponce de Leon in Florida, not too far from Mary Rita's home, so she was right there.

Mary Rita let her in and they started talking.

"Well, the funeral is paid already, we did it in advance, but I need to call the church tomorrow for the service. Bob didn't want a two day wake; he wanted one day only and the funeral next day. I know its Thanksgiving weekend and many people will be out of town. He was well loved by the car clubs people and by all our church people. If it weren't Thanksgiving Day,

NUMB

so many people would attend his funeral. I feel sorry for them because I know everyone would love to show their respects. Cynthia, do you remember our agreement, are you going to help me or I will end up in a nursing home?"

"Mary Rita, don't worry. Eve took care of everything. She gave you three days to decide what you want and I will do whatever it takes to see you safe," Cynthia said.

The funeral service was solemn but something was missing, it was Mary Rita's mind, she was thinking how to solve her dilemma, how to escape her fear of her daughter's actions. She could see herself living in a nursing home even she was in perfect mental and physical shape.

Saturday and Sunday after the funerals were normal; Mary Rita kept the doors unlocked so family and friends could go in and out.

Mary Rita and Cynthia came home from church and they had the door locks changed. Eve told them to do it, so the thieves wouldn't rob the house.

Kathleen went to her mom's house Monday to have coffee and spend some time together.

She found a note on her windshield saying that she went to Pensacola to see an attorney. Kathleen called her few times, but her mother never returned her calls.

Kathleen knew she wasn't welcomed. Somebody else spent the night with her mother after her dad's funeral. Things were getting complicated, her mother didn't trust her anymore, and she had to fight hard to get her back.

Kathleen called the sheriff and said that her mom disappeared, but the sheriff said that they couldn't do anything now. A person had to be missing for at least twenty four hours.

She drove all the way to Pensacola to look for her mother without knowing where to find her. Dan Cross, a friend of Kathleen's offered to help her, so they went to FBI and reported her mom missing and Kathleen told them the entire story.

The officers were speechless; listening to Kathleen like it was a movie developing in front of them.

Kathleen and her friend went home devastated.

The next day, the sheriff called and said that Mary Rita Wish was not missing and that they helped drive her to the airport.

Suddenly, Kathleen remembered how coming back from the funerals, she had asked Mary Rita to let her borrow her dad's car, but she said that the car was in the shop being fixed.

She believed it, so she forgot about that incident.

Cynthia and few other members of the group flew to Las Vegas to be with Mary Rita when she would marry the man she was advised to, a man she didn't care for.

It was part of the work...it was Eve's work. Before the marriage was to take place, Arthur Walker had to sign a notarized document stating that he would not request any goods, money, homes or anything connected to the wealth accumulated by Bob and Mary Wish, that he was marrying her to protect her finances and all the assets from Mary Rita's daughter, Kathleen Petrovich!

Now, that the document was signed, Eve could go on with her diabolical plan. Mary Rita already paid ten thousand

NUMB

dollars to Cynthia to help her get out of her home and she paid for six group members to join her, all because of her fear.

Eve had her plans put together, so Arthur Walker would protect Mary Rita, this way she would be under her 'husband's' protection and no one could put her into a nursing home, declaring her incompetent. This way, Eve could continue using Mary Rita's donations for her work, for her group.

Eve told Mary Rita to ask for police protection; to be sure no one could touch her.

How can I marry this man? It's only been few days after my Bob was buried, how can I do this? Who's going to understand my actions? I have never heard about such a thing in my long life. How can I do this to my family, my church friends? There has to be another way to be protected. Mary Rita asked herself, knowing there was no way to escape Eve's plans.

The air tickets had been purchased, the group members were ready to board the flight, and she knew there was no other way, but to marry that man.

Eve knew for sure that Mary Rita would be able to serve her mission this way, being married to a man that Eve would tell how to do everything needed for the mission.

Las Vegas, Nevada, Mary Rita and Arthur Walker got married December first, 2011 and Mary Rita made a verbal agreement that she would give Eve Garner ten percent of her wealth to protect her from her family.

"Now, we have to fly to Louisiana and you'll become a legal resident there," Arthur said.

"Whatever has to be done, I'll do it," Mary Rita said in a numb voice.

"I think it will be a good idea to resign from St. Anne Catholic church and record your resignation in Walton County Clerk of Court's Office in Florida," Arthur suggested.

"This way, you will not be a member of the church, a parishioner, so Father Timothy would be prevented by Catholic Church regulations from expressing an opinion on a non parishioner."

"I didn't know you were so smart. I'll do it, and it makes sense," she said.

"Actually, it wasn't my idea. We talked about it few weeks before this."

"Who talked about this?" Mary Rita asked.

"You know who; don't make me say the name," Arthur said.

His big stature made her feel safe and it gave her a security, and a feeling that no one could put her in a nursing home.

"Are you going to keep your home in Florida?" Arthur asked.

"Yes, always. I love my home and I already donated so many houses that I don't think she will want me to sell my home in Florida. I still have properties in Baton Rouge."

"We know this," Arthur replied.

"The way you say 'we' is like you are part of the leaders, are you?" Mary Rita asked.

Arthur realized he made a mistake and he tried to correct it. "I'm so involved in our group, that sometimes I feel like I'm leading the group. I know that Eve wouldn't be too happy to hear what I just said."

"Do not worry, I'm not going to tell anyone what you said, I think it's a real good thing to feel that way, to be so dedicated. I'm also as devoted as you are, we're good Christian people and God is going to award us for the work we did for the mission."

"I know how much you love God and how much you want to get communion. In order to receive communion, we have

NUMB

to be married in church. We have to see what she has to say about it. Mary Rita, it will be hard to find a Catholic priest to officiate our marriage in church but for sure, she knows how to do it. I think she did it before but for some reason, she didn't do it for her own marriage. I think she can't receive communion in any of the Catholic Churches, but I'm not so sure," Arthur said.

Arthur was right, Eve's friend, Cynthia's sister, knew a priest in Iowa and made arrangements for the wedding to take place.

"Kathleen, I'm getting married in a Catholic Church, so I can receive communion," she called her daughter on the phone to let her know she was okay.

That moment, Kathleen knew she had to find something to stop this wedding from taking place, even if she knew it wouldn't change much with her mother's legal status.

"Eddie," she called her cousin, the person that had the custody of her mother, you have to do everything in your power to prevent this wedding," and she started telling him all the things she knew about.

"Kathleen, I'll call the priest, tell me where the wedding supposed to be," Eddie said.

Kathleen told him what she knew and she called all their relatives to ask them to call and protest the wedding and to not let the priest officiate it.

So, the Iowa wedding didn't take place.

Mary Rita and Arthur Walker flew back to Baton Rouge where Mary Rita found the document that Bob and she signed in 2002 and had it revoked it, line by line.

"I have to file this revocation with the Clerk of Court in East Baton Rouge Parish, Louisiana and Walton County, Florida, both of them," she said.

"Well, you have to do what you have to do, so we can get married in church, like you want," Arthur said.

"I have to because for me, getting communion is more important than the marriage itself, but I cannot have one without the other, do not forget the reason I married you," Mary Rita said.

"I think our leader will arrange this. She knows everyone, and we have to be patient," Arthur told her.

"The place I live in now is so different than my beautiful home in Florida, but better here than in a nursing home, I guess." Mary Rita sighed.

NUMB

CHAPTER FIFTEEN

"We have to become members of the St. Andrew Catholic parish. She told me so we should do it. Once we become members, the priest will marry us in church," Arthur said.

In July 2012, Mary Rita Wish and Arthur Walker became members of that church and not too long after this, in September, the couple was married in St. Andrew Catholic Church and Father Jonathan presided.

Mary Rita's heart was a lot lighter knowing that she was accepted by her Catholic Church, she could get communion being married and no one could remove her from her home and put her in a nursing home, her eternal fear.

"Mary Rita," Eve said. "You're going to start a new life now, you're a free woman and you and Cynthia can take care of our mission, as her husband died also."

"I know and I feel so sorry for her," Mary Rita said.

"Don't be sorry, they never had a good marriage like yours, she is relieved now. She can spend time the way she wants, goes everywhere she wants, the same as you."

"The only difference is I had the best marriage anyone could wish for and I could do everything I wanted my entire life. My Bob never told me what to do; he is the love of my life even if he went to heaven to be with our father."

"What about Arthur? He is a handsome man, tall and well built," Eve insisted.

"Eve, for me he is a body guard, not a man, not a husband, when I have to look at him I see him as my employee, not a man. There is nothing, I mean there are no feelings, between him and I."

"Well, I hoped for more, but you're right about Bob. He was an exceptional human being even if he didn't like me or Paul, my husband. It was a curse between us from the first moment we met and it never changed. I'm grateful I didn't have the same experience with you, my friend. Oh, and we have to have you sign the bill of sale for Bob's trucks and your red Cadillac," Eve said.

Mary Rita grabbed a chair and she absolutely threw herself on it. How could she have forgotten that night!

A week before Bob died, Eve came to Florida with her team and she invited herself for dinner. Eve had an incredible talent to talk for hours getting people to fall asleep under her eyes. She talked so much that Mary Rita was almost falling asleep at the table. Bob's condition was taking so much of her energy, but she was glad to use her energy to take care of her loving husband.

"Well, you were so tired, but remember, we have to get the cars out of here. I have a paper saying that you'll allow Arthur Walker to drive Bob's truck and Paul will drive the red Cadillac, here are the papers, you only have to sign it at the bottom. Do not worry, I know what I'm doing," she said and she pulled out few pages.

Mary Rita signed it.

The pickup truck and the red Cadillac, the new and beautiful Cadillac, both were gone and now she wants me to sign the sale document. She did say she was going to buy my Cadillac for twenty five thousand dollars but she never gave me the payment.

NUMB

Next day, Eve picked her up and they went to a notary to legalize the documents. Mary Rita looked at the value of the red Cadillac and she saw twenty five thousand dollars, saying that she'd already received the payment. Mary Rita signed and she knew she would never see a dime from selling her favorite car.

The same thing happened for the pick up truck, seven thousand dollars that she never got.

She thought Eve considered it presents for helping her stay safe in her house. Mary Rita didn't question herself twice; the donations went on and on....

The checks were flying from one 'need' to another one, a mortgage here, a mortgage there, a house sold for a lot less value, another one sold there...

The two duplexes with apartments to rent, Bob's car garage, everything had been sold for prices that even the lucky buyers were wondering if the next day, those properties were going to be taken away from them even if they paid the asking price. All the sales, all the checks were given away for needy and the poor and no one could convince her to stop.

Arthur kept saying to Mary Rita what he was told to say, "Your daughter is going to poison you. So when we go to Florida to pay your bills, I'll throw away all the food from your refrigerator and we have to make a dummy doll, your stature, we have to buy a blonde wig and she wants you to put it on a chair in front of a window because someone will shoot at it. When you see what will happen, then you'll believe why we work so hard to save you."

As soon as they arrived at Mary Rita's home in Florida, Arthur opened the freezer and threw away all the food from there.

It took awhile to make the dummy but it turned out to be a realistic doll and Mary Rita put it in the window.

One day when Eve came to visit and she didn't see the dummy in the window. She threw a fit, she yelled at Mary Rita that she didn't deserve to be protected and all the things the group did for her.

As soon as Eve left the house, Mary Rita never moved that dummy from its place, at the window, sitting on a chair!

Another day, Mary Rita realized how hard it was to live with someone she had nothing in common with. They were married, but it wasn't a consummated marriage. The difference in age was an important factor and not having feelings for each other was making them more like roommates. Arthur never tried to touch her more than the obligatory kiss he gave her at their wedding.

They were going to shows together, and one time when they were visiting Mexico, Mary Rita wanted to walk and see the beautiful scenery laid in her path. "I had noticed that since we got off the street car, you prefer to wait for me to come back from where I'm visiting. Are you tired? If you are, wait for me here. I would prefer to be together though because this is a foreign place. I don't speak the language but I'll understand."

"Walking is not my favorite activity. I prefer to wait for you," he said.

"I had no idea you suffered like my Bob did, short of breath, heart conditions. You better be careful," Mary Rita warned.

"I'm okay. I don't have any heart problems, but I have to wear a body suit so I cannot walk long distances," he said.

"What kind of body suit? I don't get it."

"Mary Rita when I was in the service, the truck I was driving got hit and a fire started. My body was burned really badly and since then, I have to wear a body suit and walking is uncomfortable for me. It was the worst time of my life, but

NUMB

I'm grateful it didn't burn my face and my neck. Not too many people know about it even if I don't care much. Now you know why I don't walk much."

It was the first time Mary Rita felt sorry for the man in front of her; the first time she felt his pain, even if she couldn't stand him as a person. How could she have known about him wearing a body suit if she never saw him naked? "Oh, I'm so sorry to hear such a thing. The doctors couldn't do anything to make it better?"

"What could be better than being alive and walking? I feel so grateful for being alive."

She stared at him and wondered again, what kind of man he really was inside. "I'll be back soon. I'm going to the place that sells necklaces. I saw something similar to a beautiful, unique necklace my Bob gave me, years ago."

"I'll be here, just be careful," Arthur said.

Mary Rita left and on the way to the jewelry shop, she thought that any person listening to their conversation would think they were a nice, loving couple. The words exchanged in between them seemed to have feelings when they were just being polite.

Mary Rita thanked God for being in a relationship where her memories didn't have to be altered, where her love for her Bob was alive.

But sometimes she wanted the relationship she was in with Arthur to be friendlier, without raising voices; she wasn't used to having someone yelling at her.

When one day, Arthur lost his temper without her doing anything wrong or even being close to him, she told him very politely, "You have no right to yell at me and if this happens again, I'll complain about it."

And she did tell Eve, his boss about his behavior. Eve listened to her and after few minutes, she called Arthur and talked to him.

A few months later, Mary Rita noticed that Arthur stopped yelling at her, so she asked Eve what she'd told him that stopped his bad behavior.

"Well," she answered. "He knows better how much we need you here and if he ever does it again and you tell me, he has to give me fifty bucks every time he does it. It was that simple."

Mary Rita knew the real translation of what she said was that he was going to lose his ' job' the job of being Mary Rita's husband, her protector...

Mary Rita had all these thoughts in her mind when she entered the jewelry shop and once she saw the beautiful art work; she became less sad and her heart didn't feel as heavy. The shop set up and the experience she had reminded her of her loving husband and made her want to stay inside the shop forever. Outside, it was getting darker so she had to leave. Mary Rita was sure Arthur was going to yell at her for staying so long and she was surprised to see his reaction.

"I thought something bad must have happened to you. I'm glad you're back and safe, let's go back to the hotel," he said without any sign of anger in his voice.

Eve's warning worked!

As soon as her mother's marriage was officiated in Church in Baton Rouge, Kathleen, her daughter, her son in law and all her colleagues, friends, relatives started checking on line for things to help Mary Rita get out of that group.

NUMB

Kathleen never stopped looking for solutions to help her mother but after spending more than a hundred thousand dollars, she gave all her worries and her fights, her searches, she put everything in the hands of God, saying that she did the most she could, but it would take God's power to move the mountain that was her mother.

Attorney's fees, FBI visits and endless means to figure it out what and how to do it.

The FBI answered her complaints and informed her that she wasn't the only person who'd complained about the questionable Eve Garner but unless a victim came forward, they could do nothing.

Yes, all this ended for Kathleen the day she talked to God and decided enough was more than enough.

She was looking to fix things that were under evil's influence and she didn't want to get the key to that entrance anymore, the key to the dark side, she'd had enough.

Mary Rita was back in Baton Rouge working for the mission, and she was told to not walk to far from the place where she lived.

Being right across from church, she felt like it was a safe area for her to be, a beautiful grotto with the Virgin Mary, a small bench where people could relax, meditate or pray.

It was a great place to say a Rosary, so she sat down to enjoy her time alone.

An hour later, Mary Rita saw Eve, Paul and Arthur out in the street, driving like they were looking for someone.

Arthur parked his car on a side of the church and Mary Rita felt sure he could see her. But she was sure they were looking for something else or someone else, not her. She really enjoyed the shade of the grotto and the trees that covered the area. It was a Saturday afternoon, a beautiful Saturday. The church doors opened, so Mary Rita went inside and sat right in the front pew where she never sat before, never. It was a change in her ritual and she was trying to see what her feelings were by sitting there, to see what other people see when being that close to the altar.

The peace coming from being in the presence of God, the purity of those moments were interrupted by Eve as if she didn't respect the sanctity of the church. She came directly to Mary Rita and she was absolutely steaming. "You have to get home now. No mass for you, we almost had to call the police for help. We asked a pastor if he saw you, but someone we asked saw you in church and told us."

"The church gate was locked but the garden gate was opened, so I wanted to pray and relax in that beautiful corner," Mary Rita tried to excuse herself.

"Without telling us where you go, this is unacceptable. You have to write a check for a thousand dollars for the pastor and the check has to be done in my name because the priest would prefer cash better than a check," Eve said.

Mary Rita learned another lesson, to not go anywhere without telling where she was going, or pay big money...

Another day she was talking with Eve and they were discussing about a recent death in their vicinity.

"No one understands what I go through when I'm praying for all the sufferings, the sick and the dying people, how much I have to stand and pray," Eve said.

"I remembered what you told me one time," Mary Rita said.

"What did I tell you?" she asked.

"You told me and I think there other people in the room when you said that God told you to go gambling at the casino, to recover all the energy you put in prayers and that it was

NUMB

the only way you should relax and enjoy yourself. I'm still confused about this but once in a while, I like it too, but I don't play like you do, I never lost or won top dollars," Mary Rita said.

"This is absolutely true, it's the only way I can recover my energy that I use when praying for all those situations and those dying people," she said.

The day when Eve took her from church, Mary Rita was so upset that she wasn't allowed to attend the Saturday Mass. This event marked her with certain questions and few things started to surface in her mind.

The more money she gave away, the thinner her checking account became, but she had to be part of the group till the 'end' the goal, the mission to see all things accomplished and the main goal to be reached. But only few people knew what the real goal was and how much more money and donations were still needed to see that goal and everything had to be done in the name of God.

No one knew better than Eve how much money or how many more properties Mary Rita still had. When her devoted men and women moved Mary Rita from her Florida home, she offered to put all the important documents in Paul Garner's safe and Mary Rita was feeling grateful to have a safe place for all her bank documents for her properties, houses, land, everything she had. So, Eve and her husband knew her financial situation better than Mary Rita did, more detailed. The group needed her alive and present to use everything till the last drop!

"My red Cadillac is a 2005 and now driven by my 'boss' and once in awhile, she is taking me out for a ride," Mary Rita told Cynthia one day.

"I know and I see it, what a beautiful car," she said.

The time spent in Baton Rouge was used as the 'boss' was dictating, reading tons of books and watching some TV, but Mary Rita was way too active and energetic to linger around the apartment. She was living now in a three room apartment and all her good furniture, clothes, jewelry were misplaced or gone. "I'm content with what I have, it seems like God wants me here, to serve his purpose, so I will do my best with what I have," Mary Rita told Cynthia.

"I know, me too. We've known each other for so many years and I feel like you're a sister for me. We have always worked together, either here or in Florida."

"And together, we work for Eve and her mission. Cynthia, sometimes I have some doubts about what is going on with us. I doubt where all the money and the properties went but when I see few people helped here and there, I stop wondering and ask our God for forgiveness. Don't you think I live almost like a monk in a monastery?"

"Not when she takes you gambling!" Cynthia said laughing.

"You're right, but I was talking about what I'm doing everyday: praying, reading and all over again. I'm not a TV watcher, maybe sometimes if there is something really nice but other than that my life is pretty much what I said. Do you think I complain about it? Absolutely not. It is my obedience to God, He wants me here for His purpose, and I'm His tool. Do you feel the same way?"

"My daughters feel like helping Eve and the mission but sometimes their husbands say no and after showing them the reasons why they do not agree, they kind of slow down helping, especially Irene. But they still do, finding ways to hide things from their husbands. But that is

NUMB

another story. I can see how much you and Arthur run away from each other. I remember when Bob told you to not marry him but you had to do it to protect yourself from being isolated and being put in a nursing home. At least my daughters would never do this to me. Your Kathleen is a good girl but she thinks we all just want your wealth! Of course, the mission needs our money, yours and mine, but the group protects us from the vultures. I mean everyone doesn't see what we see. We have our own visions sent to us by God; we know what He wants us to do. Those people don't have our faith; they are blinded by the world's temptations. We aren't and that's why we have to stay away of those people, like your Kathleen and some of my sons in law. Mary Rita, I'm glad I convinced you to meet Eve, don't you feel like your new life has a better meaning now, helping so many people in need?"

"Cynthia, you said it so nicely that you've made me feel like a saint now. You said it better than Eve. It is good for my mind to hear this once in a while; it gives my life a sense and a purpose. Thank you for your words of wisdom, at this moment my doubts are bothering me less."

"You have doubts, you? I can't believe it; you're the best member we ever had. Your dedication is by far the most loyal to our cause."

"Yes, I had my doubts. I was wondering where all the donations went. I wanted to see the fruits of our money, to see real people being helped and to see the mission started."

"Don't ever doubt it, everything is done with God in our hearts, she knows whom to help and when and how. She is an angel sent to Earth. We're strong, godly women and we're ready to serve Him."

CHAPTER SIXTEEN

"Eve, may I ask you something?" Mary Rita asked.

"Go ahead, ask me."

"Does Arthur want me to buy him a new car?"

"Why do you think so?"

"Because he takes me to all the car dealerships, everywhere we go and he asks me stupid questions."

"Actually, I told him that you'd buy him a brand new car because he married you. No man would marry an old woman and protect her from her family without a reward. I promised him you'd buy him a new car."

"But I don't have the money for a new car and I don't want to buy him anything. Eve, you know better than anyone that I don't care about him and he doesn't care about me either. We are two strangers living in the same space because we agreed to."

"I know but people around us don't and it is a lot better for the sake of our mission to pretend that you're a couple. You better buy him the car he wants," Eve ordered. Then reminded her what to not forget she had to pay a price for being 'free' a different kind of freedom and not be in a nursing home.

The books Eve gave to Mary Rita to read were religious books and some of them she already read twice. Time was going slow and when her thoughts became alive and painful, she loved to think about the good times she had in her life,

NUMB

not too long ago. The fun she had with Kathleen and Christina, the daughters that she loved, her family, the grandchildren, her place in Santa Rosa Beach, her paradise. The St. Anne Church, friends, the passion she had raising funds to build the new, larger church, the recognition from the Pope, the award from her business but above all, images of her life with the man she loved her entire life, Bob, were more vivid than ever. Mary Rita's heart started beating faster, her love making her feel like a young woman in love with the man of her life. She didn't want those images to fade; she wanted them to stay with her till the end of her life. What a man, what a husband and what a father he was.

Eve interrupted Mary Rita's dreams by saying, "Mary Rita, it's about time for your annual check up, are you ready?"

"Of course, when is my appointment?"

"Tomorrow at 8 am, you already had the blood work done, tomorrow is the exam, and I know you're healthy and strong."

"I hope so; I'll be ready to go," Mary Rita said.

The next morning, Mary Rita entered the doctor's office smiling. The doctor performed a routine exam, read the blood test and everything seemed to be perfect until he checked her left breast. He stopped for a second, went back to the records, and read something to be sure that wasn't a recurrence of an old condition. As soon as he finished reading the records, he examined her breast again and said, "Mary Rita there is something we have to pay attention to and do some investigation, because there is a lump that wasn't there before. I'll suggest a procedure that will tell us what we're dealing with. Let's get the procedure scheduled if you agree with my suggestion, do you?"

"Of course, I'd like to know what it is," Mary Rita said, thinking what the lump could be. She had never had major health issues and she was blessed with good genes, so she wasn't too much concerned about the lump.

She was directed to a lab where the doctor explained her how the procedure would be done and what to expect. Once the doctor started to pull liquid from her left breast, he was amazed what a brave woman she was. Mary Rita was holding her fists tight and the entire time she talked to God, praying and keeping her mind occupied. Bob was there with her, in her mind, holding her hand.

The result wasn't the one she wanted to hear—Cancer! Mary Rita was really taken by surprise, she didn't expect to hear that word, it could be a life changing word, a life changing diagnosis... a life threatening diagnosis.

The lump had to come out followed by other treatments, so it wouldn't spread to the other tissue surrounding the lump. The doctor explained the procedure, the following treatments, the side effects, and the benefits of getting rid of the cancerous tumor.

"I'm ok, you can schedule the surgery, the sooner the better," she said without even thinking twice.

The doctor and his nurse were amazed by how strong Mary Rita was and they couldn't believe her reaction when she heard the situation.

Mary Rita went home and she talked to Eve about the situation.

As soon as Eve realized that Mary Rita had to have surgery done, she knew that if she were in the hospital, it would be easier to be visited by her family and this wasn't what Eve wanted. Her 'disciples' had to be under her supervision, she wouldn't allow any external influences to influence her people. "Mary Rita, I don't think you should be staying at the hospital after the surgery. What about if you stay at the hotel you like, the ones you stayed with Bob before?"

NUMB

"What a good idea! I like that hotel. I have good memories there, I agree with you," she said, impressed at how thoughtful her friend was.

The day of the surgery came and after everything was done, Mary Rita went to the hotel being accompanied by one of her friends. She didn't have to suffer, she did not have much pain, and the doctor gave her pain pills, knowing how painful the wound would be for the next couple of days.

Brenda Stuart, another member of the group was coming every day to check the drain tubes and to measure how much liquid came out. She was a really good nurse, doing everything the doctor instructed her to do.

Eve asked Arthur to call Kathleen Petrovich, Mary Rita's daughter and to let her know about the surgery. She wanted to be covered legally just in case something went wrong with Mary Rita. Suddenly, Eve was scared seeing that not all things went the way she wanted. She hoped her members would never have to leave the group, and if they did, it shouldn't death.

In Mary Rita's case, she knew she had no reason to worry because Mary Rita was such a healthy, strong woman, but things could happen...

"Kathleen, this is Arthur, your mother had a surgery and she is now recovering," he said, being short and concise, like he had been instructed to give the news.

"Surgery, my mom had surgery? What happened?" Kathleen was shouting at the other end, not believing what she just heard.

"She has cancer. The doctor discovered a lump in her left breast, she had a needle biopsy, and the result came back positive. The doctor suggested a lumpectomy, if I pronounce correctly, and it was done yesterday."

"Where is she now?" Kathleen asked and she wanted to find out as many details as possible.

"Do you remember the hotel your parents were staying before they purchased their house here? Well, that's where she is. That's all I have to say, goodbye." Arthur hung up the phone.

Kathleen wanted to find out more details about her mom's condition but Arthur didn't have permission to say more than this, Kathleen was grateful that she knew at least where her mother was staying.

The moment she found out about the ordeal her mother went trough, Kathleen made arrangements so she could leave and check on her mom.

She got on a plane right away and the thought of seeing her mother's 'dictators' didn't help her to feel comfortable, but seeing her mother after a long time of silence, made her trip a meaningful one.

Being alone, she let her memories come alive in her mind, thinking about all the things she did, all the fight she put up with to save her mother from that group's influence. Her struggles to win the trial in court to declare her mom mentally incompetent, like she'd been advised to do by lawyers. In order to help her mother stay away from the people who were using her pure love for God, for evil purposes.

All the time and money she spent with lawyers, doctors, counselors, the time she spent educating herself to understand what was going on with her mother, and she wasn't thinking of health issues because she was only thinking of the mental prison her mom was in. During her

NUMB

flight, she remembered one of the visits she paid for with an attorney.

That attorney pulled out a bunch of papers and gave it to her to take with her home and read, after listening to her and all the things that happened to her mother.

The next day she'd called his office and he let her ask all the questions she had. "Sir, everything you gave me to read, applies to my mother's situation to the last letter. I mean everything."

"Did you get a chance to read all of them?"

"Yes, I did, all of them. I had no idea there was a name for the situation my mother is in."

"Yes, it is called 'undue influence' and it is punishable by the law, if detected. Kathleen, this is something hard to prove and to determine if it is an undue influence case it needs and requests long, costly tests for those people that seem to be able to handle their finances and necessary decisions by themselves because only family and close friends would notice the changes in their behavior. Most of the time, seniors and disabled adults are a special target for those criminals that abuse them. It is a form of elder abuse," the attorney said, explaining in detail. "Are you still there?" Mr. Joseph asked.

"Yes, Mr. Joseph. I'm sorry but I'm speechless. I can't believe how many years I tried to get an answer to learn how to save my mom. Sir, I don't think there are too many lawyers that know this, to know how to deal with it. I'm glad I met you."

"Me too, now that you know what this crime is, it will be a lot easier to understand and to figure out what will work in your mother's case, because there are no two cases the same, the circumstances differ from one case to the anther. But all of the cases have something in common: there is a victim and a perpetrator."

"I see, in my mother's case the charlatan used my mom's will to help the poor and also, the woman has other people in the group doing what my mother does, donating everything they have in the name of God."

"It is often difficult to legally define whether the financial interactions between two individuals, one of them being a senior or a disabled adult were conducted as a matter of routine business or were based on coercion. It is clear, however, that such coercion is common. I wish I could help you more and I'm glad I had the time to talk to you."

"I'm the one glad and I appreciate your time, now I understand my mother's fear."

"Yes, the predators are sociopaths with narcissistic traits who progressively breed fear in their victims and over time, cause the elder or the disabled adult to sever relationships with family, friends and isolating them. Those predators instill suspicion in a victim, increasing his or her sense of helplessness and dependency on the perpetrator. When the victim has been adequately brainwashed into believing that no one else cares for them, then the criminal starts offering his/her precious protection. It is a complicated process to prove it is a crime. Once the victim becomes comfortable and dependant, exploiters enhance their control by isolating the victim from relatives and friends, often by restricting mail or phone calls, making the victim believe the relatives and friends are only there because they desire to exploit them. Kathleen, I could spend hours talking about the "undue influence" because I'm the one that made this law known. You're a smart woman and you already knew all this, except what the real crime is called."

NUMB

"Yes, sir, I've lived all these because they tried to get me first. When I finally resisted, even if it took me few good months and many, many tens of thousands of dollars, I knew there was something bad going on, but I had no way to prove it, because my mother's medical exam stated she had full capacity of her mental health."

"Is she really that healthy?"

"Yes, she is sharp and smart, but she is dominated by a sense of accomplishments, a sense of recognition and working that close with the poor made her feel she would receive recognition in heaven, and this is what all of us dream about. I know I do."

"I wish you good luck and to be able to get your mother out alive from the inferno she is in."

"Thank you, Sir. Thank you again. I feel like I attended a class at the law school," Kathleen said.

Now she knew how to deal with her mother's predators, she knew what to say and what not to say. She was wearing a protective screen of knowledge and this was a powerful tool. Kathleen was determined to accept any behavioral treatment Eve was going to try with her, she was ready to be humiliated, yelled at, be called bad names, anything for her mother's sake. She would be showing her mother that she wasn't there to take anything from her, least of all her freedom as she'd feared all this time.

When Kathleen arrived after an exhausting trip to the hotel, she saw her mother with tubes coming out from the bandages, her pale but beautiful face and especially, her smile; Kathleen couldn't hold her tears, even if she'd trained herself to not cry. She could feel her love hugging her mom's sick body by giving her hope.

For few seconds, Mary Rita was the mother that found her loving daughter, and their love was a real flame that was brought to life, but only for few seconds.

Mary Rita wanted to tell her daughter how much she appreciated that she came such a long way to come and see her. How much she'd missed her but all this remained silent, only their eyes could talk because Mary Rita was never left alone by the group members. There were at least four women every time Kathleen wanted to say something to her mother but she was prepared for the long haul....

When Eve came to check on Mary Rita to be sure everything was going according to her plans, she pulled a chair close to Kathleen and started blaming her for trying to put her mother in a nursing home instead of letting her work for such a noble cause. St. John Charity, and their mission, St. Faustina.

Kathleen's training was helping her lot; she did not react to Eve's provocations, she looked her in the eyes and it was worse than cursing, Kathleen's look was cold and sharp but Eve had the strength of Satan in her eyes.

Mary Rita never saw her daughter so quiet when someone was yelling at her; she always fought for her beliefs and she didn't take crap from anyone.

Mary Rita almost forgot where she was, watching the duel between her daughter and the leader, the head of the mission. She couldn't believe her eyes, to see Kathleen with her head down. No, this had never happened—it couldn't be real!

The visit was short but the love between mother and daughter could be felt by both of them even through the

NUMB

immense fear Mary Rita had of Kathleen, even if she knew her daughter would never really hurt her.

Kathleen went back to Indiana and worked endless hours to forget about the image she carried with her, the image of a suffering mother that needed her help, a help that she could not offer yet...

Mary Rita didn't talk with any of the women in the hotel room; her mind was with her daughter on her long trip.

She took the time and came all the way here to see me, to be with me, she still loves me. Of course, I'm afraid of her because who knows what she could do to me, but this didn't stop me from admitting how kind and sweet she was. How is possible to have such contrasting feelings at the same time about the same person? How come I feel so good to see that she didn't forget about me, even now when she knows I have no wealth left? It must be love, only love could do this.

Eve came back from the parking lot where she went to bring some pills for Mary Rita, but when she tried to give them to her, she refused them saying she wasn't in pain. Mary Rita didn't like to take pills that hadn't been subscribed by her doctor. Eve felt insulted, but she had no choice but to take her pills back and leave. She could sense something happened but she wasn't sure what.

The group, Eve, Paul, Arthur and Cynthia purchased a large painting of the Divine Mercy representing Jesus Christ with a colorful scarves coming from His heart. They had purchased it with money donated by Mary Rita. The painting was presented during a big ceremony. The Knights of Columbus were there and lots of people attended the procession around the church and venerated the Savior. Mary Rita couldn't attend the procession, so Eve showed her a film of it. The procession was lovely and bright. Everyone there seemed so happy to be blessed by it. To see the Divine Mercy up close.

Mary Rita found out a few days later through Kathleen that the painting came from the Diocese and it had been sent to different Catholic Churches to be seen and venerated, it wasn't purchased by Eve Garner at all.

Mary Rita felt startled by this lie and she then thought about the many other lies she'd been told. She knew then that she had to get out of Eve's group, away from her influence...she just didn't know how she could do it.

The time came when she was supposed to go to her Florida home, pay the bills and check on the house. Arthur drove her to Florida and he had a room reservation at the hotel because Mary Rita's home had no internet connection and he wanted to use it.

She was happy he wasn't staying at her house. Before he headed to the hotel, he had to do what he was instructed to do, so he started throwing away all the food in the house, again. He emptied everything, the refrigerator, freezer, and pantry.

Eve told Mary Rita that Kathleen would do anything to see her dead and she was convinced that Kathleen has poisoned the food.

Mary Rita knew her daughter would never poison the food or anything like this, she knew this was impossible.

Arthur left and said he would bring breakfast soon.

That day was another gift from God sent to Mary Rita. She had no idea that Kathleen was at her home, the one next door with two of her friends from Canada, Rose and her daughter. Kathleen's friends were staying for the winter.

Kathleen knew her mother was in her house and she wanted so badly to be with her. Rose came up with the idea to invite Mary Rita over, to spend some time together, but

NUMB

Kathleen wasn't sure if she would want to come, she knew the fear was still there.

To their surprise, Mary Rita invited them to come to her because Arthur wasn't there and even if he came back, she didn't care, not a big deal.

So, Kathleen and Rose brought some wine, snacks, soda and they went next door to be with Kathleen's mother.

What a joy! Mary Rita welcomed her guests with open arms and it was the best thing she ever did because that visit marked the healing of the relationship between mother and daughter.

Laughing and remembering all the fun and the good times they had during their lives, it made Mary Rita feel blessed and loved.

Their laughter could be heard from the driveway, so when Arthur finally came back he was surprised to see guests having really good time with Mary Rita. "Oh, I'm glad you have company," he said "Hi, Kathleen!"

"Hi Arthur, this is my dear friend from Canada, Rose."

"Nice to meet you Rose, I'm Arthur," he said.

He was invited to drink some wine and have some snacks and soon, everyone had a good time. Mary Rita did not remember ever seeing Arthur other than grumpy, so she was surprised to see that he could be a nice person if he wanted, or if he had to be.

Not too long after that, he left and went back to the hotel he was staying at.

Kathleen and her friend, Rose went to spend the rest of the evening at Kathleen's home, next door.

Mary Rita went to bed early, being tired and not having any food but snacks for the entire day. She blamed herself that she let Arthur throw away all the food in her house, but at least she had an amazing good time with her daughter and her friend. She knew Rose for many years and she remembered how they used to spend five months of the year, the cold months of the year in Florida. She was happy that her daughter had such a loyal company, a good friendship.

Late at night, a loud noise woke Mary Rita up, it was a frightening noise. She went directly to her kitchen and realized the alarm went off, right away she called the police and the person that answered the phone told her to not hang up the phone and to stay with her on the phone till the police crew got there. This is what she did, being so grateful the person offered to stay with her on the phone.

The police crew came and the nice police man was kind as he looked and checked each corner of her house. He couldn't find anything, anywhere, so advised he her to call if something else happened and he left.

Mary Rita now looked at her home phone and she saw the red light flashing, she had two voicemails on her answering machine, both from Arthur; she listened to them:

"Mary Rita, open the door, can you hear me, open the door," this was at midnight, the second voicemail one was a minute after: *"I know you can hear me, open this door now!"* His furious voice was shouting over the phone.

Mary Rita called the hotel where Arthur was staying to be sure he was there and checked to see if Arthur used her credit card and when she found out that he didn't, she told them that she didn't give permission to anyone to use her credit card. So the next day or whenever Arthur would check out, he would have to use his own credit card.

She checked the bolt again, holding the door and went to bed.

Mary Rita slept a little bit longer than her normal hours being exhausted from the events of the last night.

NUMB

She pushed the button from the inside the garage to open the garage door and a high fire, a foot high fire was burning right at the corner of the house where she had a large plant. She grabbed the water hose and started putting the fire out. Her daughter came right away and helped her to finish putting it out.

Kathleen went to the 8:30 am Mass and she noticed Arthur was there but she didn't talk to him. After the Mass, Arthur came to Mary Rita's home and said, "I'm going back to Baton Rouge and I'm leaving you."

Mary Rita couldn't have had a better day, to start with such good news. She would be finally free, her prayers had been heard.

At that moment, she had only a twenty dollar bill in her pocket and no car.

Kathleen took her to a dealership and Mary Rita put a down payment for a car on her credit card and she felt brand new again.

"Mom, how are you going to pay all these bills? For the new car, the mortgage you took on your home for you know who?" Kathleen asked.

"Don't worry, I'll sell my last piece of land and I'll pay my bills, thank God I'm healthy and alive. Kathleen, I never thought I'd live long enough to see this day! He's gone and Eve is gone they'll never come back because I'm broke, no more money to donate. Do you remember the waterfront lot? Well, somebody seems to be interested to buy it. I'll let you know if it goes through."

Kathleen had to go back to Indiana to take care of her house and her business, but mother and daughter made plans to spend time together. She knew that if her mother needed financial help, she would always be there to help.

Kathleen saved all the documents of the complaints, doctors' reports, copies of the checks given away for St. John Charity, all the bank statements showing the huge amount of money spent by her on one side and her mother on the other side. Attorneys, lawyers, houses purchased, sold, renovated, donated, all the documents of the cars sold without getting a dime for, trucks, furniture, jewelry, a lifetime of hard work wasted for an nonexistent cause; a cause of a Satanic, sick mind that was able to manipulate hundreds of people, ruining them and their families.

Kathleen was determined to not let this happen to someone else.

"Kathleen," Mary Rita said to her daughter when they were talking on the phone, and feeling proud of her daughter for what she intended to do. "I'll help you in what you're going to do. I'll be your witness every time it is needed. I'll tell the truth. I have so many friends, or better said, I *had* so many friends, most of them my age, widows that lost their husbands and they could be such easy targets for predators like Eve and her entire cult. Do you think I'll ever have my dear, real friends believe in me again and will they ever be able to understand why I did what I did? I can only pray to God to tell the truth, to make them accept me back because I love them all. Yes, I said I love them all. Even a few days ago, a friend from St. Anne Catholic Church told me what happened after the daily Mass she attended. You won't believe this. The lady told me that Arthur had spread a rumor that I came back home to Florida to die, that I'm terminal and I don't have too much longer to live. People started talking and one of the women sitting at the table, having coffee said negative words about me. It happened to be Cynthia, the woman that I was ready to give my life for! I always thought she was the only loyal friend I was left with. She was here in Florida to check on her

NUMB

house in Ponce de Leon, if you remember, she had a house there."

"Mom, stop. You're talking way too fast. Start again and slowly. I'm confused now, your best friend from Baton Rouge, the best friend in Florida. The same woman that introduced you and dad to the cult leader, the woman that knew everything about your dedication to God that knew how much you loved God, this is the one that talked like this about a lifetime of soul torture? I'm sorry mom, but I cannot comprehend what you said, I need time to digest all this....give me a second!"

CHAPTER SEVENTEEN

"Mom, I have an appointment with a doctor that knows all about you and whose name was on the papers that the court served you with years ago. I know I lost the case but God gave you back to me. What about if go together to Baton Rouge and see if he can see you for few minutes?"

"Dr. Krauss, his name was on those papers, to see me for what? Do you think he can help us? Is he going to examine me? I'm better than ever and happier I can say."

"Yes, he will help us. He doesn't need to examine you; he knows how smart you are..."

"I promised I'll do everything necessary to see those people in jail. I'll go with you."

Mother and daughter went to Baton Rouge and the doctor spent almost a full hour talking to both of them. At the end of the visit, he had only one question for Mary Rita, "How did you get out?"

Mary Rita knew the answer but talking to a doctor, she didn't want him to think she was one of those 'religious nuts' so she answered, "I don't know, I just got out. I had very little money left is why I think?"

Mary Rita knew that her answer, the real answer she should answer was...The Prayers, *all the relatives and friends that prayed day and night for my salvation.* She knew he was a strong Catholic believer, but she didn't want him to change his impression about her.

NUMB

Before leaving, Dr. Krauss said, "Mary Rita's case has to be on TV so people learn about this kind of situation. I would call them atrocities. Kathleen, let me give you a phone number." He grabbed his prescriptions pad then crossed a line to void it. He wrote a name and a phone number and gave it to Kathleen. "Do you still have all the documents from the CIA?" he asked.

"Yes sir, I brought all of them for the FBI interview."

"Perfect, let me know what they intend to do."

"I promise. Thank you so much," Kathleen said.

Mary Rita hugged him and she had tears in her eyes. "Dr. Krauss, thank you for helping my daughter and me. You did a lot more than my attorneys."

"I did it with all my heart, my mother could fall in the same trap you did, but I'm sure now that these criminals will never try to get in touch with you again. Stay strong and healthy."

"Thank you again, I will!" Mary Rita promised.

Kathleen called the number the doctor gave her and it seemed like it was one of her lucky days. The person that answered the phone invited them, Mary Rita and Kathleen to come to the office of the local TV station.

They went there, met with the person in charge, and after that, he looked through the papers then asked if he could make copies from their documents. He couldn't stop from saying that he had a relative who knew Eve Garner and her 'tribe' and she had very negative words to describe her experience. He seemed interested about the story and asked if they could come be back the next day for a TV interview.

Kathleen was supposed to be at FBI building at the time he suggested this, so they tried to figure out how to make it work.

The TV person asked if they would like to be interviewed there, on the spot. First, Kathleen and her mother thought about their appearances, hair, make up etc. but they decided it was a lot more important to have the interview than their looks.

That interview was aired after two weeks of production. Everyone in Baton Rouge and surroundings became aware of the cult and what could happen to anyone.

Kathleen was satisfied with the results of her trip, Satan was unarmed, vulnerable, unmasked and this was what mother and daughter wanted...mission accomplished!

Years and years of cruel mental abuse, isolation and fear were all gone; it was time to gain friends back.

Paula and Cathy were wonderful friends from St. Anne Catholic Church that tried hard to help Mary Rita during the crisis and they never lost their trust in her. Even when Mary Rita didn't invite them to go inside her home, they understood the situation and accepted it. Good friends do not need explanations; they only love you the way you are.

Now it was Mary Rita's turn to pay back their loyal friendship.

"Kathleen, do you remember when I had a buyer for the water front lot and it didn't work out, he changed his mind? Well, I sold it and like you said, I took payments. You see, now I listen to you because I know what a good real estate agent you are. You always told us, your dad and me, how to do all the transactions we did, and when we didn't listen to you, it wasn't a good thing. But I can learn even at my age."

"Mom, you're young, you don't look your age and you know it; everyone tells you this every day."

"Is true and what is even more important is that I don't feel my age."

NUMB

"Oh, Mom you don't even act your age. I'm glad you sold that land and now you're financially okay. You can pay all the bills and still have some extra money to save. I'm proud of you and I don't think another woman that had to endure what you did, would come out alive from that trap. You're a hero, a less wealthy hero, but a hero. I love you mom. I don't think I have to say this, I said it before anyway, but if you ever need my financial help, you know I will help you."

"Me too, and if I'm a hero, you saved me, you pulled me out from the hell, I never liked to use that word, but it is exactly what it was. The flames of hell were burning my health and my life and separated me from you and the world. I cannot say that I believe more in God now than I did before, because it wouldn't be true. I believed in Him all my life but some dark forces took advantage of my strong faith."

"I'm so glad to hear how positive your words are, Mom. I think sometimes I need your encouragement, you know kids, marriage, business...."

"I'm not worried about all that, because if you were able to save a lost soul like me, the rest is a piece of cake. You're dealing with a normal world, not the dark side, and everyone in our family is a strong believer. All these incidents only need to be discussed and solved, because the rest is love."

"Mom, I always loved you but lately, I feel like I want you to live closer to me."

"You never know, let me get a little older and then I'll start thinking," Mary Rita said smiling and she made her daughter laugh.

A few months later, Mary Rita was again, deeply involved with her church, St. Anne's. She'd met a lovely couple there, JB and his wife, Francine. Then Francine started having some health problems and Mary Rita wanted to help. She wanted to help because she was helped too, and her strong faith was telling her to love her neighbor like she loved herself.

Mary Rita's health was now the best she'd had. Many who knew her were impressed by the way she looked and the way she acted. Mary Rita knew JB, he was one of the most reliable parishioners, doing things to help the church and those that needed his help. His beautiful, sweet wife, Francine, was suffering lately, her body was giving up. The wheelchair she was using made it difficult to use the beautiful home they had, so they both decided to sell their home and build a new one, completely wheelchair accessible.

"I'm glad you decided to do this, it will be so much easier for Francine to get around the house, and she will really enjoy it," Mary Rita said.

"I hope so, it's getting harder and harder for her to do things by herself," JB said.

"I can help. I have nothing else to do, going to Mass, twice a day, if I can. I swim every day in my pool and help my daughter with her hotel in Indiana. Let me talk to Francine and see if she wants me to help her. Are you okay with me being in your home?"

"Mary Rita, I never stay around women when they come and visit my wife." He smiled. "I would do anything for her. I hate to see her suffering."

"Well, let me talk to her and see what she says."
The next day Mary Rita went over to their house.
"Francine, how are you doing? I talked to your husband and now I would like to ask you if you want me to help you when you need help. What do you think?" Mary Rita was afraid she would be rejected because of her past.

NUMB

Francine had the kindest smile on her face and she said, "I would like you to come and spend some time with me. You're such a positive person and I enjoy being with you."

Mary Rita had tears of happiness, as she did not expect such sweet generosity and kindness. Francine gave her faith again.

Mary Rita spent a lot of quality time with Francine and everyone could see how beneficial their friendship was. Francine's spirits were calm and joyful even if her body was claiming her health, she invited ladies to have lunch in their absolutely amazing home. The home was on the golf course and it was one of the most beautiful homes Mary Rita had ever visited.

But it wasn't the home it was the spirit of their home that made people feel welcomed and loved.

"Is your home on the market or are you waiting for spring?" Mary Rita asked her.

"Yes, it is and when the other home that we're building is done, we'll move there. It will be completely wheelchair accessible and it will make JB's life easier. He doesn't say anything but I know it is hard for him to take care of me."

"He loves you so much that I don't think you're right. Everything he does is for you and only for you, everyone can see that."

"Mary Rita, tomorrow I invited few ladies from our church for lunch and everyone accepted our invitation, hope you'll be here."

"Of course, thank you for inviting me." Mary Rita was thinking how special this woman was. She knew why Francine invited the ladies to come for lunch. She did it for her, so these women would get to know her better, maybe accept her situation and understand what she'd went through.

Few days after their conversation, Mary Rita found out that Eve Garner, the Satan, the diabolic cult leader, died of cancer at sixty seven years old.

The evil woman couldn't escape her fate, she died and now, she could go and be in hell, where she came from.

"Kathleen, Eve passed away," she announced as she released a huge sigh.

"I'm relieved and I know I shouldn't say this, but I am!" Kathleen admitted.

Both, mother and daughter had a moment of silence when all the events they went through washed over them both and after that... those troubles were put behind a door to never be opened again, sealed forever.

Soon, Mary Rita received a letter from FBI that her case was still under investigations but that the main person of their criminal investigations had passed away.

A water issue surfaced at Mary Rita's home and needed repairs that would require quite some time. The couple from church, Francine and JB invited her to come and live there for the time the repairs were done.

She accepted right away. She could really help Francine and spend time with her, creating funny situations so she would forget about her pains.

"JB, I would like to be clear from the beginning. I have to pay my bill every time we go out to eat. I'm not a guest, I'm a friend and I appreciate the hand you gave to me when I needed it, so please let's be friends."

NUMB

Francine had the best time of her life while Mary Rita was there, enjoying her energetic and smiling friend. She was very attached to her friend and they looked like two sisters sharing love between them. It was a blessing and Francine showed this on her face.

JB found himself less stressed out and he was able to find few minutes to relax.

The time came when Francine had to go and be with the Lord. The church people, friends and family, neighbors came and paid their respects.

Not too long after Francine's death, their home got sold and JB was invited to share Mary Rita's house, till his new house was finished. It was Mary Rita's turn to help.

"It couldn't be a better time than now actually, because I'll go to Indiana for eight months, so you can stay here by yourself. I'm the lucky one, because you can take care of things when I'm gone. Francine would approve."

"Thank you, I'll do it," he said.

Mary Rita's life was coming back with full strength, she was loved, she had friends and her health was excellent.

"How's everything?" she asked JB on the phone. "Are you ok? Do I still have a house?" Mary Rita joked.

"Yes, you do. I have good news for you, my house is almost ready, and when you come back, I'll move in my new home."

"I'm happy for you and really sad for me."

"Sad, what do you mean?" he asked.

"Well, it was good to have someone I trust being in my home but I'm happy for you."

"Mary Rita you said that we are best friends and I'll take care of your home every time you go somewhere, or every time you stay with Kathleen. You know how close our homes are from each other, we can walk if we want...."

~ 360 ~

"Not with the humidity we have," she teased. "But you're right, thank you for everything. I'll be home soon and I cannot wait to see some movies. You did a good job with that home theater, I love it."

"When you come home, we'll watch some."

"Perfect, see you soon."

The conversation ended but Mary Rita was looking forward spending time with a reliable companion, a friend that helped her feel secure and welcomed. She knew her new life just began with a wonderful, pure friendship, a friendship for life.

Time was flying but at the same time, it was bringing joy and there was no sadness and desperation, pain and suffering.

"Mom, I called to let you know that your dear nephew made all the arrangements for your birthday."

"He did? I didn't think would be an easy task to put together all the details for my unique ninetieth birthday. As a reminder and please tell everyone that will come to celebrate with me: this is not a birthday party, this is a celebration of our victory against everything bad in our lives, and it's a victory of God. We are going to celebrate His work and our love. I want all of us to feel this way, I sure do. No presents, just a mass card that I'll read every day and Kathleen, thank you for all the years that you spent trying to save me. I have robbed you of your most beautiful years and I know you forgave me, because you knew that everything I ever did was in the name of God."

"Oh Mom, I just love you so much," Kathleen replied with tears.

"We're going to have the most amazing ninetieth celebration and looking toward my hundredth one. I love you and all those whose prayers saved me. I'm grateful to have a

NUMB

really good friend in my life, someone reliable, a good Christian man, JB."

Notes from Mary Rita's family and friends at her 90th Birthday Anniversary

"When asked to write a few sentences about Mary Rita Wish I thought what attributes I would say to describe her.
Since she has been my friend for over 50 years, I feel I am in a position to be honest and totally unbiased.
My best friend walks in sync with God; she lives her faith 24/7. She has and does perform acts of kindness and generosity on a daily basis.
I watched her take a fledging business and bring it to the best in the nation status.
She is Intelligent, courageous and funny. But of all the many things that make up this remarkable woman the one that shines brightest is that certain radiance she exudes, an inner joy that touches all.
She is my best friend and the world is a better place because of her."

Joan Cronin

"Mary Rita Wish has more charm than should be allowed one person. Her work ethic is now rare; her love and support of the Catholic Church has never wavered despite its many problems.
I've known Mary Rita Wish for 30 years and she has always been a joy and lots of fun, regardless of family problems. But there was a glitch (briefly considering her 90 years). So read all about it in 'NUMB'!

Charlotte Compbell

"Mary Rita Wish has been my dear and close friend for nearly 50 years. My husband, Ernie and I consider our friendship with Mare and Bob a huge blessing as we owe so much of our
Tupperware success to them.
Mary Rita's caring and sharing of her superb business expertise, her kindness and dynamic personality is responsible for many stories for which we are all grateful.
Thanks for the wonderful memories. Love you forever.

Minerva (Min) Liberatore

"It makes me very sad to think someone taking advantage of my grandma the way these people did. I'm just glad she got away from them and she can spend time with her family again. Love you gram!"

Granddaughter Genia

"You have always been a great aunt and I admired you for your ability to achieve."
Ever since I was a little girl, I thought my aunt, Mary Rita Wish, was the classiest lady I knew. She always carried herself with grace, pride and confidence, wore the most up to date cloths and drove a convertible.
Even had a silver Christmas tree with rotating lights (sorry I dropped a plastic toy in one of them when I was younger and it broke..... this is my confession). Even today, at her young age of 90, I still think of her as the classiest lady I know."

Your niece, Rose (Carone) Benson

NUMB

"Aunt Mar, you're an inspiration, all our love."

Ron, Teri and Ronnie

Mary Rita has been known to be the Tupperware Lady to many but to me she's been my "Pretty Grandma." She is truly the best person to be around. I would not have been half the person I am today without her.
I am blessed to have her as my grandmother/ second mother as she raised me several times while I grew up. I cannot say enough good, fantastic things about her.
She gives till she bleeds and loves like no other. To have her as a part of my life has been the best blessing I could have ever asked for.

Shawn Hayes

"Thank you for being a strong female role model for our family! You broke through the glass door and paved the way for the females in this family as well as many others.
Have many wonderful memories as a child visiting you at the Tupperware Distribution Center as well as Destin! Thanks for all you have done for this family."

Debbie Carone the 1st

Mary Rita Wish has a soul of gold and a brilliant mind. We all should learn from her.

Ed Carone Junior

"And God will open wide the gates of heaven for you to enter into the eternal kingdom of our Lord and Savior Jesus Christ." 2 Peter 1:11

NUMB

Mary Rita And Bob Wish

Mary Rita Wish

NUMB

G.V. CORA

I'm a woman wearing many hats: Mother, wife, grandmother, business owner, aesthetician, handmade crafts maker, and many more, but the one that I added lately to my long list is "author" and it brings me joy and freedom to live in different worlds.

This new "hat" helps me get my words to those who need them, helping people see their problems with different eyes, to find solutions for situations that seem life threatening or hopeless.

My husband, Eugene Voiculescu and I, live in Santa Rosa Beach, Florida. Our two children are grown up and we are also happy grandparents. Life is good!

Thank you for reading my books,
G.V. Cora

OTHER BOOKS BY G.V.CORA

Escape
The Note
Skin and Beauty Wisdom
The Gift (To be released April 2019)
The Mercenary (To be released in 2019)

G.V. CORA